George Duncan

Marilynne Robinson is the author of the modern classic *Housekeeping,* winner of the PEN/Hemingway Award, and *Gilead,* winner of the Pulitzer Prize. Her book, *Mother Country,* was a National Book Award finalist for nonfiction. She teaches at the University of Iowa Writers' Workshop.

Also by Marilynne Robinson

Fiction
Gilead
Housekeeping

Nonfiction
Mother Country: Britain, the Welfare State and Nuclear Pollution

The
DEATH
of ADAM

Essays on Modern Thought

MARILYNNE ROBINSON

Picador
New York

www.picadorusa.com

Picador® is a U.S. registered trademark and is used by St. Martin's Press under license from Pan Books Limited.

For information on Picador Reading Group Guides, as well as ordering, please contact Picador.
Phone: 646-307-5626
Fax: 212-253-9627
E-mail: readinggroupguides@picadorusa.com

The author wishes to thank Katherine Stall for her assistance; Robert and Peggy Boyers, the editors of Salmagundi, in which "Darwinism" and "Puritans and Prigs" first appeared, in slightly different form; and Linda Spalding and Michael Ondaatje, the editors of Brick, where "Facing Reality" first appeared. "Psalm Eight" was published in Communion, edited by David Rosenberg (Anchor Books, 1996), and "Dietrich Bonhoeffer" in Martyrs, edited by Susan Bergman (Harper San Francisco, 1996). "Puritans and Prigs" was collected in The New Salmagundi Reader, 1996. Grateful acknowledgment is also made to the National Book Foundation, under whose auspices "Family" was presented as an address; and to the University of Iowa Libraries and the Lila Wallace—Reader's Digest Foundation, cosponsors of the colloquium on nineteenth-century American history, where "McGuffey and the Abolitionists" was presented.

Book design by Melodie Wertelet

Library of Congress Cataloging-in-Publication Data

Robinson, Marilynne.
 The death of Adam : essays on modern thought / Marilynne Robinson.
  p. cm.
 ISBN 0-312-42532-5
 EAN 978-0-312-42532-6
  1. United States—Civilization—1945-—Philosophy. 2. United States—Civilization—European influences. 3. Theology—United States—History. 4. Calvinism—United States. I. Title.

E169.12.R583 1998
973.92—dc21
               98-18021
                 CIP

First published in the United States by Mariner Books, an imprint of Houghton Mifflin Company.

10 9 8 7 6 5 4 3 2

For
Frank Conroy
and
Connie Brothers

CONTENTS

The
DEATH
of ADAM

INTRODUCTION

THESE ESSAYS were written for various uses and occasions over a number of years. They have characteristic preoccupations — religion, history, the state of contemporary society — and they are, all of them, contrarian in method and spirit. They assert, in one way or another, that the prevailing view of things can be assumed to be wrong, and that its opposite, being its image or shadow, can also be assumed to be wrong. They undertake to demonstrate that there are other ways of thinking, for which better arguments can be made.

I often look at primary texts, books generally acknowledged to have had formative impact, because they are a standard against which other things can be judged, for example the reputations of these same works, or the reputations of those who wrote them, or the cultures that produced and received them, or the commentaries and histories which imply that their own writers and readers have a meaningful familiarity with them. If the primary text itself departs too far from the character common wisdom and specialist wisdom (these are typically indistinguishable) have ascribed to it, then clearly some rethinking is in order.

In these essays I launched on what looks in retrospect to have been a campaign of revisionism, because contemporary discourse feels to me empty and false. I assumed, I was educated to believe, that I would live my life in a civilization of expanding comprehension. The old lost myth of civilization is that it unfolds, that it opens up the realizations of which it is capable, that it instructs itself. Obviously this is in some degree an idealization. But there seemed good grounds to hope that I would learn from the collective life new things about aesthetics, and justice, and language, and social order — about the human project, the human collaboration, about the expression of human exceptionalism in the arts and sciences that declare the strange exhilarations of our strange life on earth. Granting evil, which it seems a dangerous error to consider solvable, human civilizations have created abundant good, refining experience and circumstance into astonishingly powerful visions and dreams, into poems and music which have fallen like a mantle of light over our mere human weakness.

What use are these things, after all? We live in an age of neo-Hobbism, and this is considered a respectable question. Of course, absent these human tentatives there is no way to speak of "use," a word that implies the preferential subordination of some conditions or outcomes to others — which implies value, in other words. If all that has happened on this planet is the fortuitous colonization of a damp stone by a chemical phenomenon we have called "life," then there is no case to be made for utility. If our myths and truths are only another exotic blossoming, the free play of possibility, then they are fully as real and as worthy of respect as anything else. Or if use or value in this demythologized context signifies the

adaptation of a creature to its circumstances, however gratuitous they may be, then even the universal human predisposition to create and value myths must be assumed to be a form
of adaptation, therefore true in the sense and in the degree
that these myths make an effective response to some exigency
of being.

It all comes down to the mystery of the relationship between the mind and the cosmos. Those who would employ
reductive definitions of utility or reality credit their own
perceptions of truth with fundamentalist simple-heartedness,
brooking no allusion to complexities and ambiguities and
countervailing experience. But if the mind is able to tell us
what is true, why not credit its attempts at higher truth? And if
its intuitions in these matters seem often to be in error, even to
those who do not by any means wish to dismiss them, are not
its intuitions always very substantially in error even in matters
of science or economics? Is it not in fact a very naive conception of reality, and of its accessibility to human understanding,
that would exclude so much of what human beings have always found meaningful, as if by this means fallibility or error
or delusion could be localized and rejected?

It seems to me that there is now the assumption of an
intrinsic fraudulence in the old arts of civilization. Religion,
politics, philosophy, music are all seen by us as means of consolidating the power of a ruling elite, or something of the kind.
I suspect this is a way of granting these things significance,
since we are still in the habit of attending to them, though
they are no longer to be conceded meaning in their own
terms. If they have, by their nature, other motives than the
ones they claim, if their impulse is not to explore or confide
or question but only to manipulate, they cannot speak to us
about meaning, or expand or refine our sense of human expe-

rience. Economics, the great model among us now, indulges and deprives, builds and abandons, threatens and promises. Its imperium is manifest, irrefragable — as in fact it has been since antiquity. Yet suddenly we act as if the reality of economics were reality itself, the one Truth to which everything must refer. I can only suggest that terror at complexity has driven us back on this very crude monism. We have reached a point where cosmology permits us to say that everything might in fact be made of nothing, so we cling desperately to the idea that something is real and necessary, and we have chosen, oddly enough, competition and market forces, taking refuge from the wild epic of cosmic ontogeny by hiding our head in a ledger.

I want to overhear passionate arguments about what we are and what we are doing and what we ought to do. I want to feel that art is an utterance made in good faith by one human being to another. I want to believe there are geniuses scheming to astonish the rest of us, just for the pleasure of it. I miss civilization, and I want it back.

I propose that we look at the past again, because it matters, and because it has so often been dealt with badly. I mean the past as a phenomenon has been dealt with badly. We have taken too high a hand with it. By definition it is all the evidence we have about ourselves, to the extent that it is recoverable and interpretable, so surely its complexities should be scrupulously preserved. Evidence is always construed, and it is always liable to being misconstrued no matter how much care is exercised in collecting and evaluating it. At best, our understanding of any historical moment is significantly wrong, and this should come as no surprise, since we have little grasp of any present moment. The present is elusive for the same reasons as is the past. There are no true boundaries around it, no limit to the number of factors at work in it. When contact between indigenous people in America and the earliest European explorers led to the catastrophic destruction of the native population of this continent by disease, on one side there were whatever transient circumstances of climate or geology permitted and then prevented the movement of people between the Americas and Eurasia; and, on the other side, the Crusades, the plagues, the development of dense urban civilizations in Europe, every circumstance that had toughened Europeans to pathogens that would be deadly to people with another history. As European "history," this depopulation was not intended, understood, or remembered. Yet it is certainly fair to assume that the history of European settlement of North America, with all that has entailed, would have been radically different if there had been twenty times as many indigenous people here to resist the encroachment. We now can easily imagine someone somewhere urging along mutation in a bacterium with the thought of improving an industrial process or carrying out some limited, decisive act of war. We can imagine an error, and unintended consequences on a global scale. Modern economic, political, and technological history would be fully implicated in that event. The idea that all history is parochial should be understood to mean only that all history is defective. It must not be taken to justify the very kind of error that makes the enterprise so often futile or dangerous, and surely not to suggest that the problem can be solved or avoided, rigorous as the attempt to do so must be.

I do not wish to suggest in these essays that the past was better than the present, simply that whatever in the past happens to have been of significance or value ought to be held in memory, insofar as that is possible, so that it can give us guidance. Then, too, nostalgia, reaction, and denial, all of which assume a meaningful sense of the past, are potent energies in any civilization at any time. To be sane and manageable they ought to have a solider base than unconstrained fantasy, or prejudice or malice or tendentiousness. This is as much as to say that truth should be adhered to, to the very significant degree that truth can be established. The recovery of the past is now treated as an arcane science, a little like the science that provides the newspapers with a steady stream of diets and cures and newly identified syndromes in terms of which we are to reform our lives and revise our understanding of ourselves. We are content not to know how the discovery is made that yogurt promotes longevity, for example, or that Jefferson was insensitive to the issue of slavery. We are always happy to assume objectivity and competence, though each dazzling hypothesis awaits displacement by the next, the whole project somehow deriving prestige from its very insubstantiality. Meanwhile, many myths abide, so firmly established in the common mind that no one thinks to challenge them, not even the people who write history. This is not a new phenomenon. History has always been self-serving, polemical, and, very often, simply slovenly. The historians I will look at in the course of this introduction satisfy any ordinary definition of cultural literacy, even to the point of illustrating its perils. So when I find fault I am not suggesting decline. The vices of the present appear in many cases to be failed correctives to the vices of the past.

It has formed some part of my intention in these essays to raise very fundamental questions about the way our intellectual life, in the narrowest and also the widest sense, has been lived and is being lived now. I am not alone in finding it short on substance, even though some part of it is sternly devoted to the rectification of old wrongs, and some part to the rehabilitation of old values. In this culture, we do depend heavily on the universities to teach us what we need to know, and also to sustain and advance knowledge for the purposes of the society as a whole. Surely it was never intended that the universities should do the thinking, or the knowing, for the rest of us. Yet this seems to be the view that prevails now, inside and outside the academy.

I do not wish to imply that the universities constitute an elite, as they are often said to do. On the contrary. A politician who uses a word that suggests he has been to college or assumes anyone in his audience has read a book is ridiculed in the press not only for pretentiousness but for, in effect, speaking gibberish. Many editors are certain that readers will be alarmed and offended by words that hint at the most ordinary learning, and so they exercise a kind of censorship which is not less relentless or constraining for being mindless. Language which suggests learning is tainted, the way slang and profanity once were. Rather than shocking, it irks, or intimidates, supposedly. It is not the kind of speech anyone would think to free because it is considered a language of pretension or asserted advantage. People writing in this country in the last century used a much larger vocabulary than we do, though many fewer of them and their readers were educated. I think it is the association of a wide vocabulary with education which has, in our recent past, forbidden the use of one. In other words, the universities now occupy the place despised classes held in other times and cultures in that they render language associated with them unfit for general use.

So the universities have become hermetic. At the same time they have lost confidence and definition. Perhaps because the universities preside over our increasingly protracted adolescence, and are associated with the arbitrary chores of grade-getting, and with football and parties, the stigma which has long attached to any book or poem read in high school has spread to the curriculum of the colleges. Graduate students talk of Dickens seminars in which nothing of Dickens is read, art history seminars in which no art is looked at. It is as if these were subjects we master and advance beyond, and would be embarrassed to return to, like freshman composition. The curriculum itself is not the issue. However a curriculum is put together, its elements are assumed to satisfy standards which distinguish them as especially significant products of civilization. The problem is that there is something about the way we teach and learn that makes it seem naive to us to talk about these things outside a classroom, and pointless to return to them in the course of actual life. In other words, whatever enters the curriculum becomes in some way inert.

What used to be meant by "humanism," that old romance of the self, the idea that the self is to be refined by exposure to things that are wonderful and difficult and imbued with what was called the human spirit, once an object of unquestioned veneration, has ended. Both institutional education and all the educating aspects of the civilization — journalism, publishing, religion, high and popular culture — are transformed and will be further transformed until the consequences of this great change have been absorbed. Education as it was practiced among us historically reflected its origins in the Renaissance, when beautiful human creations were recovered from the obscurity of forgotten languages and lost aesthetics, or of prohibition or disapprobation or indifference, and were used to demonstrate the heights which human beings can attain. It is not unusual now to hear religion and humanism spoken of as if they were opposed, even antagonistic. But humanism clearly rested on the idea that people have souls, and that they have certain obligations to them, and certain pleasures in them, which arise from their refinement or their expression in art or in admirable or striking conduct, or which arise from finding other souls expressed in music or philosophy or philanthropy or revolution.

When people still had sensibilities, and encouraged them in one another, they assumed the value and even the utility of many kinds of learning for which now we can find no use whatever. It was not leisure that was the basis of culture, as many have argued, but the profoundly democratic idea that anyone was only incidentally the servant of his or her interests in this world; that, truly and ideally, a biography was the passage of a soul through the vale of its making, or its destruction, and that the business of the world was a parable or test or temptation or distraction and therefore engrossing, and full of the highest order of meaning, but in itself a fairly negligible thing.

Literacy became virtually universal in Western civilization when and where it began to seem essential for people to be able to read the Bible. All the immeasurable practical benefits that came with mass literacy, its spectacular utility, awaited this unworldly stimulus. Clearly mere utility is not sufficient to sustain it at even functional levels, though the penalties of illiteracy are now very severe. Reading, above the level of the simplest information, is an act of great inwardness and subjectivity, and this is why and how it had such a profound meaning while it did — the soul encountered itself in its response to a text, first Genesis or Matthew and then *Paradise Lost* or *Leaves of Grass.* Great respect for the text and great respect for, and pleasure in, the reader's subjectivity flourished together. Now they are disparaged together. Dickens must pass through a filter of specialists who can tell us what we must see when we read him. Neither his nor our singularity is of value, nor are we to imagine his spirit acting on ours.

The idea is very well established now that people have areas of competence from which they should not wander, and into which others should not stray. This results in a sort of intellectual desertification, an always more impoverished stock of ambient information to give context to any specific work. For those of us who live in the atmospheres of general educated awareness, and form our views of the world from what we find in respectable nonspecialist sources — and this means every expert of every kind whenever he or she is reading outside his or her area of expertise — the dearth of good information must necessarily be reflected in false assumptions brought to bear within areas of presumed competence. Americans are astonished to realize that Karl Marx and Abraham Lincoln were contemporaries, let alone that Lincoln and much of literate America would have read Marx, who published articles on European affairs for years in Horace Greeley's *New-York Daily Tribune,* and that Marx wrote about Lincoln. They are amazed that Marx also wrote a contemporary account of the Civil War, passionately taking the side of the North. This is only one illustration of the great fact that we have little sense of American history in the context of world history. Given our power and influence, which seem only to grow as disorder and misfortune afflict so many populations, it seems a sad failure that we have not done more to make the world intelligible to ourselves, and ourselves to the world. Shared history is certainly one basis for understanding.

Our Pilgrims, for example, were at least the fourth Calvinist settlement to be attempted in the New World. Three French attempts at colonization had been undertaken half a century earlier, one in Brazil and two in Florida. Jean Cauvin, whom we call John Calvin, was a Frenchman, and his influence was felt first in France. Calvinism was a singularly international movement because its adherents were often forced to seek shelter outside their own countries. Over time, there were Dutch exile churches in England, Italian and French and Dutch exile churches in Germany, French and English exile churches in Switzerland, English exile churches in Holland, French exile churches in England. When the Pilgrims and the Puritans came to North America, they were reenacting a highly characteristic pattern that the people with whom they identified had already carried on for two generations. It is important to our understanding of our origins to realize that they were precisely not provincial, or bound by one cultural perspective, but were a late offshoot of a religious and intellectual movement which arose and developed in continental Europe.

If history has any meaning or value, as we must assume it does, given our tendency to reach back into the past (or what we assume to have been the past) to account for present problems, then it matters to get it right, insofar as we can. Granting the problems of history, some are less insuperable than others. We may never know the full consequences of the introduction of the potato into Europe, or appreciate as we should the impact of a trade route or a plague. We can, however, read major writers, and establish within rough limits what they did and did not say. Since Plato and Aristotle, the names of major writers have been a sort of shorthand for cultural history. While the significance of such figures has its limits, it is also true that their influence has been very great indeed — certainly considerable enough to warrant our reading them. Think how much less stupefying the last fifty years might have been if people had actually read Marx. It seems to have been regarded as a species of disloyalty to acquaint oneself with the terms of that catastrophic argument that engrossed the world for so long, except by the people who called themselves Marxists. And they pioneered this strange practice, so prevalent now, of reading *about* a writer they did not read. They wrote about Marx endlessly, in language arcane and abstruse as his never was, and at the same time astonishingly devoid of basic information, for example about what he wrote and where he was published, and how long and how widely the terms now associated with him were in use before he adopted them. And now that we are supposedly talking to the Russians about democracy, how useful it would be if anyone had actually read Jefferson, or Lincoln.

In several of the essays in this book I talk about John Calvin, a figure of the greatest historical consequence, especially for our culture, who is more or less entirely unread. Learned-looking books on subjects to which he is entirely germane typically do not include a single work of his immense corpus in their bibliographies, nor indicate in their allusions to him a better knowledge than folklore can provide of what he thought and said. I have encountered an odd sort of social pressure as often as I have mentioned him. One does not read Calvin. One does not think of reading him. The prohibition is more absolute than it ever was against Marx, who always had the glamour of the subversive or the forbidden about him. Calvin seems to be neglected *on principle*. This is interesting. It is such a good example of the oddness of our approach to history, and to knowledge more generally, that it bears looking into. Everything always bears looking into, astonishing as that fact is.

History has a history, which is not more reassuring nor less consequential than the figures and events it records or constructs or reconstructs, or erases. Calvin, whoever he was and is, walked in the fires of controversy and polemic for centuries, flames of a kind that generally immortalize rather than con-

sume. Yet Calvin somehow vanished. If history means anything, either as presumed record or as collective act of mind,
then it is worth wondering how the exorcism of so potent a
spirit might have been accomplished, and how it is that we
have conspired in knowing nothing about an influence so profound as his is always said to have been on our institutions, our
very lives and souls.

The British historian Lord Acton, writing at the beginning
of this century, did not perform this feat of exorcism alone,
but it is fair to assume that he had a hand in it, because his
influence was very great. In a book titled *History of Freedom*
he included "The Protestant Theory of Persecution," an essay
which asserts that Protestantism and especially Calvinism are
uniquely associated with illiberalism and repression. He argues
— more precisely, he declares — that, while Protestants did
not in fact engage in persecution at nearly the same rate
Catholics did, their theology required it, while Catholic theology did not. Therefore Protestantism is peculiarly the theology
of persecution.

Whether this argument would have merit in any case is a
question which will be subordinated here to the question of
the adequacy of the writer's apparently elaborate demonstration that there really was a "theory of persecution" in Protestant theology, and especially in Calvin's writings. One is
staggered at first by the amount of sheer Latin in Acton's
footnotes, which might be taken to imply rigor, and a facility
with this formidable tongue sufficient to make him indifferent to the existence of some very serviceable translations of
Calvin's Latin writings into English. Acton was famous in his
time for his great erudition. But if one's eye happens to rest for
just a moment on this effusion of fine print, the most terrible
doubts arise. For example, the following statement rests on a
passage from *Institutes of the Christian Religion,* Calvin's first and

most famous work of theology. The passage, which Acton cites in a footnote, absolutely does not justify Acton's characterization of Calvin's thought, and is in fact famous or notorious for saying precisely the opposite of what Acton implies it says in the following account of it.

> Calvin was as positive as Luther in asserting the duty of obedience to rulers irrespective of their mode of government. He constantly declared that tyranny was not to be resisted on political grounds; that no civil rights could outweigh the divine sanction of government; except in cases where a special office was appointed for the purpose. Where there was no such office — where, for instance, the estates of the realm had lost their independence — there was no protection. This is one of the most important and essential characteristics of the politics of the reformers. By making the protection of their religion the principal business of government, they put out of sight its more immediate and universal duties, and made the political objects of the State disappear behind the religious end. A government was to be judged, in their eyes, only by its fidelity to the Protestant Church. A tyrannical prince could not be resisted if he was orthodox; a just prince could be dethroned if he failed in the more essential condition of faith.

And more to the same effect. But here is the passage from Calvin quoted in Acton's footnote. I include in italics the paragraph which immediately precedes it in the *Institutes,* because it is highly germane, and I supply language Acton omitted from the passage itself, also in italics, insofar as the difference in word order between the Latin and the translation allows them to be set apart.

But however these deeds of men [that is, the overthrow of Old Testament kings] *are judged in themselves, still the Lord accomplished his work through them alike when he broke the bloody scepters of arrogant kings and when he overturned intolerable governments. Let the princes hear and be afraid.*

But we must, in the meantime, be very careful not to despise or violate that authority of magistrates, full of venerable majesty, which God has established by the weightiest decrees, even though it may reside with the most unworthy men, who defile it as much as they can with their own wickedness. For, if the correction of unbridled despotism is the Lord's to avenge, let us not at once think that it is entrusted to us, to whom no command has been given except to obey and suffer.

I am speaking all the while of private individuals. For if there are now any magistrates of the people, appointed to restrain the willfulness of kings (as in ancient times the ephors *were set against the Spartan kings or the* tribunes *of the people against the Roman consuls or the* demarchs *against the senate of the Athenians* and perhaps, as things now are, such power as the three estates exercise in every realm when they hold their chief assemblies), I am so far from forbidding them to withstand, in accordance with their duty, the fierce licentiousness of kings, *that, if they wink at kings who violently fall upon and assault the lowly common folk, I declare that their dissimulation involves nefarious perfidy, because they dishonestly betray the freedom of the people of which they know that they have been appointed protectors by God's ordinance.*

Obviously, there is no mention of institutional religion here at all, and certainly not of the Protestant Church, which, at the time Calvin wrote these paragraphs, could hardly be said to have existed, and never did exist as the monolith Acton seems to conjure. The justifications given here for resistance to tyranny are precisely political — defense of "the freedom of the people." Since he finds his chief examples of "magistrates of the people" in pagan governments, clearly Calvin does not consider the political state essentially Christian, let alone Protestant, nor imagine that God acts only to vindicate the rights of the church. Calvin does not discuss the consequences of the absence of offices entrusted by God with the defense of the people, as Acton implies; instead he says the three estates "in every realm" hold the power of restraining kings, and must assert it. Acton's interpretation of the passage is fanciful at best, and could be used as evidence that his Latin was really very poor, if his deletions were not so effectively deployed to disguise the actual drift of Calvin's argument.

The footnote does draw attention to the fact that the long sentence which ends the second Latin paragraph quoted by Acton concludes with the word *veto*. This is a rhetorical strategy of emphasis and irony. *Veto* is the word the Roman tribune of the people spoke to forbid an action of the Senate which he took to be hostile to the interests of the plebeians. In this instance Calvin says *non veto*, "I do not forbid" — the action of a senate in defense of the "lowly common folk." This is curious language from Calvin, who makes very little use of the first person, and who, as a young fugitive writing anonymously, was hardly in a position to forbid or assent to anything. The use of the word here could be a joke, or a threat, or a promise, or all three at once. In using it, Calvin puts himself in the role of a pagan and entirely political "magistrate of the people."

Since Acton's subject is the history of freedom, it is as the enemy of freedom that Calvin is especially reviled by him. He says, ". . . [Calvin] condemned all rebellion on the part of his friends, so long as there were great doubts of their success. His principles, however, were often stronger than his exhortations, and he had difficulty in preventing murders and seditious movements in France. When he was dead, nobody prevented them, and it became clear that his system, by subjecting the civil power to the service of religion, was more dangerous to toleration than Luther's plan of giving to the State supremacy over the Church." This erudite man would have known that Calvinists never controlled the French "civil power," that the civil power served religion precisely in destroying Calvinists, just as it had always served religion in destroying heretics and dissenters.

Acton was an English Catholic reared in Italy. His mother and wife and a significant part of his education were German. He was the student and friend of Johann von Döllinger, a Munich professor and church historian famous for his attacks on the papacy, which were occasioned by the promulgation of the doctrine of papal infallibility in 1870. Acton also strongly opposed this doctrine, though he did not leave the church, as Döllinger did, to join the Old Catholic movement which arose in Germany at that time. He did, however, end the publication of an important English Catholic journal, which he edited, rather than accede to the claim of the church that Catholic writers must be governed by its views and teaching. Döllinger, who trained Acton in new German historical methods, was the author of books on Luther and the Protestant Reformation which are said to be very severe. Aside from the direct influence of Döllinger's work on Acton, the fact that both of them were vehemently critical of their own church might have predisposed them to emphasize their ultimate loyalty by engaging in still more vehement criticism of other churches. Acton wrote to William Gladstone, hyperbolically, that in the Catho-

lic church "[w]e have to meet an organized conspiracy to establish a power which would be the most formidable enemy of
liberty as well as of science throughout the world." To be worse
than this, the other traditions would have to have been very
bad indeed.

I suspect Acton's influence may be reflected at least indi-
rectly in Jonathan Israel's *The Dutch Republic: Its Rise, Greatness, and
Fall 1407–1806* (1995). In his discussion of the Dutch War of Independence from Spain, Israel says:

> 'Freedom' was adopted by William the Silent and his
> propagandists as the central justifying principle of the Re-
> volt against Spain. In his manifestos of 1568, explaining his
> taking up arms against the legitimate ruler of the Nether-
> lands, William referred, on the one hand, to the Spanish
> king's violation of the 'freedoms and privileges' of the
> provinces, using 'freedom' in this restricted sense; but he
> also claimed to be the defender of 'freedom' in the ab-
> stract, in the modern sense. He maintained that the people
> had 'enjoyed freedom in former times' but were now be-
> ing reduced to 'unbearable slavery' by the king of Spain.

Though Calvinism played a decisive role in the origins and
history of the Dutch Republic, no work of Calvin's appears in
Israel's bibliography. Presumably he is unaware that he has
described precisely the kind of revolt justified by Calvin in the
passage from the *Institutes* quoted above. He attributes to Calvinism the influence of "clear doctrines," but it seems not to
have occurred to him to wonder what the content of those
doctrines might have been. But the shadow of presumed Calvinist illiberalism — Acton says "the order it defended or
sought to establish was never legitimate or free" — hovers

over his interpretation of the culture of the Republic. The point is made repeatedly that the famous liberty of the Dutch had its dark side — on one hand, women may have enjoyed unprecedented status, freedom of movement, and autonomy, but, on the other hand, prostitution was suppressed. It seems we are always obliged to choose our poison.

Simon Schama, in *The Embarrassment of Riches: An Interpretation of Dutch Culture in the Golden Age* (1988) also assumes Calvinist illiberalism, and assigns the enlightened aspects of the culture to other influences. He says, for example, "Calvinist suspicions and anxieties did not . . . monopolize the cultural response to Jews and Judaica. Humanist scholars, many of whom were busy reviving Hebrew as one of the three indispensable classical languages, were capable of softening the divisions between one faith and another in the interests of scholarly community." He would have learned from closer acquaintance with the history of the Reformation period that the study of Hebrew was a religious and especially a Calvinist discipline. It was Calvin himself who instituted the study of the three languages in the academy that he established for the training of clergy in Geneva years before there was a Dutch Republic. Ministers educated in his tradition studied Hebrew as a part of their training until the middle of the present century. Schama's characterization of the Calvinist view of the Old Testament is thoroughly misinformed, nor is there any sign elsewhere of acquaintance with the theology. No work of Calvin's is listed in his bibliography.

Acton's influence is very visible in the work of the prolific American religious historian Roland H. Bainton. In an essay titled "Protestant Persecutors," published in 1935, his nine-page discussion of Calvin is fortified, to all appearances, by sixty-eight footnotes, almost all of them simply citations of volume and page numbers in the *Calvini Opera,* the forbidding nine-teenth-century Swiss edition of his complete works in the original Latin and French. By comparison, Acton seems tenderly solicitous of the reader. Of the three discussions of Calvin in English cited by Bainton, one is an article of his own and another is Acton's *History of Freedom.* Almost all the rest are in German, which tends to disguise the fact that Calvinism has had a long and uniquely significant history in English-language culture and theology, reflected not least in the availability of translations of most of the texts Bainton refers to. Bainton is writing for Americans, who then still included the largest concentration of Calvinists ever to exist on earth, as he would have known, being himself a Congregationalist. Yet he writes as if he were describing a theology and an ethos not only wholly alien to them but also beyond their competence, over their heads. This Duke-and-the-Dauphin style of scholarship is really very funny. We can see in it the importance of the persistence of yokelism among us, and of our ever unbridled deference in the face of pretension.

Bear in mind that Calvin approved the execution of *only one man* for heresy, the Spanish physician known as Michael Servetus, who had written books in which, among other things, he attacked the doctrine of the Trinity. One man is one too many, of course, but by the standards of the time, and considering Calvin's embattled situation, the fact that he has only Servetus to answer for is evidence of astonishing restraint. Consider Luther and the Peasants' War. Consider the Inquisition. Out of this anomaly, this one execution, has come all the writing about Calvin's zeal for persecution, till he above all others is associated with it. Bainton says, "Calvin brought Protestant persecution to a head. He began where Luther left off. Euphemisms disappeared. Calvin did not pretend that persecution is not constraint of conscience. He did not worry about any conscience save his own which compelled him to vindicate the divine majesty." He continues, "Heresy was for him, as for the Middle Ages, a sin against Christendom . . . He felt as keenly as Augustine the sin of schism and could not but regard heresy as an offense against Christian society." But Bainton offers no evidence that anyone else took another view. "Heresy" is, after all, a word freighted with just such assumptions.

Geneva in the time of Calvin had in fact reformed its laws so that religious infractions could not receive a penalty harsher than banishment. Servetus came there perhaps for this reason, having escaped from imprisonment by the Inquisition in Vienne. (Oddly, this escape is one of the things he was charged with in Geneva.) Then the Genevans broke their own law by trying and burning him. Disheartening as that fact is, it nevertheless indicates that Calvinist Geneva was eschewing a practice which was, and for centuries had been, commonplace all over Europe — as Geneva was well aware, since their coreligionists elsewhere were chief among those being burned.

Bainton sees Calvin's use of the Old Testament as a device for evading the Sermon on the Mount — "The gentle Savior who said, 'Love your enemies' was prefigured by David, who sang 'Do I not hate them, O Lord, that hate Thee?'" Bainton says, "This resort to the Old Testament necessitates also a picture of God as ruthless and arbitrary . . . In the service of such a God we must crush all considerations of humanity." This is, of course, Bainton's reading of the Old Testament, certainly not Calvin's, and it is an alarmingly hostile one. Calvin wrote a commentary on Psalm 139, the psalm which Bainton quotes here. In it he says, "We are to observe . . . that the hatred of which the Psalmist speaks is directed to the sins rather than the persons of the wicked. We are, so far as in us lies, to study peace with all men; we are to seek the good of all, and, if possible, they are to be reclaimed by kindness and good offices: only so far as they are enemies to God we must strenuously confront their resentment." He says, "David's example should teach us to rise with a lofty and bold spirit above all regard to the enmity of the wicked, when the question concerns the honour of God, and rather to renounce all earthly friendships than falsely pander with flattery to the favour of those who do everything to draw down upon themselves the divine displeasure." Surely it is fair to wonder why Bainton did not consult the *Calvini Opera* before denouncing Calvin's bloody-mindedness. A better scholar would certainly have known that this verse was not traditionally taken to "crush all considerations of humanity." Augustine wrote a gloss on the psalm also. He takes David to mean, "I hated in them their iniquities, I loved Thy creation. This it is to hate with a perfect hatred, that neither on account of the vices thou hate the men, nor on account of the men love the vices."

Bainton does note that Calvin would not countenance the breaking of icons, an excess sometimes engaged in by people who claimed his influence. He notes that Calvin restrained the Comte de Coligny, a powerful supporter in France, from acting to defend the Protestants there by saying, "Better that we should perish a hundred times than that the name of Christianity and the Gospel should be subject to such a reproach." Yet he says, "If Calvin ever wrote anything in favor of religious liberty it was a typographical error," like Acton, offering no instance of his supposed frothing intolerance except the trial and execution of Michael Servetus.

Acton worked free of what might seem to be the common-sense connection between the tendency of a theology to encourage persecution and the actual numbers of the victims of its agents and enthusiasts. Historically speaking, this is a non-sensical way to proceed. I suspect it has its origins not in comparative religion — if either Acton or Bainton were competent to make meaningful comparisons, they were not inclined to make them — but in those new German historical methods that were so influential at the time. Max Weber, perhaps the most effectively dismissive of all the writers on Calvinism, was another exponent of these new methods. His *The Protestant Ethic and the Spirit of Capitalism* associated Calvinism with a joyless, ascetic acquisitiveness, which, so long as it had a basis in theology, reflected anxiety about one's salvation, and, when it lost its religious rationale, outlived it joylessly, making of modern life an iron cage, an insupportable tedium. Weber allows that there has been capitalism since Babylon. In his view Calvinists did not invent it, but they accelerated its development. They created its modern *spirit* with their asceticism, their anxiety for worldly proof of divine favor, their adaptation of Luther's concept of vocation to create a powerful work ethic. (Curiously, Weber ranks beside these influences certain advances in methods of bookkeeping.) His proof of a special relationship between Calvinists and capitalism was that in Germany, at the time he wrote, Calvinists were more prosperous than Lutherans and Catholics, and were overrepresented in the universities and the professions. A yet more brilliant sociologist might have found other possible explanations for these facts.

By comparison with Lutherans, Calvinists lack *gemütlichkeit* — they are not good fellows. Weber says you can see this in their faces. This is the new historical method. This is how *spirit* becomes a term suitable for use in economic analysis. I suppose I am unfair in saying that for Weber a prejudice is a proof. He offers none of the usual criticisms of capitalism in itself — that it is exploitive, that it is crisis prone, that it creates extremes of wealth and poverty. His criticism is that, in its "modern" form, those who prosper from it do not enjoy their prosperity. He knows and says that Calvin did not encourage the accumulation of wealth, and that he insisted the "church" — in this sense, the elect — do not prosper in this world. He does what Acton does. They both argue that a social group defined by them as the people who adhere to or have been acculturated by a particular theology, are, with generalizable and world-historical consistency, peculiarly inclined to behave in ways precisely contrary to the teaching of that theology — tolerantly, in Acton's case (though he would never acknowledge that, in practical terms, a relative disinclination to persecute does equal tolerance), and, in Weber's case, acquisitively and in the manner of those attempting to achieve salvation by works — the very thing Calvin strove most ardently to discourage. For Acton, the supposed spirit of the theology makes the actual conduct of Calvinists in the world of no account. For Weber, the supposed spirit in which they act in the world makes the theology of no account. Surely it is fair to wonder if any of this amounts to more than personal animus — which was the preferred historical method of much of the Western world at the beginning of this bitter century.

I know Weber's book has been long and widely thought to merit respect. Try as I may, I can find no grounds for this view of it. (He, like Acton, is said to have been spectacularly learned. He wrote analyses of the ethics and social forms of Confucianism, Taoism, Hinduism, Buddhism, and ancient Judaism. But then, if he used the *gemütlichkeit* method, he may have found this fairly light work.) In fairness to Weber, he considered his conclusions in *The Protestant Ethic and the Spirit of Capitalism* to be merely tentative, likely to be superseded when "comparative racial neurology and psychology shall have progressed beyond their present and in many ways very promising beginnings."

In these essays I consider questions that influence, or are influenced by, the way we think about the past, and therefore the present and the future. Cynicism has its proof texts. An important historical "proof" very current among us now is that Thomas Jefferson wrote the Declaration of Independence unconscious of the irony of the existence of slavery in his land of equality. The most ordinary curiosity would be a sufficient antidote to the error of imagining that Jefferson was such a knave or fool as this notion implies. Jefferson attacked slavery as a terrible crime in the first draft of the Declaration, in which he said of the English king:

> He has waged cruel war against human nature itself, violating its most sacred rights of life and liberty in the persons of a distant people who never offended him, captivating and carrying them into slavery in another hemisphere, or to incur miserable death in their transportation thither. This piratical warfare, the opprobrium of INFIDEL powers, is the warfare of the CHRISTIAN king of Great Britain. Determined to keep open a market where MEN should be bought & sold, he has prostituted his negative for suppressing every legislative attempt to prohibit or restrain this execrable commerce.

The passage was edited out before the document was approved, and published by Jefferson in his autobiography, with the remark that its excision was owed to the pusillanimity of the Congress, who feared offending friends in England. If those interested in Jefferson's thought were interested enough to look at what he wrote, they would find the powerful attack on slavery in his *Notes on Virginia,* and more elsewhere to the same effect. Granting the difficulties of the question, it is surely useful to bear in mind that Jefferson, in the Declaration of Independence, did explicitly assert the "sacred rights of life and liberty" of the enslaved people, as an aspect of their human nature. Now he and his period are undergoing aggressive reinterpretation on the grounds that they lacked just this insight, to the disparagement of ideals we once found moving and useful. All this occurs on the strength of seemingly universal ignorance of important and accessible fact, an ignorance which blossoms as quasi-scholarship and seeds the wind. How are we to read someone capable of such gross blindness and hypocrisy as Jefferson must have been? With hostility or condescension, or not at all. More precisely, still not reading him, we will now regard him with ill-informed condescension rather than with our traditional ill-informed respect. This change is already palpable and full of consequence. An honorable ideal sounds to us now like patent self-deceit, like the language of complacent oppression.

Surely it is fair to ask what benefit justifies the polemical use of defective information. For it is characteristic of the long campaign of dysphemism otherwise known as the public discussion of American history that its tone is one of a moral superiority to its subject so very marked as to make ridiculous any other view of a matter than the one that is most effectively dismissive — Thoreau's mother laundered his shirts. A complex view of history must necessarily reincorporate in it lovely and creditable things, simply because the record attests to them, as well as to venality and hypocrisy and vulgarity. It is clearly true that the reflex of disparagement is no more compatible with rigorous inquiry than the impulse to glorify. And it is simply priggish to treat ambiguity as a synonym for corruption.

Once, and for millennia, people painted human figures on their jars, carved them into their city gates, made pillars and pilasters of them, wove them into tapestries, painted domed heavens full of them, made paintings of them bent over books or dreaming at windows or taking their ease on the banks of rivers. Human figures decorated lamp stands and soup tureens and the spines of books. Now they seem never to be used decoratively, as things pleasing in themselves. Advertising uses them to part us from our money, implying that we should compare ourselves and our lot to the supposedly acquirable condition of well-being these insinuating images represent to us. They are vendors or cadgers who, in their subtler way, only want to get a foot in the door. We defend ourselves from the appeal they have for us, just as, if they were flesh, we would resist, or take offense at, their earnest gaze and their firm handshake.

It seems to me that, when we lost our aesthetic pleasure in the human presence as a thing to be looked at and contemplated, at the same time we ceased to enjoy human act and gesture, which civilization has always before found to be beautiful even when it was also grievous or terrible, as the epics and tragedies and the grandest novels testify. Now when we read history, increasingly we read it as a record of cynicism and manipulation. We assume that nothing is what it appears to be, that it is less and worse, insofar as it might once have seemed worthy of respectful interest. We routinely disqualify testimony that would plead for extenuation. That is, we are so persuaded of the rightness of our judgment as to invalidate evidence that does not confirm us in it. Nothing that deserves to be called truth could ever be arrived at by such means. If truth in this sense is essentially inaccessible in any case, that should only confirm us in humility and awe.

DARWINISM

AMERICAN CULTURE has entered a period in which atavism looks to us for all the world like progress. The stripping away of humane constraints to liberate great "natural" forces, such as capital flow or the *(soi-disant)* free market, has acquired such heady momentum that no one even pauses to wonder whether such forces are indeed particularly "natural." The use of the word implies a tendentious distinction. Billions of dollars can vanish into the ether under the fingers of a bad young man with a dark stare, yet economics is to be regarded as if it were lawful and ineluctable as gravity. If the arcane, rootless, disruptive phenomenon we call global economics is natural, then surely anything else is, too.

Rivers flow to the sea — this fact implies no obligation on our part to abet them in it, to eliminate meanders and flood plains. If economics were natural in this sense, presumably moderating, stabilizing mechanisms would be intrinsic to its systems. But economics is simply human traffic in what people make and do and value and need, or think they need, a kind of epitome of civilization. It is the wealth of nations, and also their fraudulence and malice and vainglory. It is no more reliably benign or rational than any other human undertaking. That is to say, it requires conscious choice and control, the making of moral and ethical judgments.

Primitive, sometimes called classical, economics has long lived symbiotically with Darwinism, which sprang from it. Darwinists have always claimed that they were simple scientists, pursuing truth even in the face of outrage and rejection, even at the cost of dispelling myths upon which weaker souls preferred to remain dependent. It seems fair to allow that Darwinism might have evolved long enough on its own to have become another species of thought than the one in which it had its origins, though nature provides no analogy for change of that kind. Yet we find the recrudescence of primitive economics occurring alongside a new prominence of Darwinism. We find them separately and together encouraging faith in the value of self-interest and raw competition. Furthermore, we find in them certain peculiar assumptions which are incompatible with their claims to being objective, freestanding systems. One is progressivism, which is implied everywhere in primitive economics, and denied everywhere in contemporary Darwinism.

The idea of progress implies a judgment of value. We are to believe the world will be better if people are forced into severe and continuous competition. If they work themselves weary making a part for a gadget assembled on the other side of the earth, in fear of the loss of their livelihoods, the world will be better for it. If economic forces recombine and shed these workers for cheaper ones, the world will be still better. In what sense, better? To ask is to refuse to accept the supposedly inevitable, to deny the all-overriding reality of self-interest and raw competition, which will certainly overwhelm us if we allow ourselves some sentimental dream of a humane collective life. This economics implies progress and has no progress to show.

Contemporary Darwinism shuns the suggestion that the workings of natural selection are progressive, perhaps in resistance to the old error of assuming that humankind is the masterpiece of evolution. To do so would be to discover special value in peculiarly human attributes, to suggest, for example, that mind is something toward which evolution might have tended. That would be to legitimize the works of the mind, its most characteristic intuitions, concerning, for example, ethics and religion. Yet we are told by Darwinists to celebrate the wondrous works of natural selection, the tangled bank. Its authority must be received, its truth made the measure of all truth, because heaven and earth are full of its glory. To claim creation as the signature act of whatever power one prefers is clearly to overstep the bounds of scientific discourse. The intention is to demonstrate that there are emotional satisfactions in this worldview, which is at least to acknowledge the claims of one distinctively human longing. Characteristically, however, Darwinists, like primitive economists, assume that what is humane — I use the word here, unexceptionably, as I believe, to mean whatever arises from the desire to mitigate competition and to put aside self-interest — is unnatural, and therefore wrong.

The debate between Darwinism and religion is and has always been very strange. I wish to make a distinction here between evolution, the change that occurs in organisms over time, and Darwinism, the interpretation of this phenomenon which claims to refute religion and to imply a personal and social ethic which is, not coincidentally, antithetical to the assumptions imposed and authorized by Judaeo-Christianity. Darwin's theory was published in 1859, two years before the inauguration of Abraham Lincoln. His achievement would be impressive if even a tiny core of scientific insight survived such an explosion of new understanding of the nature of things as has occurred in the last century and a half. It is important to remember, however, that evolution as I have defined it was observed and noted even in antiquity. In 1850 Alfred Tennyson had published *In Memoriam,* the long poem in which he ponders the dark implications of an evolutionary origin of man and creation, and arrives at a reconciliation of this theory with a new understanding of divine providence. In 1852 Matthew Arnold published "Empedocles on Etna," in which evolution is represented as exposing religion as mere human illusion. The tendency to confuse Darwin with Prometheus obscures the fact that his ideas, too, have an ancestry, and an evolution, and, most certainly, a genus.

What, precisely, this theory called Darwinism really is, is itself an interesting question. The popular shorthand version of it is "the survival of the fittest." This is a phrase coined by the so-called Social Darwinist, Herbert Spencer, in work published before the appearance of the *Origin of Species* and adopted — with acknowledgment of Spencer as the source — in later editions of Darwin's book. There is an apparent tautology in the phrase. Since Darwinian (and, of course, Spencerian) fitness is proved by survival, one could as well call the principle at work "the survival of survivors." This is not, strictly speaking, tautological, if the point is to bless things as they are, insofar as they are a matter of life and death. (The words "competition" and "struggle" are grossly euphemistic, since what is being described in Thomas Malthus's *Essay on the Principle of Population* [1798], the winnowing that inspired Darwin, was the withholding of very meager sustenance from those who would die without it. Nothing more heroic was called for than closing one's hand, or turning one's back, both of them familiar and congenial exercises in Darwin's time, and both of them what Spencer was commending when he coined this phrase.)

If we are to take this notion of natural selection as a chaste, objectively functioning scientific principle, however, the issue of tautology is not so easily resolved. Since those who are alive tend to make up the majority of any population, one cannot really be surprised to find their traits predominant, and their offspring relatively numerous. At the same time, one cannot be sure that they have not found the broad path to extinction, like so many creatures before them, doomed by traits that cannot at this moment be called incompatible with their survival, given the fact of their survival. In other words, the theory understood in these terms is notably weak in its ability to generalize, describe or predict. Life forms do change, and there is an orderliness in their existence over time, notably in the phenomenon of species, whose origins Darwin did not, in fact, explain, or even claim to have explained. That the drifting of the forms of life corresponds in significant ways to the drift of the content or configuration of their genetic endowment is not a fact whose meaning is self-evident. The change to be observed is change, not necessarily refinement or complication, and not even adaptation, because it is often maladaptive. In *The Descent of Man*, Darwin notes, "Natural Selection acts only tentatively." Behold the great Law that governs nature.

It appears to me that the conjunction which allowed evolution to flourish as Darwinism was the appropriation of certain canards about animal breeding for the purpose of social criticism, together with a weariness in European civilization with Christianity, which did cavil, if anything did, at the extraordinary cruelty of industrial and colonial civilization. Malthus wrote his *Essay on the Principle of Population* to demonstrate the harmful consequences of intervening between the poor and their death by starvation. In his *Autobiography,* Darwin says:

> [In 1838] I happened to read for amusement [!] Malthus on *Population,* and being well prepared to appreciate the struggle for existence which everywhere goes on from long-continued observation of the habits of animals and plants, it at once struck me that under these circumstances favourable variations would tend to be preserved, and unfavourable ones to be destroyed. The result of this would be the formation of new species. Here, then, I had at last got a theory by which to work . . .

It would appear he made Malthus's grim thesis, that alleviation of misery only results in greater misery, darker still by concluding that those who die deserve to, as the embodiments of unfavorable "variations." In *The Descent of Man* he treats human fecklessness as atavism, and perhaps that is part of what he means here. But as a consequence of the progressive character of change brought about by the process of destruction he describes as occurring within and between populations, survival is always a function of *relative* fitness. There is no such thing as intrinsic worth. No value inheres in whatever is destroyed, or destructible. In *Origin of Species* he says:

> In each well-stocked country natural selection acts through the competition of the inhabitants, and consequently leads to success in the battle for life, only in accordance with the standard of that particular country. Hence the inhabitants of one country, generally the

smaller one, often yield to the inhabitants of another and generally the larger country. For in the larger country there will have existed more individuals and more diversified forms, and the competition will have been severer, and thus the standard of perfection will have been rendered higher.

Those who have wondered how it can be that larger countries so consistently dominate smaller ones will find their answer here — bigger countries have better people in them. Insights like this one must have sweetened the pill of Darwinism considerably for those among the British who felt any doubts about the glory of Empire. Especially to be noted is the progressivist spin Darwin puts on Malthus. A more populous country implies for him one in which there is more severe attrition, therefore a more highly evolved people. That is to say, success depends not on numbers but on the severity of competition that is the presumed consequence of large population. Brutal conditions at home legitimize domination abroad. Surely this is the worst of all possible worlds. But my point here is that the idea of progressive evolution through natural selection occurred to Darwin as a consequence of reading about endemic starvation in the populations of wealthy countries. He elaborated it into a theory of national aggression.

If Darwin retreated, in one context or another, from the assertion that there is in fact such a thing as progress in evolution among the plants and animals, he nevertheless consistently assumed that human beings were "perfected" by the struggle for survival. In *The Descent of Man* he makes quite clear what form this progress takes. He says:

At some future period, not very distant as measured by centuries, the civilized races of man will almost certainly exterminate, and replace, the savage races throughout the world. At the same time the anthropomorphous apes . . . will no doubt be exterminated. The break between man and his nearest allies will then be wider, for it will intervene between man in a more civilized state, as we may hope, even than the Caucasian, and some ape as low as a baboon, instead of as now between the negro or Australian and the gorilla.

Darwin speaks frequently about higher and lower races of man, and he also says that there is little difference in mind or temperament among the races of men. Mind is not a consideration for him, so this causes him no embarrassment. It is true of Darwinism in general that the human mind, and those of its creatures which are not compatible with the Darwinist worldview, are discounted as anomaly or delusion. Elsewhere Darwin remarks, with striking obduracy, "If man had not been his own classifier, he would never have thought of founding a separate order for his own reception." The fact that we alone are capable of describing order in nature is not a significant distinction in his view, but instead a source of error, even though the human brain is taxonomically singular, and should therefore set us apart if our sciences and civilizations did not. Darwin freely concedes to the savages (as to the ants) courage and loyalty and affection. He describes an anthropologist's overhearing African mothers teaching their children to love the truth. These things do not affect the confidence with which he assigns them to the condition of inferiority, which for him is proved by their liability to extermination by the civilized races.

In his useful book, *Darwinian Impacts: An Introduction to the Darwinian Revolution* (1980), D. R. Oldroyd, defending the phrase "survival of the fittest" from the charge that it is tautological, proposes that the reader "consider a simple case of natural selection arising from the struggle for existence." It is the "struggle" that led to the extermination of the native people of Tasmania by European settlers in the nineteenth century. "One group (to their lasting *moral,* but not biological shame) survived; another group failed to survive. Surely it is perfectly clear that this may be explained in terms of some criterion of fitness (say the possession of fire-arms) that is quite separate from the *contingent* fact that the Europeans *did* survive. Thus we can readily see this example as an empirical exemplification of the principle of natural selection or the survival of the fittest." He goes on to discuss the change in coloration of the English peppered moth, omitting to provide the list of contributions made by Anglo-Tasmanians to global well-being which might assuage our doubts about the persuasive force of this simple case, this systematic destruction of unarmed people. Darwinism is, intrinsically, a chilling doctrine.

Rejection of religion was abroad in Europe in the nineteenth century, just as evolution was. Ludwig Feuerbach and Friedrich Nietzsche are two noted debunkers who flourished in Darwin's lifetime, and Karl Marx is another. Marx, the gentlest of them, said, "*Religious* suffering is at the same time an expression of real suffering and a *protest* against real suffering. Religion is the sigh of the oppressed creature, the sentiment of a heartless world, and the soul of soulless conditions. It is the *opium* of the people." Whether the protest against suffering makes suffering harder to relieve, as he argues, or simply makes it harder to ignore, weariness with the sigh of the oppressed creature is easy to document in the thought of the time, and the mode or avenue of such sentiment was religion.

Whether Darwin himself intended to debunk religion is not a matter of importance, since he was perceived to have done so by those who embraced his views. His theory, as science, is irrelevant to the question of the truth of religion. It is only as an inversion of Christian ethicalism that it truly engages religion. And in those terms it is appropriately the subject of challenge from any humane perspective, religious or other. Insofar as ethical implications are claimed for it, it is not science, yet historically it has sheltered under the immunities granted to science. The churches generally have accepted the idea of evolution with great and understandable calm. The God of Abraham, Isaac, and Jacob, or of Luther, Calvin, and Ignatius of Loyola, or of Dietrich Bonhoeffer, Simone Weil, and Martin Luther King, is no Watchmaker. To find him at the end of even the longest chain of being or causality would be to discover that he was a thing (however majestic) among things. Not God, in other words. Daniel Dennett's *Darwin's Dangerous Idea* (1995) declares from its irksomely alliterative title onward that the complex of assertions I have described as Darwinism is vigorously alive. Dennett asks, "If God created and designed all these wonderful things, who created God? Supergod? And who created Supergod? Superdupergod? Or did God create himself? Was it hard work? Did it take time?" This is my point precisely. It is manifestly not consistent with the nature of God to be accessible to description in such terms. Even Dennett, who appears to have no meaningful acquaintance with religious thought, is clearly aware that to speak of God in this way is absurd.

If one looks at the creation narrative in Genesis one finds no Watchmaker, as the Darwinists would have us believe, but a God who stands outside his creation, and calls it into being by, in effect, willing its existence. This terse account does as little to invoke the model of a human artisan as it could do. The creation and blessing of everything, from light to the great sea creatures to whatever creeps on the earth, is done in the same formulaic terms. It all has the same origin, and it is all good. There is no suggestion of hierarchy in the order in which things come into being any more than in the language that names them, with the exception of man/woman, who are made in God's image and given dominion over the rest of creation.

The narrative stabilizes essential theological assertions, first of all, that God is not embodied in any part of creation. He is not light, nor is he the sun, as the gods of other ancient peoples were thought to be. He is in no sense limited or local. He is not the force of good or order struggling against forces of evil or chaos, but the sole creator of a creation that is in whole and in part "very good." There are no loci of special holiness, humanity aside, and nothing evil or alarming or unclean. The sun and moon are simply "lights" and the markers of days and seasons. The alternation of day and night are not the endless recurrence of a terrifying primal struggle but the frame of a great order, identified by the repeated reference to evening and morning with the ordering of creation itself. All these things articulate a vision of being which is sharply distinct from those expressed in competing ancient cosmogonies. The narrative, with its refrain, tells off the days in a week, and culminates in the Sabbath, which is, therefore, as fundamental a reality as creation itself. It is as if God's rest were the crown of his work. This is a very powerful statement of the value of the Sabbath, so essential to the life of the Jews, and it seems to me it probably accounts for the fact of the narrative's describing creation as the business of a week.

Certainly this cosmogony describes a natural order which is freestanding and complete, with rainfall and seasons established, as well as the fecundity of all living things. In *Human, All Too Human,* Nietzsche says:

In the imagination of religious people all nature is a sum-
mary of the actions of conscious and voluntary creatures,
an enormous complex or *arbitrariness.* No conclusion may
be drawn with regard to everything that is outside of us,
that anything will *be* so and so, *must* be so and so; the
approximately sure, reliable are *we,* — man is the *rule,* nature is *irregularity* —

This statement is wrong, point for point, as a characterization of the world of the Genesis cosmogony, which is not
in the least degree animistic or demon-haunted or dependent
for its functioning on divine intervention. If ancient people had
consciously set out to articulate a worldview congenial to science, it is hard to imagine how, in the terms available to them,
they could have done better. And in fact, Judeo-Christian culture has been uniquely hospitable to science.

But the point to be stressed is that religious people — by
definition, I would say — do not look for proof of the existence
of God, or understand God in a way that makes his existence
liable to proof or disproof. It is naive to talk about proof in that
way, which is why Darwinists need not apologize for their
failure to prove the existence of the process of natural selection, which they freely concede they have not done. That attempts at proofs of God's existence have been made from time
to time, under the influence of the prestige of Aristotle, or of
early science, does not mean that religious belief has sought or
depended on that kind of affirmation, as any reader of theology
is well aware. Faith is called faith for a reason. Darwinism is
another faith — a loyalty to a vision of the nature of things
despite its inaccessibility to demonstration.

The Creationist position has long been owned by the Religious Right, and the Darwinist position by the Irreligious Right.

The differences between these camps are intractable because they are meaningless. People who insist that the sacredness of Scripture depends on belief in creation in a literal six days seem never to insist on a literal reading of "to him who asks, give," or "sell what you have and give the money to the poor." In fact, their politics and economics align themselves quite precisely with those of their adversaries, who yearn to disburden themselves of the weak, and to unshackle the great creative forces of competition. The defenders of "religion" have made religion seem foolish while rendering it mute in the face of a prolonged and highly effective assault on the poor. The defenders of "science" have imputed objectivity and rigor to an account of reality whose origins and consequences are indisputably economic, social, and political.

Creationism is the best thing that could have happened to Darwinism, the caricature of religion that has seemed to justify Darwinist contempt for the whole of religion. Creationism has tended to obscure the fact that religion — precisely as the hope of the powerless and the mitigator of the abuse of the weak — has indeed come under determined attack by people who have claimed the authority of science, and that Darwin's work was quite rightly seized upon by antireligionists who had other fish to fry than the mere demystification of cosmogony. I am speaking, as I know it is rude to do, of the Social Darwinists, the eugenicists, the Imperialists, the Scientific Socialists who showed such firmness in reshaping civilization in Eastern Europe, China, Cambodia, and elsewhere, and, yes, of the Nazis. Darwin influenced the nationalist writer Heinrich von Treitschke and the biologist Ernst Haeckel, who influenced Hitler and also the milieu in which he flourished.

If there is felt to be a missing link between Darwinism and these distinctive phenomena of modern history, it is because we pretend that only Darwin's most presentable book would have had circulation and impact. Reading *The Descent of Man,* one finds Darwin the obsessive taxonomist marveling that Hindus, who are apparently so unlike Europeans, are in fact also Aryans, while Jews, who look just like Europeans, are in fact Asiatics. This sort of language is a reminder of the kind of thinking that was going on in Europe at that time, which Darwin's cheerful interest in the extermination of races, and his insistence on ranking races in terms of their nearness to the apes, could only have abetted.

Daniel Dennett alludes delicately to the sources and history of Darwin's thesis. He says, "The grim Malthusian vision of his social and political forces that could act to check human overpopulation may have strongly flavored Darwin's thinking (and undoubtedly has flavored the shallow political attacks of many an anti-Darwinian) [Shallow? Gentle reader, is this sufficient? Is this fair?], but the idea Darwin needed from Malthus is purely logical. It has nothing at all to do with political ideology, and can be expressed in very abstract and general terms." The idea Darwin took from Malthus was of a continuous cull. Darwin's understanding of the phenomenon was neither abstract nor general. The economic and social programs which claim the authority of Darwin have tended to apply this idea, in one way or another, to human society, in a manner he himself might well have approved, considering that he discovered it in its application to human society. The notion that this idea could have "nothing at all to do with political ideology," presumably because it is "purely logical," is the thinking of a true fundamentalist. Dennett seems unaware that zealots of every sort find every one of their tenets purely logical. Discussing the ongoing Malthusian "crunch," which means that only some organisms in a population will leave progeny, Dennett says:

Will it be a fair lottery, in which every organism has an equal chance of being among the few that reproduce? In a political context, this is where invidious themes enter, about power, privilege, injustice, treachery, class warfare, and the like, but we can elevate the observation from its political birthplace and consider in the abstract, as Darwin did, what would — must — happen in nature.

This language is evasive, and also misleading. As we have seen, if by nature we are to understand the nonhuman world, that is by no means the only setting in which Darwin saw his principle at work. If, as Darwin argues, the human and nonhuman worlds are continuous and of a kind, then Dennett implies a distinction that is in fact meaningless. Since Dennett insists that an ethic is to be derived from Darwinism, our concern is not properly with what happens in nature — since, in any case, it *must* happen — but with the interactions among people in society, concerning which choice is possible. I think we all know that we cannot look to nature for a model, unless we are able to find equity in predation, as, in this century particularly, certain people have in fact claimed to do.

The notion of "fitness" is not now and never has been value neutral. The model is basically physical viability, or as the political economists used to say, physical efficiency. In *The Descent of Man,* Darwin says:

> With savages, the weak in body or mind are soon eliminated; and those that survive commonly exhibit a vigorous state of health. We civilized men, on the other hand, do our utmost to check the process of elimination; we build asylums for the imbecile, the maimed, and the sick; we institute poor laws; and our medical men exert their ut-

most skill to save the life of everyone to the last moment. There is reason to believe that vaccination has preserved thousands who from a weak constitution would formerly have succumbed to smallpox. Thus the weak members of civilized society propagate their kind. No one who has attended to the breeding of domestic animals will doubt that this must be highly injurious to the race of man. It is surprising how soon a want of care, or care wrongly directed, leads to the degeneration of a domestic race; but excepting in the case of man himself, hardly anyone is so ignorant as to allow his worst animals to breed.

This is pure Malthus. So is the demurral: "[We could not] check our sympathy, even at the urging of hard reason, without deterioration in the noblest part of our nature . . . We must therefore bear the undoubtedly bad effects of the weak surviving and propagating their kind . . ." None of this is abstract or general or innocent of political history or implication. The *Descent of Man* (1871) is a late work which seems to be largely ignored by Darwinists now. The persistence of Malthusian influence in such explicit form indicates not only the power but also the meaning of its influence in Darwin's thinking. And of course its relevance is clearer when Darwin has turned his gaze, as Malthus did, to human society.

It does bear mentioning in this context that the full title of his first book is *On the Origin of Species by Means of Natural Selection, or the Preservation of Favoured Races in the Struggle for Life*. However generously this title is interpreted, clearly it does not assume that biological systems evolve by chance and not design, as Darwin is always said to have done. It clearly implies that whatever is is right, and — even less tenably — that whatever is is the product of raw struggle, and — still less tenably —

that there is a teleology behind it all, one which favors and preserves. Darwinists seem unable to refrain from theology, as the supplanters of it. The old God may have let the rain fall on the just and the unjust alike, but this new god is more implacable in his judgments, and very straightforward, killing off those who die, to state the matter baldly. What need of this theology except to imply that there is wisdom and blessing and meaning in "selection," which the phenomenon itself does not by any means imply? If the temperature on earth rose or fell by five degrees, this same god would curse where he had cherished and love what he had despised, which is only to say that natural selection must indeed be thought of as blind, from the preserving and favoring point of view, if consistency is to be respected at all.

Surely we must assume that a biosphere generated out of any circumstances able to sustain life is as good as any other, that if we make a desert of this planet, for example, and the god of survival turns his countenance upon the lurkers and scuttlers who emerge as fittest, under the new regime, we can have no grounds for saying that things have changed for the worse or for the better, in Darwinist terms. In other words, absent teleology, there are no grounds for saying that survival means anything more or other than survival. Darwinists praise complexity and variety as consequences of evolution, though the success of single-celled animals would seem to raise questions. I am sure we all admire ostriches, but to call a Darwinist creation good because it is credited with providing them is simply another version of the old argument from design, proving in this use of it not the existence of God but the appropriateness of making a judgment of value: that natural selection, whose existence is to be assumed, is splendid and beneficent, and therefore to be embraced.

I am aware that many Darwinists do not argue that the complexity of organisms is a mark of progress in evolution, yet the idea is implicit in their model of adaptation. It is difficult to read about an amoeba, or for that matter a hydrogen atom, without beginning to doubt the usefulness of the word "simplicity." Rather, the universe itself seems to have evolved so far beyond simplicity, before there was any planet Earth or any sun to rise on it, that the only question is, how will complexity be manifest? Shut up in a cell or a spore, it is clearly still complexity. In other words, there is something archaic in the Darwinist assumption that there was anything simple to begin from, and that complexity was knocked together out of accident and circumstance, as a secondary quality of life. And it is consistent with this same archaism that its model for interaction among creatures is simpler than anything to be found anywhere in experimentally accessible nature. In considering how a black hole might lose mass, the simplest account is to be preferred, no doubt. But this is simplicity of a very rarefied kind. We are of one substance with these roaring phenomena our mathematics stumbles in describing.

In any case, the passage from *The Descent of Man* quoted above, which undertakes to account for the physical superiority of the savages, suggests extraordinary limits to Darwin's powers of observation and reflection. If it was true, so far into the era of the contact of savages and Europeans, that the health of the former was still comparatively good, it was true despite the disasters of invasion and colonization and slavery and the near and actual extinctions on this continent and elsewhere brought about by the introduction of European diseases. Darwin notes these effects of the contact of civilized and savage at length in other contexts. He is remarkably inconsistent. He assumes elsewhere, as I have noted, that it is the high rate of attrition within nations that makes them successful in their "struggles" with the less-favored races.

And if it was true that savages throve relatively well it was because they did not live in their own filth in vast conurbations, did not breathe air heavy with brown coal smoke, did not expose themselves to lead or mercury or phosphorus poisoning, did not hold torches to the feet of children to force them to crawl up narrow chimneys or set five-year-olds to work in factories or brickyards, did not sell one another opium tonic to hush the crying of babies. Malthus pondered at length the fact that the mass of the population of Europe, and especially Britain, lived continuously in a state of near starvation. There were two instances of outright famine in Ireland, an agricultural country, in the first half of Darwin's century. In neither case did any crop fail but potatoes, the staple food of the poor, who were virtually the whole of the population. Vastly more than adequate food to end the famine was exported for sale by nonresident landowners while death by starvation swept over the country. Relief was given only to those who had eaten the potatoes they would have put aside to plant a new crop, so the famine went on and on. No doubt the fittest survived, scrawnier for the experience, and not terribly presentable by comparison with the savages. Darwin is simply repeating a commonplace in finding benevolence the villain in the matter of European "degeneracy." History does not at all support the idea that benevolence was ever an important enough phenomenon to have done measurable harm, if, for the sake of argument, we concede it that power.

That human beings should be thought of as better or worse animals, and human well-being as a product of culling, is a willful exclusion of context, which seems to me to have remained as a stable feature of Darwinist thought. There is a worldview implicit in the theory which is too small and rigid to accommodate anything remotely like the world. This is no doubt true in part because acknowledging the complexity of the subject would amount to acknowledging the difficulty of demonstrating the usefulness of the theory. Those best suited to survive do no doubt survive in their descendants, all things being equal, as they rarely are. The point is that, in the matter of interpretation, judicious and dispassionate consideration of all factors would be required to establish with certainty why an organism seems to be successful in evolutionary terms in any specific case. While Darwin argues, in one context, that traits such as generosity and self-sacrifice enhance group survival, though not the survival of the individual organism, in others he clearly sees these same traits as defeating the process of selection at the level of the social group. In the first instance he wishes to prove that such motives and emotions are biologically based and analogous with those of animals because they promote survival, and in the second to argue that their effect is contrary to the workings of nature because it prevents the elimination of the weak or defective. His conclusions seem merely opportunistic. Contemporary Darwinism appears generally to discount group survival as a factor in the operations of natural selection.

Darwinism is harsh and crude in its practical consequences, in a degree that sets it apart from all other respectable scientific hypotheses; not coincidentally, it had its origins in polemics against the poor, and against the irksome burden of extending charity to them — a burden laid on the back of Europe by Christianity. The Judeo-Christian ethic of charity derives from the assertion that human beings are made in the image of God, that is, that reverence is owed to human beings simply as such, and also that their misery or neglect or destruction is not, for

God, a matter of indifference, or of merely compassionate interest, but is something in the nature of sacrilege. Granting that the standards of conduct implied by this assertion have rarely been acknowledged, let alone met, a standard is not diminished or discredited by the fact that it is seldom or never realized, and, especially, a religious imperative is not less powerful in its claims on any individual even if the whole world excepting him or her is of one mind in ignoring it and always has been. To be free of God the Creator is to be free of the religious ethic implied in the Genesis narrative of Creation. Charity was the shadow of a gesture toward acknowledging the obligations of human beings to one another, thus conceived. It was a burden under which people never stopped chafing — witness this unfathomably rich country now contriving new means daily to impoverish the poor among us.

Darwinism always concerns itself with behavior, as the expression of the biological imperatives of organisms. Though, historically, it is truer to say that this feature of the theory arose from rather than that it ended in a critique of traditional ethical systems, Darwinism is still offered routinely as a source of objective scientific insight on questions like the nature of human motivation and the possibility of altruism. As I have said, the views of contemporary adherents on these matters are darker than Darwin's own. The theory has been accommodated to Mendelian genetics, yielding the insight that it is not personal but genetic survival for which the organism strives, a refinement which does not escape the tautology implicit in the popular version of the theory, but does add a little complexity to the myth of the battle of each against all, which, however it may thrill sophomores, cannot account for the existence of social behavior in animals. The redefinition of survival enlarges the theater of possible selfish behavior. "Selfish" is a word apologists use without hesitation or embarrassment, because they remain committed to the old project of transforming values, and therefore still insist on using ethically weighted language in inappropriate contexts. It is no more "selfish" for an organism to abide by its nature, whatever that is, than for an atom to appropriate an electron. Certainly finding selfishness in a gene is an act of mind which rather resembles finding wrath in thunder.

In any case, the slightly expanded definition of selfishness is not without problems. This would be a somewhat sweeter world than the one we have if it were true among human beings, at least, that the flourishing of kin and offspring were nearer our hearts than any other interest. As it is, I propose that since this hypothesis cannot survive the evidence to be gathered from reading any newspaper, it ought not to be allowed too great an influence in the formation of social policy. Anecdotal evidence is of the highest order of relevance — evidence gathered inductively would be a better phrase, if the mass of relevant data were not infinitely great, therefore peculiarly vulnerable to misinterpretation as a result of the design of specific inquiries or of bias in the observer, and therefore not really deserving of a more dignified name than anecdote. Studies that proceed by excluding variables are of no use in discovering patterns that signify adaptation to the complexities of the natural order. In zoos we can learn little more than that animals experience boredom and depression.

Observations of human behavior can only be meaningful if they are made in real-world conditions, with an understanding of all factors at play in every instance, and on a scale great enough to allow for every sort of deviation of individuals and groups, and their circumstances, from what might be appropriately described as a norm. To do this would be impossible, of course. But surely science cannot extrapolate with authority from evidence which is only what happens to be available, especially when its appropriateness as evidence is very doubtful. Cats and dogs are quite closely related, but a lifetime of studying dogs would not qualify anyone to speak with authority on the ways of cats. So with the whole earthly bestiary which has been recruited to the purposes of the proper study of mankind.

I fell to pondering Darwinism while reading an essay by Robert Wright in *Time,* in an issue of the magazine that featured Bill Moyers's televised discussions of the Book of Genesis. Wright's essay, titled "Science and Original Sin," delivers the "verdict of science" on human nature, while generously allowing that the biblical view is not entirely misguided. I would never wish to suggest that Wright speaks for science, a word he uses synonymously with Darwinism. His essay is mired in logical problems virtually sentence by sentence. But its appearance in a major mass publication, offered as an antidote, apparently, lest we be misled by the respectful attention paid to Genesis into forgetting that Science had displaced its fables with Fact and Truth, indicates the persisting importance of the theory, and the form in which it has its life among the general literate public.

The essay is full of Darwinian eccentricities. Wright says, "Such impulses as compassion, empathy, generosity, gratitude and remorse are genetically based. Strange as it may sound, these impulses, with their checks on raw selfishness, helped our ancestors survive and pass their genes to future generations." To whom on earth would this sound strange except to other Darwinists? Most human beings live collaboratively and have done so for millennia. But Darwinists insist that "selfishness" is uniquely the trait rewarded by genetic survival. So while Wright does concede a biological basis to the traits we call humane and civilized, he puts them in a different category from the more primary traits (in his view) of selfishness and competition. It is not at all clear to me how some biologically based survival mechanisms have priority over others. Wright goes on to say, as Darwinists do, that we are kind to our kin, those custodians of our genetic immortality. "This finickiness gives our 'moral' sentiments a naturally seamy underside. Beneath familial love, for example, is malice toward our relatives' rivals." So our beguiling attributes can be reduced to the little meanness that governs all. It seems inevitable that, over time, doctrines and worldviews would recruit those to whom they make sense, who would therefore, generation after generation, and given the tendency of creatures to herd with their kind, become less and less capable of assuming a posture of critical distance. I cannot report from my own experience and observation that the malice he describes underlies family love. There is a tendency to consider, as he does in this case, pathological behavior as the laying bare of impulses that are in fact universal, so that any quantity of data can be refuted by a single example of behavior that would seem to illustrate his point. This kind of thinking makes all experience that contradicts its assumptions into the product of illusion or self-deception. A splendid way to win every argument.

The idea of illusion is very important to Darwinian thinking, and I am at a loss to understand how it can function legitimately in a Darwinist context. It is often used to reinterpret behavior to make it consistent with the assumptions of the observer. Wright says that when we send money to help victims of a famine on another continent, our "equipment of reciprocal altruism . . . is being 'fooled' by electronic technology into (unconsciously) thinking that the victims of famine are right next door and might someday reciprocate." Well, perhaps. This may be truer of Wright's equipment than of mine. The elaboration of this nonsensical machinery, whose function, I would suggest, is not the behavioral one of converting selfishness into generosity but the rhetorical one of converting generosity into selfishness, looks to me like anything but science. If behavior is genetically based, then the only insight one can have into the content of the genes that govern behavior is in manifest behavior, which, like it or not, includes generosity.

Wright does make one very valuable point. He says, "There remains one basic, unbridgeable divergence between religious doctrine and Darwinism: according to *Genesis,* nature is in essence benign . . . Only when man fell to temptation did the natural world receive a coating of evil. But according to Darwinism, the evil in nature lies at its very roots, instilled by its creator, natural selection. After all, natural selection is chronic competition untrammeled by moral rules. Heedless selfishness and wanton predation are traits likely to endure. If these things are sins, then the roots of sin lie at the origin — not just of humankind but of life." In the degree that we have persuaded ourselves of the truth of this peculiar "science," we have lost a demiparadise, in which there was a knowledge of good as well as of evil. I do not intend this as a defense of religion. I do not share the common assumption that religion is always in need of defending. What is needed here is a defense of Darwinism.

Why generosity and morality, whose ordinary, commonplace utility need hardly be defended, should be given secondary and probationary status is a question I think is best answered in terms of the history of Darwinism, or of the kind of thinking of which it is one manifestation. Utility, after all, should be a synonym for benefit, from the point of view of promoting survival. And behaviors should be looked at indifferently for their survival value, not screened to assure that they satisfy the narrowest definition of self-seeking before they can be regarded as natural and real. The rejection of religion by Darwinism is in essence a rejection of Christian ethicalism, which is declared to be "false" in terms of a rhetoric that pointedly precludes or disallows it. This is manifestly illogical.

Daniel Dennett quotes Friedrich Nietzsche frequently and with admiration as a writer with a profound understanding of Darwinist thinking and its implications. He deals with the problem of the historical consequences of Nietzsche's work by remarking that he "indulged in prose so overheated that it no doubt serves him right that his legion of devotees has included a disreputable gaggle of unspeakable and uncomprehending Nazis." Elsewhere he says, combining optimism with understatement, "fortunately few find [Nietzsche's idea of a will to power] attractive today." The following is a passage from Nietzsche's *Ecce Homo:*

> Let us look a century ahead, let us suppose that my *attentat* on two millennia of anti-nature and the violation of man succeeds. That party of life which takes in hand the greatest of all tasks, the higher breeding of humanity, together with the remorseless destruction of all degenerate and parasitic elements, will again make possible on earth that *superfluity of life* out of which the dionysian condition must again proceed. I promise a *tragic age:* the supreme art in the affirmation of life, tragedy, will be reborn when mankind has behind it the consciousness of the harshest but most necessary wars *without suffering from it* —

Nietzsche's many defenders always scold as naive the suggestion that he should be taken to mean what he says, that he is not just being "overheated." What is most striking to me is the profound similarity between this language and Darwin's in *The Descent of Man.* Not that Nietzsche had to know Darwin's work directly. I do not wish to blame Darwin for Nietzsche, and there is no need to. This passage is entirely conventional except for the detail of heroizing the unpoetic business of breeding and, especially, culling.

One Nazi who was surely comprehending, and who still seems to be highly reputable — I use the term "Nazi" in the strict sense, to mean a member of the Nazi Party in the time of Hitler and an active supporter of his regime — is the Darwinian biologist Konrad Lorenz. In 1943 Lorenz wrote about the decline of humans in civilization: "In a very short time the degenerative types, thanks to their larger reproductive rates and their coarser competitive methods toward the fellow members of the species, pervade the Volk and the state and lead to their downfall, for the same biological reasons that the likewise 'asocial' cells of a cancerous growth destroy the structure of the cellular state." In 1940 he wrote: "From the very beginning the Nordic movement has been emotionally opposed to this 'domestication' of humankind, all its ideals are such as would be destroyed by the biological consequences of civilization and domestication I have discussed." In 1973 he wrote:

It is one of the many dilemmas into which mankind has maneuvered itself that here again, what humane feelings demand for the individual is in opposition to the interests of mankind as a whole. Our sympathy with the asocial defective, whose inferiority might be caused just as well by irreversible injury in early infancy as by hereditary defects, endangers the security of the nondefective. In speaking of human beings, even the words 'inferior' or 'valuable' cannot be used without arousing the suspicion that one is advocating the gas chamber.

How true. I quote Lorenz only to illustrate that his views can be derived from Darwin or from Nietzsche with equal plausibility. The fact that these ideas are fully within the intellectual range of the average blowhard is very far from exculpating their distinguished proponents.

The "two millennia of anti-nature" of which Nietzsche speaks is the Christian era. They are to be undone through "remorseless destruction," making up for time lost, presumably, to the practice of mercy while that myth held sway. I hope for the sake of Christianity that it was indeed a constraint on cruelty, on balance. Certainly it was often enough a pretext for it. The thing to note here is that it is not the failure of Christianity but its success, in terms of its own highest values, for which it is despised. And it is despised because it is "anti-nature," that is, it has fostered degeneracy and parasitism. The antireligious animus is directed at a "falseness" which inhibits the instinct of cruelty. It is another expression of the belief — for which no proof is imaginable — that human goodness is not natural, and therefore is neither beneficial, nor, if the truth were known, even truly good. This is the impetus of the attack on religion, the rejection of the belief, encoded in the terms of myth, that goodness is not only present in creation but is the essence of it. This attack is an impulse of fierce, fastidious aversion directed at humankind, which alone is capable of "degeneracy."

Let us, as a thought experiment, imagine that all those disreputable Nazis who admired Nietzsche were not uncomprehending after all; that, being culturally and historically closer to Nietzsche than Daniel Dennett, and intimate with his language, they were actually the better interpreters. Let us say that they found in passages like the one quoted above an imperative to act as the agents of nature and to effect the splendid restoration foreseen by Nietzsche. The result was, of course, a hideous crime, which issued in so many kinds of catastrophe that we will never see the end of them. History would then have demonstrated, certainly, the superior naturalness of the very values Nietzsche so passionately derides, if naturalness can be taken to imply consistency with the survival of nature. Perhaps we ought not to be treating these questions of value as if they were purely theoretical, but should instead consider drawing tentative conclusions from experience and observation.

Surely it is useful to note affinity. Dennett remarks of Darwin's contemporary and supporter Herbert Spencer that he was responsible for "an odious misapplication of Darwinian thinking in defense of political doctrines that range from callous to heinous." Why do these innocent scientific ideas veer so predictably toward ugliness and evil? I would suggest they do so because they systematically disallow the legitimacy of benign, or for that matter merely neutral, motives and behavior. They are not designed to arrive at any other result. Dennett notes, in his circuitous way, that Darwin did not disavow Spencer, publicly or privately. He interprets this as a regrettable omission. But since Spencer's odious views were already in print while Darwin was still at work on *Origin of Species*, it seems appropriate to consider the implications of the very great probability that influence in fact went from Spencer to Darwin.

Then there is Sigmund Freud, a good Darwinist who has had as much to do with shaping the modern soul as any one man. Himself a compulsive mythologizer, he rejected the myths of Judeo-Christianity, and replaced them with his own luridly dismal accounts of primal cannibalism and so on. In keeping with the absurdity of this strain of intellectual history, this great debunker insists the events he sets at the beginning of human civilization actually happened. In *Civilization and Its Discontents* he says of religion, "Its technique consists in depressing the value of life and distorting the picture of the real world in a delusional manner — which presupposes an intimidation of the intelligence. At this price, by forcibly fixing them in a state of psychical infantilism and by drawing them into a mass-delusion, religion succeeds in sparing many people an individual neurosis. But hardly anything more." It is characteristic of Freud to personify abstractions and to attribute to them motive and strategy. I know of no one else but Hesiod who is so inclined to this way of thinking.

In any case Freud restates the commonplace that religion is delusional, that it is external to the "real world" — though clearly very actively employed in it. And how does this undeluded scientist view the world? Well, "the ego detaches itself from the external world. Or, to put it more correctly, originally the ego includes everything, later it separates off an external world from itself. Our present ego-feeling is, therefore, only shrunken residue of a much more inclusive — indeed, an all-embracing — feeling which corresponded to a more intimate bond between the ego and the world around it." This is the "oceanic feeling" he associates with religion, his version of Wordsworthian clouds of glory. He is expounding romanticism with the poles reversed, so that maturity as "shrunken residue" is a condition superior to the "intimate bond between the ego and the world." Clearly in his own terms it is arbitrary to call one sense of things truer than the other, though it might have seemed daring, and therefore true, in a culture weary of romanticism.

As for the sentimental joy associated with feeling a bond with the world, the Freudian psyche has no place for it. "The program of becoming happy, which the pleasure principle imposes on us, cannot be fulfilled," though we must try. "Happiness, in the reduced sense in which we recognize it as possible, is a problem of the economics of the individual's libido." I will not pause here over the absolute awfulness of this language, a machinery of imposition and imprecision worthy of a Kafka story. I wish only to point out the utter asociality of the self in the Freudian world. Presumably the existence of others is implied in the concept "libido." The Freudian psyche operates under the constraints and imperatives now to be found in the Darwinist's "selfish gene," with the difference that the psyche has no interest in genetic survival. In *The Future of an Illusion,* Freud ridicules the idea that one might love one's neighbor as oneself, a commandment Jesus quotes from Leviticus, on the grounds that it is contrary to human nature. This is the great peculiarity of this school of thought, that it wishes to make an ethic of what it presents as an inevitability, when, if inevitability were a factor, no ethic would be needed.

Freud's star has dimmed, at last. But his theories were propagated so widely for so long, with so great a degree of certainty of their value, that they survive the demise of his reputation and flourish among us as received truths. They are remarkably meager and charmless. Their lack of scientific foundation, their prima facie implausibility, and their profound impact on modern thought, prove together that we can in fact choose myths which will function for us as myths, that is, that will express visions of reality which form values and behavior. This thought is more frightening than reassuring, though if Freud had not been able to adapt the great influence of Darwin and Nietzsche to his purposes, and if they had not themselves been codifiers of widely held attitudes, Freudian theories would never have achieved the status of myth. Since we do in fact have some power of choice, however, what in the world could have moved us to choose anything so graceless and ugly? Darwinians to this day watch for murder in baboon colonies. Altruism was thought to have been sighted among the penguins, but a study of the question found that they did indeed reliably feed their own offspring and not others, so the shimmering possibility of altruism slipped out of our beaks, as it were, and into the arctic waters of the biological imperatives common to humankind and penguins. Surely there was some wisdom in the old story that we are exceptional among the creatures. George Williams, honored among the Darwinists, wonders briefly in his book *Adaptation and Natural Selection* what function there could be for human "cerebral hypertrophy." Obviously it serves to allow us to learn our limitations from the penguins.

Ironically, Darwin, Nietzsche, and Freud have all benefited from a myth of origins. Even now, the idea that they astonished a world of settled belief with brave new insight, and that they dispelled the gloom of an unvalued present life by turning their piercing gaze resolutely to Truth and Nature, makes giants of them — and, more regrettably, makes history a suitable backdrop for this opera, at whatever loss to verisimilitude. In 1932 Albert Einstein wrote an open letter to Sigmund Freud titled "Why War?" In it he asked:

> Is it possible to control man's mental evolution so as to make him proof against the psychoses of hate and destructiveness? Here I am thinking by no means of the so-called uncultured masses. Experience proves that it is rather the so-called "Intelligentzia" that is most apt to yield to these

disastrous collective suggestions, since the intellectual has no direct contact with life in the raw, but encounters it in its easiest synthetic form — upon the printed page.

Freud replied:

We have been guilty of the heresy of attributing the origin of conscience to this diversion inwards of aggressiveness. You will notice that it is by no means a trivial matter if this process is carried too far: it is positively unhealthy. On the other hand if these forces are turned to destruction in the external world, the organism will be relieved and the effect must be beneficial. This would serve as a biological justification for all the ugly and dangerous impulses against which we are struggling. It must be admitted that they stand nearer to Nature than does our resistance to them for which an explanation also needs to be found.

Freud took his heresy from Nietzsche. This account of the origins of conscience was at the center of Nietzsche's theory of the "transvaluation of values," by which the noble types who ruled mankind were made to accept constraints on their behavior by the craftiness of priests. Nietzsche says "*conscience . . . is the instinct of cruelty turned backwards after it can no longer discharge itself outwards. Cruelty here brought to light for the first time as one of the oldest substrata of culture and one that can least be thought away.*" Freud is quoting back to Einstein one of those books which Einstein blames for propagating "disastrous collective suggestions." He is refusing, also, Einstein's characterization of the cult of hate and destructiveness as psychotic — the "organism" will benefit from the release of these impulses upon the "external" world. (It is eerie how alien from the self the world is for Freud.) Pathology is the

consequence of the *restraining* of these impulses. They in themselves are natural and biologically justified.

Note that Freud speaks of humankind as an "organism"
on which conscience is artificially imposed. This implies that
whatever conscience might tell us about obligations to others,
or respect for them, is unnatural and also at odds with our
own well-being. History had proved, and was about to prove
again, that the well-being of human organisms is not served by
the unrestrained release of aggression. It is as if Freud truly
were not persuaded of the reality of the external world, as if he
did not understand the simple fact that aggression is followed
by retaliation in the great majority of cases. And when it is not,
it still impoverishes the world, on which, oceanic feelings aside,
one does indeed depend for what traditionalists would call the
good things in life. As realists would point out, one depends on
it for life itself.

It is bizarre in the circumstances, with the horrors of World
War I a recent memory and the Nazi era under way, that Freud
would consider the attempt to resist hatred and destructiveness to be as much in need of explanation as the desire to act
on them. To say the least, this strongly implies a refusal to find
value in human life. Note that Freud refers the question to
study, to explanation, not to common experience or common
sense or common decency. He is telling Einstein that the "In-
telligentzia" are indeed the appropriate arbiters of these great
questions, no doubt because human beings are misled by
such artificial phenomena as conscience. Einstein's query and
Freud's reply make the politics of this "science" very clear.
Utter moral passivity, and a presumption in favor of aggressive
violence, together with an almost perfect lack of imagination
for the reality of other "organisms" — who can doubt that
Pericles proceeded from other assumptions?

It is a persistent characteristic of the school of thought

called Darwinism to resist finding a biological basis for true social behavior, that is, behavior designed to exploit the benefits and satisfactions of attending to collective well-being, of valuing others irrespective of issues of survival. But then the grievance against civilization from which the theory sprang was precisely that it has prevented survival from being a pressing consideration for many people most of the time. All the forms in which this freedom has been celebrated, all the arts and sciences and philanthropies, are only possible because civilization is intrinsically sociable and collaborative. And human beings everywhere create civilizations. The prophet Zechariah, in his vision of Jerusalem restored, says, "Old men and old women shall again sit in the streets of Jerusalem, each with staff in hand for very age. And the streets of the city shall be full of boys and girls playing in its streets." This fine, plain peace and human loveliness are the things we are learning not to hope for.

For old Adam, that near-angel whose name means Earth, Darwinists have substituted a creature who shares essential attributes with whatever beast has been recently observed behaving shabbily in the state of nature. Genesis tries to describe human exceptionalism, and Darwinism tries to discount it. Since Malthus, to go back no farther, the impulse has been vigorously present to desacralize humankind by making it appropriately the prey of unmitigated struggle. This desacralization — fully as absolute with respect to predator as to prey — has required the disengagement of conscience, among other things. It has required the grand-scale disparagement of the traits that distinguish us from the animals — and the Darwinists take the darkest possible view of the animals. What has been rejected is the *complexity* of the Genesis account, in favor of a simplicity so extreme it cannot — by design, perhaps — deal with that second term in the Biblical view of humankind, our destiny, that is, the consequences of our actions. It is an impressive insight, in a narrative so very ancient as the Genesis account of the Fall, that the fate of Adam is presented as the fate of the whole living world. I have heard people comfort themselves with the thought of the perdurability of cockroaches, a fact which does not confute the general truth of the view that our species is very apt to put an end to life on this planet.

Surely *this* makes us exceptional among the animals. Surely this complicates the idea that we are biologically driven by the imperatives of genetic survival. Surely it also complicates the idea that competition and aggression serve the ends of genetic survival in our case, at least. Perhaps our unique moral capacities were designed to compensate for our singular power to do harm — clearly some corrective has been needed. There is a mad cheerfulness in Darwinism, a *laissez-faire, enrichissiez-vous* kind of optimism that persists with absolutely no reference to history or experience. So we find Freud, in the smoldering ashes of Europe, ready to study the question of why the impulses of hatred and destructiveness should be restrained. We have Robert Wright finding hope for a future Eden of human self-transcendence in the appearance of Buddha (born 563 B.C.E.) and Jesus (born 4 B.C.E.). If the rate of appearance of salvific figures were to have continued without deceleration, there would have been three more by now — which is only to say I find this a frail hope. We have Daniel Dennett and Stephen Jay Gould offering hymns to the new Darwinist vision, as if there were anything the least bit new about it.

Evolution has been debated in America for most of this century in the unfortunate terms of the Scopes trial, in which the State of Tennessee asserted its right to forbid the teaching of Darwinism in the public schools. William Jennings Bryan, lawyer for the prosecution, wrote a concluding statement to the Scopes trial jury, which he did not deliver and which was published after his death. It is an interesting document, a moment worth pondering in the transvaluation of American values. Bryan, a former secretary of state, was a pacifist, an anti-Imperialist and a progressive, and a rapturous Presbyterian. He was a graduate of Illinois College and a product of the near utopian culture of idealism and social reform established in the Middle West in the decades before the Civil War. Religious passion was a great impetus to enlightened reform in that culture, which sprang directly from the Second Great Awakening, and which appealed freely to the Bible to give authority and urgency to its causes. He is described as a populist, which implies some pandering to the mob, but his speeches express a high-mindedness that, especially by present standards, is positively ethereal. To understand the tone of them, it is necessary to remember that his tradition of "fundamentalism" had behind it abolitionism, the higher education of women, and the creation of the public school system. There is a sadness in Bryan's tone, a kind of casting about, that suggests an awareness of the fact that the ethos of reform was dying out, that after almost a hundred years the old biblical language of justice and mercy was finally losing its power.

Bryan won his case, insisting on the right of a Christian populace not to subsidize the teaching of an inimical doctrine. The problems of this approach are obvious, but he was mortally ill and weary and might have done better under other circumstances. His was a Pyrrhic victory if there ever was one, bringing down a torrent of journalistic ridicule that is usually said to have killed him, and appearing to close, from the point of view of intelligent people, an issue that was then and is now very much in need of meaningful consideration. This is not altogether his fault. His argument, putting aside its appeal to religious majoritarianism, anticipates questions Einstein would raise in his letter to Freud a few years later. These are real questions, not to be dismissed by the invocation of science, and not to be ignored because they were posed in terms that seem archaic to us now.

Bryan makes no distinction between evolution and Darwinism, the philosophical or ethical system that has claimed to be implied by evolution. Perhaps the distinction is not important to him because he is a biblical literalist who insists on the truth of the six-day creation. It requires a little effort, that being the case, to remember that his attack on Darwinism came from the *left,* from the side of pacifism and reform. His argument against Darwinism is essentially political (though he does note that the origin of species was not accounted for, or the theory of natural selection demonstrated). Like Einstein, he associated war with the enthusiasms of the intelligentsia, specifically with the huge influence of Friedrich Nietzsche in the universities. We are all familiar with the anomaly of the success of Fascism in the most cultured countries of Europe, with the anomaly of the high percentage of Ph.D.'s in the SS, and with the startling zeal of learned men in pursuing scientific activities of one sort and another meant to affirm the Nazi worldview. Without wishing to seem to descend to shallow rationalism, I propose that there might in fact be a reason for all this — that Einstein, and also Bryan, may have had a point.

Clarence Darrow, the defense attorney in the Scopes trial, had, the previous year, defended Leopold and Loeb, two young men found guilty of the gratuitous murder of a child. Bryan quotes Darrow's arguments in extenuation of the crime. They are rather bizarre, but so were the times. Leopold, he said, as a young university student, had misread Nietzsche, while Loeb was the victim of hereditary criminality, passed down to him by an unknown ancestor. Darrow was eager to concede the brilliance of Nietzsche, although he read to the court passages "almost taken at random" which he felt were liable to such misreading as his "impressionable, visionary, dreamy" client had made of them. He said, "There is not any university in the world where the professor is not familiar with Nietzsche, not one . . . If this boy is to blame for this, where did he get it? Is there any blame attached because somebody took Nietzsche's philosophy seriously and fashioned his life upon it? . . . Your Honor, it is hardly fair to hang a nineteen-year-old boy for the philosophy that was taught him at the university." Darrow hastened to assure the court that he did not blame the philosopher, the professors, or the university.

This is very murky business. Of course it is the duty of a lawyer to make the best defense he can of his clients, and the problem must have been especially difficult in this notorious case, where the accused were gifted and privileged and the crime was without motive in any ordinary sense. Bryan used Darrow's defense of Leopold to argue that schools and universities should not have books in them that might corrupt "the souls entrusted to them." This is clearly the wrong conclusion to draw, though, of course, perfectly consistent with the prosecution of Scopes. But Bryan asks a question that seems, from the perspective of subsequent history, hauntingly prescient "[W]ould the State be blameless if it permitted the universities under its control to be turned into training schools for murderers?" This is a very extreme, almost preposterous question, and yet among the most cultured people in Europe something very like this happened. It was not unforeseen — the "disastrous collective suggestions" of which Einstein spoke flourished among the intelligentsia.

Then what to conclude? What magic is there about the word "modern" that makes us assume what we think has no effect on what we do? Bryan wrote, "Science has made war so hellish that civilization was about to commit suicide; and now we are told that newly discovered instruments of destruction will make the cruelties of the late war seem trivial in comparison with the cruelties of wars that may come in the future." This being true, how could a cult of war recruit many thousands of intelligent people? And how can we now, when the fragility of the planet is every day more obvious, be giving ourselves over to an ethic of competition and self-seeking, a sort of socioeconomic snake handling, where faith in a theory makes us contemptuous of very obvious perils? And where does this theory get its seemingly unlimited power over our *moral* imaginations, when it can rationalize stealing candy from babies — or, a more contemporary illustration, stealing medical care or schooling from babies — as readily as any bolder act? Why does it have the stature of science and the chic of iconoclasm and the vigor of novelty when it is, *pace* Nietzsche, only mythified, respectablized resentment, with a long, dark history behind it?

The strain in Western civilization that is expressed in Malthus/Darwin/Nietzsche/Freud has no place in it for the cult of the soul, that old Jacob lamed and blessed in a long night of struggle. There is a passionate encounter with the cruelty of the world at the center of Judeo-Christian experience. So far as we can tell, only we among the creatures can even form the thought that the world is cruel. We are the species most inclined to adapt the environment to ourselves, so perhaps noting the difference between what is and what, from a human point of view, ought to be, is simply a function of our nature, a recognition of the fact that we have choices, that we can improvise. If, as the Darwinists assure us, there is only the natural world, then nothing can be alien to it, and our arrangements, however extravagantly they depart from the ways of other creatures, can never be called unnatural. It is certainly one of the oddest features of a school of thought that denies human exceptionalism as its first premise that it finds so much of human behavior contrary to nature — and objectionable on those grounds. Such an idea can only have survived as part of a self-declared scientific worldview because it allows the making of value judgments, the oldest project of this line of thought. If life had only such meaning as arose from within it, then people could practice philanthropy and give themselves over to mystical visions and harden themselves to their own interests and passions without fear of rebuke. The persistent use of the idea of unnaturalness by people who insist there is only nature suggests that their model of reality is too constricted to permit even its own elaboration. This is true because it is first of all — as premise, not as conclusion — a rejection of things demonstrably present in the world, for example, human fellow-feeling. The idea of the antinatural, of decadence and priestly imposition, gives Darwinism its character as a cause.

This school of thought — ordinarily referred to as modern thought — tells us nothing more urgently than that we are wrong about ourselves. We are to believe we are the dupes of the very reactions that make us judges of circumstance, and that make us free in relation to it. Obviously, if we must act in our own interest, crudely understood, we have few real options. But if we act from a sense of justice, or from tact or compassionate imagination, then we put the impress of our own sense of things on the external world. If this is another version of the will to power, it is in any case the kind of power that religion, and civilization in its highest forms, has always sought to confer. If this is another version of self-interest, it is also a proof of the fact that the definition of that term is very broad indeed, classically friendly to paradox — "It is more blessed to give than to receive," for example, or "it is in dying we live." This does not by any means imply the moral equality of every act that can be construed as rewarding to the one who carries it out, without reference to its consequences. Nor does it imply that apparently selfless conduct is in fact merely less honest than straightforward selfishness. It means that there are rewards in experience for generosity, probably because it serves the collective well-being, but probably also because it is appropriate to our singular dignity as creatures who can act freely, outside the tedious limits of our own interests.

I am sure I would risk offending if I were to say outright that modern thought is a failed project. Still, clearly it partakes as much of error as the worst thinking it has displaced. Daniel Dennett scolds Judeo-Christianity for Genesis 1:28, in which humankind is given dominion over all the earth, as if it licensed depredation. Notions of this kind go unchallenged now because the Bible is so little known. In the recapitulation of creation that occurs after the waters have receded in the narrative of the Flood (Genesis 9:1–4), people are told, as if for the first time, that they may eat the flesh of animals. It would appear the Edenic regime was meant to be rather mild. And of course the most reassuring images of the lordliness of God in both Testaments describe him as a shepherd. Over against this we have Darwin and Nietzsche with their talk of extermination.

If it is objected — and there would be grounds for alarm if it were not objected — that the passages I have quoted above from Darwin and Nietzsche are misread by those who take issue with them, their defenders must make some little effort to be fair to the context of Genesis. It may be true historically that people have justified brutal misuse of nature on the authority of Genesis 1:28, but it is surely true that they have taken a high hand against the whole of creation on the pretext offered them by "the survival of the fittest" or "the will to power." The verse in Genesis 9 that permits the eating of animals is followed by a verse that forbids the shedding of human blood, pointedly invoking the protection of the divine image. This is the human exceptionalism which Dennett and the whole tribe of Darwinians reject as if on a moral scruple. But its effect is to *limit* violence, not to authorize it.

In nothing is the retrograde character of modern thought more apparent. These ancients are never guilty of the parochialism of suggesting that any ambiguity surrounds the word "human," or that there is any doubt about human consanguinity, though such notions would be forgivable in a people surrounded by tribes and nations with which their relations were often desperately hostile. To say this is to grant what is clearly true, that they often failed to live up to their own most dearly held beliefs. This can be looked at from another side, however. They were loyal over many centuries to standards by which they themselves (though less, no doubt, than humankind in general) were found guilty and wanting. This is a burden they could have put down. It is the burden Western civilization has put down, in the degree that it has rejected the assertion of human uniqueness. Darwin's response to objections to the idea of kinship with monkeys was, better a monkey than a Fuegian, a naked savage.

History is a nightmare, generally speaking, and the effect of religion, where its authority has been claimed, has been horrific as well as benign. Even in saying this, however, we are judging history in terms religion has supplied. The proof of this is that, in the twentieth century, "scientific" policies of extermination, undertaken in the case of Stalin to purge society of parasitic or degenerate or recalcitrant elements, and in the case of Hitler to purge it of the weak or defective or, racially speaking, marginally human, have taken horror to new extremes. Their scale and relentlessness have been owed to the disarming of moral response by theories authorized by the word "science," which, quite inappropriately, has been used as if it meant "truth." Surely it is fair to say that science is to the "science" that inspired exterminations as Christianity is to the "Christianity" that inspired Crusades. In both cases the human genius for finding pretexts seized upon the most prestigious institution of the culture and appropriated a great part of its language and resources and legitimacy. In the case of religion, the best and the worst of it have been discredited together. In the case of science, neither has been discredited. The failure in both instances to distinguish best from worst means that both science and religion are effectively lost to us in terms of disciplining or enlarging our thinking.

These are not the worst consequences, however. The modern fable is that science exposed religion as a delusion and more or less supplanted it. But science cannot serve in the place of religion because it cannot generate an ethics or a morality. It can give us no reason to prefer a child to a dog, or to choose honorable poverty over fraudulent wealth. It can give us no grounds for preferring what is excellent to what is sensationalistic. And this is more or less where we are now.

"Worship" means the assigning or acknowledging of worth. Language, in its wisdom, understands this to be a function of creative, imaginative behavior. The suffix "-ship" is kin to the word "shape." It is no wonder that the major arts in virtually every civilization have centered around religion. Darwin, always eager to find analogues and therefore inferred origins for human behavior among the animals, said that, to a dog, his master is a god. But this is to speak of religion as if it were mere credulous awe in the face of an apparently greater power and wisdom, as if there were only natural religion, only the Watchmaker. The relationship between creation and discovery — as Greek sculpture, for example, might be said to have discovered the human form, or mathematics might be said to have discovered the universe — is wholly disallowed in this comparison.

Religion is inconceivable because it draws on the human mind in ways for which nature, as understood by Darwinists, offers no way of accounting. Collaboratively, people articulate perceptions of value and meaning and worth, which are perhaps right and wrong, that is, profoundly insightful, or else self-interested or delusional, at about the rate of the best science. We tend to forget the long respect paid to the Piltdown man, a hoax whose plausibility arose from the fact that it seemed to confirm Darwinist evolutionary theory. We forget that it is only fairly recently that the continents have been known to drift. Until very recently the biomass of the sea at middle and great depths has been fantastically underestimated, and the mass and impact of microbial life in the earth has been virtually unreckoned. We know almost nothing about the biology of the air, that great medium of migration for infectious agents, among other things. The wonderful Big Bang is beset with problems. In other words, our best information about the planet has been full of enormous lacunae, and is, and will be. Every grand venture at understanding is hypothesis, not so different from metaphysics. Daniel Dennett attributes the brilliance of J. S. Bach to the fortuitous accumulation of favorable adaptations in his nervous system. Bach, of all people, is not to be imagined without a distinctive, highly elaborated conception of God, and life in a culture that invoked the idea of God by means of music. That is why his work is profound, rather than merely very clever. And it is profound. It is not about illusion, it is not about superstition or denial or human vainglory or the peculiarities of one sensorium.

We try now to establish value in economic terms, lacking better, and this has no doubt contributed to the bluntly mercenary character of contemporary culture. But economic value is extraordinarily slippery. Buying cheap and selling dear is the essence of profit making. The consumer is forever investing in ephemera, cars or watches that are made into symbols of prosperity, and are therefore desirable because they are expensive. So people spend a great deal of money for the advantages of being perceived to have spent a great deal of money. These advantages are diminished continuously by the change of styles either toward or away from the thing they have bought, which make it either commonplace or passé.

Or manufacture is taken from a setting in which adults work for reasonable wages and there are meaningful protections of the environment, and moved into a setting where children work for meager wages and the environment is desolated. This creates poverty among workers in both settings and destroys the wealth that is represented in a wholesome environment — toxins in the air or the water are great destroyers of wealth. So economic value is created at the cost of the economic value of workers who are made unable to figure as consumers, and of resources that are made unsuitable for any use. A few people may get rich, but the transaction altogether is a loss, perhaps a staggering loss. A global economy organized on these principles will be full of poor, sick, dispirited people, and shoddy goods, since they will be cheapened to suit the dwindling prosperity of the workforce, who are also the buying public. An objective accounting of value would find disaster here. Humane limits to the exploitation of people would solve the problem, but they would also interfere with competition, which is the great law of nature, supposedly, and which therefore functions as a value, because "science" has supplanted religion.

How much misery and premature death (most of it out of sight, granted) do we agree to when we accept this new economic order? Is it in any way an advance on colonialism? Do we imagine, as the colonialists sometimes did, that we are bringing benefits of civilization to the far reaches of the world? Are we not in fact decivilizing ourselves as we decivilize them? Why is there no outcry? Is it because we have cast off the delusion of human sanctity? I think we should study our silence for insight into other momentous silences in recent history.

This is not the worst of it. Now that the mystery of motive is solved — there are only self-seeking and aggression, and the illusions that conceal them from us — there is no place left for the soul, or even the self. Moral behavior has little real meaning, and inwardness, in the traditional sense, is not necessary or possible. We use analysts and therapists to discover the content of our experience. Equivalent trauma is assumed to produce more or less equivalent manifestations in every case, so there is little use for the mind, the orderer and reconciler, the artist of the interior world. Whatever it has made will only be pulled apart. The old mystery of subjectivity is dispelled; individuality is a pointless complication of a very straightforward organic life. Our hypertrophic brain, that prodigal indulgence, that house of many mansions, with its stores, and competences, and all its deep terrors and very rich pleasures, which was so long believed to be the essence of our lives, and a claim on one another's sympathy and courtesy and attention, is going the way of every part of collective life that was addressed to it — religion, art, dignity, graciousness. Philosophy, ethics, politics, properly so called. It is a thing that bears reflecting upon, how much was destroyed, when modern thought declared the death of Adam.

Facing Reality

ANYONE WHO reads and writes history or economics or science must sometimes wonder what fiction is, where its boundaries are, if they exist at all. The question implies certain distinctions, as between fiction and fact, or, more cautiously, between fiction and nonfiction. I would suggest that, while such distinctions are real, they are also profoundly relative, conditional, and circumstantial. Almost everything we have a name for exists in the universe of time and matter, and should, so it seems to me, be assumed to share certain of their essential qualities, two of these being ineluctability and profound resistance to definition.

Yet we have put together among ourselves a rigidly simple account of life in the world, which we honor with the name Reality and which, we now assure one another, must be faced and accepted, even or especially at the cost of those very things which societies we admire are believed by us to value, for example education, the arts, a humane standard of life for the whole of the community. Science fetches back from its explorations mystery upon mystery, yet somehow we feel increasingly sunk in a world of mere things, in a hard-edged Reality that disallows imagination except to exact tribute from it, in portraits which assert its own power and ferocity, or in interludes and recreations which concede by their triviality that only Reality matters. Our present model of the world is a fiction, based on notions of objectivity and of the character and implications of science which are a hundred years out of date. It is based on the flotsam and detritus and also the floor sweepings of all disciplines — psychology, penology, economics, history, all of them. From them it takes its important tone, helpful in magnifying any present obsession. For many of us it is true to say, Reality marks our ballots, even rears our children. It is such a poor contrivance that we would not believe in it for a minute if we did not want to. Yet it flourishes, because it is the servant and gatekeeper of dearer interests, a prized dependent upon which *we* in fact depend.

(I depart here from what I hope is a tone of moderation for a long moment of parenthetical candor. As a fiction writer, I feel smothered by this collective fiction, this Reality. I do not admire it or enjoy it, this work of grim and minor imagination which somehow or other got itself acknowledged as The Great Truth and The Voice of Our Time because of rather than despite its obvious thinness and fraudulence. So I will give it a bad review, in the spirit of cankered optimism which moves all indignant reviewers. Maybe I can hit it on the head, put an end to it. This is not a realistic hope. Maybe others will agree with me, and start a brilliant movement in a direction I cannot anticipate, and *they* will put an end to it. This is scarcely more realistic.

But these collective fictions matter. They have the profoundest influence on what we know and see and understand.

When they make fear the key to interpretation of history and experience, as they do so often, as ours does now, nothing contains a greater potential for releasing all the varieties of destruction. Fearfulness assumes a hidden narrative — that we are ill despite our apparent health, vulnerable despite our apparent safety. We are contemptuous of transient well-being, as if there were any other kind. Routinely discounting the preponderance of evidence is not the behavior of reasonable people, nor is devaluing present experience because it may be overtaken by something worse. I think we are not taking responsibility for keeping ourselves reasonable, individually or collectively — that we no longer admire or reward reasonableness because it has lost its place in our imagination. Now it is as if public discourse exists only to be disrupted, as if gaffes and scandals, without regard to their authenticity or significance, were the real substance of collective life, and attempts at coherent conversation about what is to be wished for or what is to be done were pretension or naiveté or a strategy of concealment, the bland surface through which the next brainless sensation is sure to erupt. When a good man or woman stumbles, we say, "I knew it all along," and when a bad one has a gracious moment, we sneer at the hypocrisy. It is as if there is nothing to mourn or to admire, only a hidden narrative now and then apparent through the false, surface narrative. And the hidden narrative, because it is ugly and sinister, is therefore true.

Lately Americans have enjoyed pretending they are powerless, disenfranchised individually and deep in decline as a society, perhaps to grant themselves latitude responsible people do not have or desire. In fact, our ability to do harm, by act or omission, is great beyond all reckoning, and greater by the measure of our refusal to accept this fact and its implications. Powerless people can hardly demand coherency of themselves, since they must always react to forces they cannot trust, whose wiles they cannot anticipate. They are safe from responsibility, safe from blame.

Before I leave the pretended shelter of this aside I will say two things more. First, individuals have collective fiction as a reality to deal with. Anyone who has brought up children knows the overwhelming power of the larger culture, and how for the peace and sanity of the family it must be in some degree accommodated. Anyone who struggles to meet the expectations the society creates must cope with emotional injury and exhaustion, or at best, very unsatisfying rewards. We are all in effect dragooned into it, enforcing compliance on ourselves, because as individuals we have few real choices, even if we know we should want them. It is hard to be critical of a society without seeming uncompassionate toward its members, yet, mysteriously, societies themselves tend not to be compassionate toward their members, and must be criticized for that reason.

Second, the art of fiction, intentional and acknowledged fiction, the kind with the author's name on it, lies outside this phenomenon of collective fiction for the most part, and often attempts by one means or another to grapple with it. But Reality, the collective fiction, has educated our audience, as surely as the pulpit educated Emerson's. It has given the writer little to build on and little of interest to explore. (I dream this might change.)

Our collective fiction is full of anxiety, empty of humor and generosity. It elaborates itself in the manner of phobia or delusion rather than vision or fancy. We find comfort in anxiety because it engrosses our attention, which we have in surplus, and are usually at a loss to employ. And anxiety is a stimulant, like love, like hatred, though generally not so prone to extravagant expression as they are, indeed even secretive, and therefore liable suddenly to produce great effects from what are apparently very small causes.

Here is one topic under which the phenomenon of anxiety can be considered. As a culture we are terrified of illness, though as people go we are rather safe from it. Perhaps to feed our anxiety, illness for us has overspilled definition and is now to be discovered everywhere, in everyone. Emotions are regarded as symptoms and treated medically, including, of course, anxiety. This is true even while the boundless resources of the society seem largely bent to the work of stimulating fear, disgust, resentment — emotions that in fact are pathological and also pathogenic. It is as if we took morphine to help us sleep on a bed of nails. Another generation would have looked for another solution.

Our terror of doctors and of medications is a generalization of the same anxiety that drives us to them, another form of hypochondriasis. Obviously both doctors and medications have the potential to do great harm, first of all because they are creatures of this civilization. Doctors responded too frequently to patients' demands for antibiotics, for example, and compromised the usefulness of antibiotics in the course of launching a spectacular advance in the evolution of bacteria. I think it is fair to assume that doctors are responding too frequently now to other demands, whose consequences will, in not too long a time, bring fresh and vivid new grounds for anxiety. We will not reflect, or draw the lessons of experience, because fearful people improvise solutions, and feel too powerless to consider a problem from the point of view of their own responsibility.

Here I should make a distinction between the fictional and the false. They are entirely different things. The givens of the collective fiction I have been describing are that societies decay;

that youth ends and the body fails; that strangers sometimes
mean us harm and friends sometimes connive in our ruin; that
things are rarely as they appear to us; that out of any present
circumstance there might arise misfortune in the face of which
we would be utterly helpless. Not a word of this is false. Common sense will confirm it all.

Nor do we indulge in the falsehood that we can make
ourselves secure, even while desperate effort is clearly assumed
to be the appropriate response to our condition. We are busy as
rodents. But this is for the most part not real purpose, merely
anxiety expending itself. Beside their root in fact, I think these
collective narratives may have something like an organic life,
in the way they invade experience and transform it to the uses
of their own survival. Anxiety-driven people are right to be
anxious. They are prone to stress and burnout, to illness and
early death. They have trouble creating satisfactory friendships
and families. What if they have misappropriated their time just
sufficiently to allow their children to become ominous strangers? What if they have made a too single-minded investment of
their lives, and then the market for their skills plunges? These
things happen — anyone who has ever glanced at a newspaper
knows it. They are right to lie awake.

The truth to which all this fiction refers, from which it
takes its authority, is the very oldest truth, right out of Genesis. We are not at ease in the world, and sooner or later it kills
us. Oddly, people in this culture have been relatively exempt
from toil and pangs and from death, too, if length of life may
be regarded as a kind of exemption. So why do these things
seem to terrify us more than they do others? One reason might
be that, as human populations go, we are old. A few decades
ago the median age was in late adolescence, and now it is deep
into adulthood. Midlife has overtaken the great postwar gen-

eration. So the very fact that we have, in general, enjoyed unexampled health has brought us in vast numbers into the years where even the best luck begins to run out. This is true of the whole Western world.

Less fortunate countries have younger populations, so the nonchalance for which youth is famous, and for which it was once admired, may be imagined to figure in their sense of things more importantly than it does in ours. It is true that they are warlike. But it is true also that a crankiness is rising in the great gray West, a brooding over old grudges and injuries, that can only alarm. I think we may have begun to see youth as Preadulthood Syndrome, a pathology to be treated with therapy and medications if it is our own, and a pestilence to be isolated if it is the youth of fecund and short-lived populations. The anxious find special terrors in unpredictability.

Jefferson said every generation has the right to make its own laws, and perhaps it has as well the right to identify illness for its own purposes. It could be that the society is too brittle just now to tolerate rambunctiousness, and not confident enough to attempt discipline or acculturation. To say that behavior is aberrant is much more powerfully coercive among us than to say an action is wrong. It implies the behavior is not really willed or controlled, and this undermines the self-confidence of the offending person. It also excuses him from responsibility, though, curiously, those taken to be the cause of his illness — his parents, usually — are assumed to have caused it through freely chosen and straightforwardly reprehensible behavior, for which blame and punishment are just and therapeutic. This makes no sense, and no one cares. The narrative is about something else, something involving fusions and displacements and improvised reconciliations among incompatible conceptions or metaphors, and we are so invested in this work that we do not choose to see the clumsiness of it.

The inconsistency probably means nothing more than that we can neither accept the idea of responsibility nor be rid of it, so we relegate it to the minor characters.

I suggest that, for us, the sense of sickness has replaced the sense of sin, to which it was always near allied, and that while we are acutely aware of the difficulties surrounding notions of good and evil, we ignore, though they are manifest, the equally great difficulties surrounding notions of sickness and health, especially as these judgments are applied to behavior. Antebellum doctors described an illness typical of enslaved people sold away from their families, which anyone can recognize as rage and grief. By medicalizing their condition, the culture was able to refuse the meaning of their suffering. I am afraid we also are forgetting that emotions signify, that they are much fuller of meaning than language, that they interpret the world to us and us to other people. Perhaps the reality we have made fills certain of us, and of our children, with rage and grief — the tedium and meagerness of it, the meanness of it, the stain of fearfulness it leaves everywhere. It may be necessary to offer ourselves palliatives, but it is drastically wrong to offer or to accept a palliative as if it were a cure.

Perhaps some part of our peculiar anxiety might be accounted for this way. Historically, cultures have absorbed those irreducible truths about the harshness of life and the certainty of death into mythic or religious contexts. The long miseries and vanquished heroics of Troy inspired the world for millennia, though there is not much in the tale to offer comfort except the spectacle of futility on an epic scale. I am not sure we have at the moment any notion of comfort in that sense, of feeling the burdens which come with being human in the world lifted by compassionate imagination. Our always greater eagerness to describe ourselves as sufferers makes us always less willing to identify with suffering as a fact of human life. It may be that we cannot bear to undermine our sense of special grievance, or our belief — consistent with the medicalization of our sorrows and in general with our ceasing to value inward experience — that they are indeed aberrant, that they say nothing meaningful to us or for us.

Our civilization believed for a long time in God and the soul and sin and salvation, assuming, whatever else, that meaning had a larger frame and context than this life in this world. Polls indicate that we in America have not really abandoned these beliefs, and that is interesting, because what I have called our collective fiction is relentlessly this-worldly, very serious indeed about material success, of all things. Success, that object of derision in every wisdom literature ever penned, not more dignified now that it is so very slackly bound to real attainment, not more beautiful now that its appurtenances generally amount to a higher tawdriness. Knowing this, we nevertheless make it stand in the place of worth. Among us, a pedestal one day is a pillory the next, because we fawn on people who would have been fortunate, in some cases grateful, simply to have escaped notice. Then we punish them relentlessly for being no more than they are and always were. This while we continue to speak very much as though success were a thing to be envied.

I think the true name for what we aspire to is nonfailure. Most of those who are household names in this strange time are objects of horror or derision, a fact which in many instances reflects our need rather than their deserving. My son came home from school once staggered by a discussion of Abraham Lincoln, whom he revered. None of the other students would be persuaded that Lincoln went into politics for anything but the money. The grandeur of his speeches merely proved the depth of his cynicism. In the same way, we can refuse evidence of actual merit, and we can discredit serious-

ness, and we can feel morally acute while we do it. Our de-
fenses against real success are invulnerable. Our hostility to
success of every kind is demonstrated afresh every day.

But nonfailure is another thing. Income and credit
shrewdly managed, desiderata learned from the better shops
and catalogs and systematically acquired — for better and for
worse, this is not much to aspire to. It is because our hopes are
in fact so very modest that we can be made to fear another
teenager with a baby might snatch them all away. It is because
we hope to acquire rather than to achieve — in the old language of religion, to receive rather than to give — that the
good we imagine can truly be taken from our hands.

Then what about religion? If we do in significant numbers
actually believe that we have a greater and a different destiny
than other created things, if we believe there is a God who
hears the cries of the oppressed and who takes almighty and
everlasting cognizance of our actions and our thoughts — I
think these views are widely held — how do we represent the
world to ourselves in terms that effectively disallow such considerations? Where did religion go? I know I risk being unfair
in characterizing television religion, because I have not paid
much attention to it. But it seems to me more television than
religion by a good margin. It is adept at exciting minor emotions and at stimulating viewer loyalty. It bears about the same
relation to religion *All My Children* bears to *King Lear.* I can see
how someone stuck at home might prefer it to golf. There is
no snobbery in saying things differ by the measure of their
courage and their honesty and their largeness of spirit, and that
the difference is profoundly one of value. Television has not
taken over the expression of religious sensibility, any more
than vendors of souvenir Eiffel Towers have deprived Paris of a
monument.

What if, in important numbers, we believe there is a God

who is mysterious and demanding, with whom one is not easily at peace? What if we believe there will be a reckoning? I find no evidence that such beliefs were felt to be discredited or that they were consciously abandoned. They simply dropped out of the cultural conversation. And, at the same time, we adopted this very small view of ourselves and others, as consumers and patients and members of interest groups, creatures too minor, we may somehow hope, for great death to pause over us. If we do still believe in the seriousness of being human, while we have lost the means of acknowledging this belief, even in our thoughts, then profound anxiety, whose origins we would be at a loss to name, seems to me an inevitable consequence. And this may account for both the narrowness and the intensity of the fiction that contains us. It is our comfort and our distraction. We are spiritual agoraphobes.

To borrow a question from Jean Genet, what would happen if someone started laughing? What if the next demographically marketed grievance or the next convenience-packaged dread, or the next urgent panacea for the sweet, odd haplessness of the body started a wave of laughter that swept over the continent? What if we understood our vulnerabilities to mean we are human, and so are our friends and our enemies, and so are our cities and books and gardens, our inspirations, our errors. We weep human tears, like Hamlet, like Hecuba. If the universe is only all we have so far seen, we are its great marvel. I consider it an honor to follow Saint Francis or William Tyndale or Angelina Grimké or Lydia Maria Child anywhere, even to mere extinction. I am honored in the cunning of my hand. This being human — people have loved it through plague and famine and siege. And Dante, who knew the world about suffering, had a place in hell for people who were grave when they might have rejoiced.

FAMILY

W E ARE ALL AWARE that "family" is a word which eludes definition, as do other important things, like nation, race, culture, gender, species; like art, science, virtue, vice, beauty, truth, justice, happiness, religion; like success; like intelligence. The attempt to impose definition on indeterminacy and degree and exception is about the straightest road to mischief I know of, very deeply worn, very well traveled to this day. But just for the purposes of this discussion, let us say: one's family are those toward whom one feels loyalty and obligation, and/or from whom one derives identity, and/or to whom one gives identity, and/or with whom one shares habits, tastes, stories, customs, memories. This definition allows for families of circumstance and affinity as well as kinship, and it allows also for the existence of people who are incapable of family, though they may have parents and siblings and spouses and children.

I think the biological family is especially compelling to us because it is, in fact, very arbitrary in its composition. I would never suggest so rude an experiment as calculating the percentage of one's relatives one would actually choose as friends, the percentage of one's relatives who would choose one as *their* friend. And that is the charm and the genius of the institution. It implies that help and kindness and loyalty are owed where they are perhaps by no means merited. Owed, that is, even to ourselves. It implies that we are in some few circumstances excused from the degrading need to judge others' claims on us, excused from the struggle to keep our thumb off the scales of reciprocity.

Of course families do not act this way, always or even typically, certainly not here, certainly not now. But we recognize such duty and loyalty as quintessentially familial where we see it. And if the institution is culturally created, what we expect of it has a great deal to do with determining what it will be in fact.

Obviously if we are to employ the idea that behaviors are largely culturally created, we must humble that word "fact." It seems very plausible to me that our ceasing to romanticize the family has precipitated, as much as it has reflected, the weakening of the family. I am sure it is no accident that the qualities of patience and respect and loyalty and generosity which would make family sustainable are held in very low regard among us, some of them even doubling as neuroses such as dependency and lack of assertiveness. I think we have not solved the problem of living well, and that we are not on the way to solving it, and that our tendency to insist on noisier and more extreme statements of the new wisdom that has already failed gives us really very little ground for optimism.

Imagine this: some morning we awake to the cultural consensus that a family, however else defined, is a sort of compact of mutual loyalty, organized around the hope of giving rich, human meaning to the lives of its members. Toward this end they do what people do — play with their babies, comfort their sick, keep their holidays, commemorate their occasions, sing songs, tell jokes, fight and reconcile, teach and learn what they know about what is right and wrong, about what is beautiful and what is to be valued. They enjoy each other and make themselves enjoyable. They are kind and receive kindness, they are generous and are sustained and enriched by others' generosity. The antidote to fear, distrust, self-interest is always loyalty. The balm for failure or weakness, or even for disloyalty, is always loyalty.

This is utopian. And yet. Certainly it describes something of which many of us feel deprived. We have reasoned our way to uniformly conditional relationships. This is at the very center of the crisis of the family, since the word means, if it means anything, that certain people exist on special terms with each other, which terms are more or less unconditional. We have instead decided to respect our parents, maybe, if they meet our stringent standards of deserving. Just so do our children respect us, maybe.

Siblings founder, spouses age. We founder. We age. That is when loyalty should matter. But invoking it now is about as potent a gesture as flashing a fat roll of rubles. I think this may contribute enormously to the sadness so many of us feel at the heart of contemporary society. "Love is not love / Which alters when it alteration finds," in the words of the sonnet, which I can only interpret to mean, love is loyalty. I would suggest that in its absence, all attempts to prop the family economically or morally or through education or otherwise will fail. The real issue is, will people shelter and nourish and humanize one another? This is creative work, requiring discipline and imagination. No one can be scolded or fined into doing it, nor does it occur spontaneously in the demographically traditional family.

Nor does it occur predictably even where it is earnestly

sought and desired. Life is in every way full of difficulty, and that is the great variable that confounds all generalization, as I am eager to concede, even while discussions of this kind oblige one to generalize.

But we have forgotten many things. We have forgotten solace. Maybe the saddest family, properly understood, is a miracle of solace. It seems to me that our multitude of professional healers and comforters are really meant to function like the doctor in a boxer's corner, there to slow bleeding and minimize swelling so that we will be able to last another round. Neither they nor we want to think about the larger meaning of the situation. This is the opposite of solace.

Imagine that someone failed and disgraced came back to his family, and they grieved with him, and took his sadness upon themselves, and sat down together to ponder the deep mysteries of human life. This is more human and beautiful, I propose, even if it yields no dulling of pain, no patching of injuries. Perhaps it is the calling of some families to console, because intractable grief is visited upon them. And perhaps measures of the success of families that exclude this work from consideration, or even see it as failure, are very foolish and misleading.

We tend to think, now, of the ideal family as a little hatchery for future contributors to the Social Security system, noncriminals who will enhance national productivity while lowering the cost per capita of preventable illness. We have forgotten that old American nonsense about alabaster cities, about building the stately mansions of the soul. We have lowered our hopes abysmally, for no reason obvious to me, without a murmur I have ever heard. To fulfill or to fall short of such minor aspirations as we encourage now is the selfsame misery.

For some time we seem to have been launched on a great campaign to deromanticize everything, even while we are eager to insist that more or less everything that matters is a romance, a tale we tell one another. Family is a narrative of love and comfort which corresponds to nothing in the world but which has formed behavior and expectation — fraudulently, many now argue. It is as if we no longer sat in chairs after we learned that furniture was only space and atoms. I suppose it is a new upsurge of that famous Western rationalism, old enemy of reasonableness, always so right at the time, always so shocking in retrospect.

Well, we have exorcised the ghost and kept the machine, and the machine is economics. The family as we have known it in the West in the last few generations was snatched out of the fires of economics, and we, for no reason I can see, have decided to throw it back in again. It all has to do with the relationship of time and money. When we take the most conscientious welfare mothers out of their homes and neighborhoods with our work programs, we put them in jobs that do not pay well enough to let them provide good care for their children. This seems to me neither wise nor economical. We do it out of no special malice but because we have lately reorganized society so that even the children of prosperous families often receive doubtful care and meager attention. The middle class are enforcing values they themselves now live by, as if these values would reduce the social pathologies of the poor, as if they were not in fact a great cause of the social pathologies of the middle class.

An employed American today works substantially longer hours than he or she did twenty-five years ago, when only one adult in an average household was employed and many more households had two adults. The recent absence of parents from the home has first of all to do with how much time people spend at work. Some of them are ambitious businesspeople or professionals, but many more patch together a living out of two or three part-time jobs, or work overtime as an employer's hedge against new hiring. Statistically the long hours simply indicate an unfavorable change in the circumstances of those who work. If an average household today produces more than twice as much labor in hours as an average household did twenty-five years ago, and receives only a fraction more in real income, then obviously the value of labor has fallen — even while the productivity of labor in the same period has risen sharply. So, male and female, we sell ourselves cheap, with the result that work can demand always more of our time, and our families can claim always less of it.

This is clearly a radical transformation of the culture, which has come about without anyone's advocating it, without consensus, without any identifiable constituency. It would be usual to imagine a conspiracy of some sort. That is a good enough reason to do otherwise. Our usual approaches have by now an impressive history of fruitlessness, as we would notice if we were at all a reflective people.

Conspiracy theories are childish and comforting, assuming as they do that there are smart people somewhere who are highly efficient at putting their intentions into effect, when history and experience combine to assure us that nothing could be more unlikely. We long imagined that the great corporations contrived against our good, but if any institution has been as staggered as the family in the last twenty-five years, it is surely the great corporation. Workers who are well paid and secure are good consumers, and in the new economy there are always fewer people who suit that description. The faltering of the economy has always been interpreted as a problem of "competitiveness" with other countries, and this notion has accelerated the cheapening of labor and the reduction of the labor force in traditional industries. That is, it has accelerated the increase of insecurity among those who work. Surely it is a tribute to the vast power of the economy that it has weathered this nonsense as well as it has.

This whole notion of competitiveness was pitched by many of its exponents as a "war" we must "win," which could surely mean nothing else than the crippling of those same foreign markets upon which our future prosperity supposedly depends. If we force wages down in competitor countries, or if we weaken their industries and lower the value of their currencies, they will simply be less able to buy from us no matter how lean we are, or how mean we are. One could say public opinion has been cynically manipulated with this talk of "challenge" and "war," but I think we should face the harder fact that a public silly enough to be persuaded by such arguments would very likely produce a class of experts silly enough to propose them in good faith.

The family as we know it in the modern West has been largely willed and reformed into existence. European culture was long distinguished by the thoroughness with which it coerced labor out of its population — slavery and industrialization, contemporary phenomena equally indifferent to such inconveniences as considerations of family, were natural extensions of feudalism, only more ambitious and ingenious in their exactions. The case has been made that childhood was invented, which it was, at least in the sense that certain societies began to feel that young children should be excluded from the workforce, and women with them, to some extent at least.

Working conditions in trades and factories were brutal into the present century. We tend to forget that women of working age were often pregnant or nursing and often obliged to leave infants and small children untended. Sometimes they gave birth on the factory floor.

Children of working age, that is, as young as five, were

spared no hardship. The British documented these horrors quite meticulously for generations, and one may read all anyone could care to read about the coffles of children driven weeping through morning darkness to the factories; children lying down to sleep in the roads because they were too exhausted to walk home at night; children dismembered by machines they were obliged to repair while the machines ran; children in factory dormitories sleeping by hundreds, turn and turn about, in beds that were never empty until some epidemic swept through and emptied them, and brought hundreds of new children, orphans or so-called child paupers, to work away their brief lives. There is nothing to wonder at, that the ideal of mother and children at home, and father adequately paid to keep them from need, was a thing warmly desired, and that for generations social reform was intended to secure this object.

By comparison with Britain, America was late in industrializing, and its agricultural economy was based on widely distributed ownership of land. Nevertheless the societies were similar enough to be attentive to each other's reform movements. The decisive innovation was the idea that one wage earner should be able to support a wife and a few children, rather than that every employable person in a household should support himself or herself and some fraction of a baby or two. The idea of the "living wage" became much more important in America, where labor was usually in demand and therefore able to command a higher price and to set other limits and conditions governing employers' access to it. Where labor is cheap, the market is flooded with it, assuring that it will remain cheap. Other goods will, over time, be withheld if they do not command a reasonable price, but the cheaper labor is, the less it will be withheld, because people have to live, and to hedge against the falling wages and unemployment which are always characteristic of a glutted labor market. These phenomena have been observed and analyzed since the seventeenth century. Now they are recrudescent like other old maladies we thought we had eliminated.

This glut of cheap labor was the characteristic state of things in England and Europe until the postwar period — and it is increasingly important among Americans now. That is why we sometimes see such anomalies as employment and unemployment rising at the same time. The two-tier economy we are developing, with accelerating inequality between those who are trained or educated and those who are not, reflects the scarcity relative to demand of skilled labor. If schemes to educate more of our workforce are carried out successfully, the increased availability of skilled labor will lower its value, and the erosion of the prosperity of those who work will simply become more widespread.

It is because the family as we have known it in this country over the last three-quarters of a century was the goal and product of reform that a radiance of idealization hung over it, and that it was so long and so confidently invoked as a common value, as a thing deserving and also requiring political and economic protection. This has had many important consequences for policy and law. Yet for some reason we are convinced at the moment that the ways of our economy should be identical with the laws of the market, and therefore we depart resolutely from norms and customs that controlled economic behavior among us through our long history of increasing prosperity. No one is more persuaded of the rightness of this course than those who claim to especially cherish the family.

Take for example the weekend, or that more venerable institution, the Sabbath. Moses forbade that servants, even foreigners, should work on the seventh day. If their wage was subsistence, as it is usually fair to assume in premodern societies, then his prohibition had the immediate practical effect of securing for them seven days' pay for six days' work. He raised the value of their labor by limiting access to it. In all its latter-day forms the Sabbath has had this effect.

Now those among us whose prosperity is eroding fastest are very likely to be at work on Sunday, because they cannot afford not to work when they have the chance, and because they cannot risk losing a job so many others would be happy to take. Absent legal or contractual or religious or customary constraints, workers without benefits or job security or income that is at least stable relative to the economy have no way of withholding their labor. Now all those constraints are gone, in the name of liberalization, I suppose. I do not recall hearing a single murmur about the effect of such changes on the family, though it is always easy to find journalistic wisdom to the effect that parents should spend more time with their children. The last great Sabbatarian institution is the school system — even the Postal Service makes deliveries on Sunday — so the quondam day of rest is now a special burden for families with young children or children who need supervision.

Of course the shops must be open on Sundays and at night because the rate of adult employment is so high and the working day is so long that people need to be able to buy things whenever they can find the time. I would suggest that such voracious demands on people's lives, felt most mercilessly by the hardest pressed, for example the employed single parent, are inimical to the family, and to many other things of value, for example the physical and mental health of such parents, though these are utterly crucial to the well-being of millions of children, and therefore of extraordinary importance to the society as a whole.

Clearly a calculation could be made in economic terms of the cost to the society of this cheapening of labor. It is no great mystery that statistics associate social problems with single-parent families. And social problems, crime for example, are an enormous expense, an enormous drag on the economy. We are conditioned to think that the issue for single mothers, say, is work or welfare. In fact the issue is decent working hours and reasonable pay. These are important people, holding the world together for children who in many instances have been half abandoned. It is grotesque that their lives should be made impossible because of some unexamined fealty to economic principles that are, if we would pause to consider, impoverishing to us all in many ways, some of them extremely straightforward.

To consider again the weekend. It is often remarked, in an odd spirit of censoriousness, that American culture was never a melting pot. We are given to know that it was wrong to have aspired to such an ideal, and wrong to have fallen short of it. There seems to me to be little evidence that the ideal ever was aspired to, at least in the sense in which critics understand the phrase. Since religion is central to most special identities within the larger national culture, religious tolerance has been the great guarantor of the survival of the variety of cultures. It was characteristic of European countries for centuries to try to enforce religious uniformity on just these grounds. If earlier generations in America chose not to follow this example, presumably they knew and accepted the consequence of departing from it, that assimilation would have important limits. This strikes me as a happy arrangement, all in all.

Now there is great anxiety about the survival and recognition of these cultures of origin. I suggest that this sense of loss, which reflects, it seems, novel and unwelcome assimilation, is another consequence of the disruption of the family I have been describing. Civic life is expected to be ethnically neutral, and at the same time to acknowledge our multitude of ethnicities and identities in such a way as to affirm them, to make their inheritors all equally glad to embrace and sustain them. These are not realistic expectations. One acquires a culture from within the culture — for all purposes, from the family.

And acculturation takes time. I suggest that those groups who feel unvalued are the very groups who are most vulnerable to the effects of the cheapening of labor, least able to control the use of their time. They look for, or are promised, amendment in the correction of images and phrases, in high school multicultural days and inclusive postage stamp issues. Such things can never supply the positive content of any identity.

The crudeness of public institutions in their attempts to respond to these demands is clearly in large part due to the fact that they are wholly unsuited to the work that is asked of them. Obviously they cannot supply the place of church or synagogue. The setting apart of the weekend once sheltered the traditions and institutions that preserved the variety of cultures. French Catholics and Russian Jews and Dutch Protestants could teach morals and values wholly unembarrassed by the fact that the general public might not agree with every emphasis and particular, and therefore they were able to form coherent moral personalities in a way that a diverse and open civic culture cannot and should not even attempt. It seems to me likely that the openness of the civic culture has depended on the fact that these groups and traditions have functioned as teachers of virtue and morality, sustaining by their various lights a general predisposition toward acting well. When the state attempts to instill morality, the attempt seems intrusive and even threatening precisely because that work has traditionally been reserved to family, community, and religion, to the institutions of our diversity, a thing we have cherished historically much better than we do now, for all our talk. Or rather, our talk arises from a nervous awareness that our traditional diversity is eroding away, and we are increasingly left with simple difference, in its most negative and abrasive forms.

I do not think it is nostalgia to suggest that it would be well to reestablish the setting apart of time traditionally devoted to religious observance. If there is any truth in polls, the American public remains overwhelmingly religious, and religion is characteristically expressed in communities of worship. To take part in them requires time. It may be argued that there are higher values, for example the right to buy what one pleases when one pleases, which involves another's right to spend Saturday or Sunday standing at a cash register or to compel someone else to stand there. If these are the things we truly prefer, there is no more to be said. But the choice is unpoetical and, in its effects, intolerant. When we were primitive capitalists we did much better. Now people in good circumstances have their Saturdays and Sundays if they want them. So observance is an aspect of privilege, though the privileged among us tend to be the least religious. No wonder the churches are dying out.

Those among us who call themselves traditionalists, and who invoke things like "religion" and "family" in a spirit that makes these honest words feel mean and tainted, are usually loyal first of all to a tooth-and-nail competitiveness our history does not in fact enshrine. Religion and family must shift as they will when there is a dollar at stake. But the exponents of these notions are no better economists than they are historians. Reforms meant to raise the price of labor! they will say. Think of the cost to the employer! But what is the cost to the employer of this steady impoverishment of the consumer — who is, after all, simply someone else's employee, spending what he dares of what he earns? This wisdom has prevailed for twenty years and more. Its methods are not in fact traditional, and their results are not good.

Well-compensated labor tends to be marketed selectively, and this protects its market value. Badly compensated labor tends to overwhelm demand, and this erodes its market value. Or, one might say, cost rations access, thereby enhancing the price for which work can be sold. This was the effect of the minimum wage law, while it was meaningful. But high levels of employment at low wages create more low-wage employment, for example in services like fast food and child care, services which reflect the fact that people have sold a great deal of their time for relatively little money. Since these services fill needs created by low-wage employment, they must keep their own costs low, and this is an inevitable downward pressure on the pay of their own employees. The accelerating disparity of wealth among us is no great mystery. But it is even now inspiring recondite speculations, electrifying learned brains to the point of reanimating ideas anyone might have thought long and utterly dead, of sclerosis or spleen or intractable primitivity.

I think the history of ideas is easily as peculiar as anything that exists on our planet, that its causalities are whimsical altogether. We know that Communism was a theology, a church militant, with sacred texts and with saints and martyrs and prophets, with doctrines about the nature of the world and of humankind, with immutable laws and millennial visions and life-pervading judgments about the nature of good and evil. No doubt it failed finally for the same reason it lasted as long as it did, because it *was* a theology, gigantic and rigid and intricate, taking authority from its disciplines and its hierarchies even while they rendered it fantastically ill suited to the practical business of understanding and managing an economy. It seems to me that, obedient to the great law which sooner or later makes one the image of one's enemy, we have theologized our own economic system, transforming it into something likewise rigid and tendentious and therefore always less useful to *us*. It is an American-style, stripped-down, low-church theology, its clergy largely self-ordained, golf-shirted, the sort one would be not at all surprised and only a little alarmed to find on one's doorstep. Its teachings are very, very simple: There really are free and natural markets where the optimum value of things is assigned to them; everyone must compete with everyone; the worthy will prosper and the unworthy fail; those who succeed while others fail will be made deeply and justly happy by this experience, having had no other object in life; each of us is poorer for every cent that is used toward the wealth of all of us; governments are instituted among men chiefly to interfere with the working out of these splendid principles.

This is such a radical obliteration of culture and tradition, let us say of Jesus and Jefferson, as to awe any Bolshevik, of course. But then contemporary discourse is innocent as a babe unborn of any awareness of culture and tradition, so the achievement is never remarked. It is nearly sublime, a sort of cerebral whiteout. But my point here is that unsatisfactory economic ideas and practices which have an impressive history of failure, which caused to founder that great nation California, which lie at the root of much of the shame and dread and division and hostility and cynicism with which our society is presently afflicted, are treated as immutable truths, not to be questioned, not to be interfered with, lest they unleash their terrible retribution, recoiling against whomever would lay a hand on the Ark of Market Economics, if that is the name under which this mighty power is currently invoked.

There is a great love of certitude implicit in all this, and those impressed by it often merge religious and social and economic notions, discovering likeness in this supposed absolute clarity, which is really only selectivity and simplification. Listening to these self-declared moralists and traditionalists, it seems to me I hear from time to time a little satisfaction in the sober fact that God, as our cultures have variously received him through the Hebrew Scriptures, seems to loathe, actually abominate, certain kinds of transgression. Granting this fact, let us look at the transgressions thus singled out. My own sense of the text, based on more than cursory reading, is that the sin most insistently called abhorrent to God is the failure of generosity, the neglect of widow and orphan, the oppression of strangers and the poor, the defrauding of the laborer. Since many of the enthusiasts of this new theology are eager to call themselves Christians, I would draw their attention to the New Testament, *passim.*

I have heard pious people say, Well, you can't live by Jesus' teachings in this complex modern world. Fine, but then they might as well call themselves the Manichean Right or the Zoroastrian Right and not live by *those* teachings. If an economic imperative trumps a commandment of Jesus, they should just say so and drop these pretensions toward particular holiness — which, while we are on the subject of divine abhorrence, God, as I recall, does not view much more kindly than he does neglect of the poor. In fact, the two are often condemned together.

I know those who have taken a course in American history will think this merger of Christian pretensions and bullyboy economics has its origins in Calvinism and in Puritanism. Well, Calvin and the Puritans both left huge literatures. Go find a place where they are guilty of this vulgarization. Or, a much easier task, find a hundred or a thousand places where they denounce it, taking inspiration, always, from the Bible, which it was their quaint custom to read with a certain seriousness and attention. We have developed a historical version of the victim defense, visiting our sins upon our fathers. But I will say a thing almost never said among us: we have ourselves to blame.

Communism demonstrated the great compatibility of secularism with economic theology, and we may see the same thing now in the thinking of many of our contemporaries. On the assumption that American society is destined to extreme economic polarization, certain brave souls have written brave books arguing that those who thrive are genetically superior to those who struggle. They have higher IQs.

So we are dealing with a Darwinian paradigm, again, as people have done in one form or another since long before Darwin. The tale is always told this way — the good, the fit, the bright, the diligent prosper. These correspond to the creatures who, in the state of nature, would survive and reproduce. But — here our eyes widen — civilization lumbers us with substandard types who reproduce boundlessly and must finally swallow us up in their genetic mediocrity, utterly confounding and defeating the harsh kindness of evolution. This peril once posed itself in the form of the feckless Irish. But they became prosperous, enjoying, one must suppose, a great enhancement of their genetic endowment in the process, since I have never heard that the arts and professions have had to stoop to accommodate their deficiencies. This theory is so resilient because it can always turn a gaze unclouded by memory or imagination on the least favored group in any moment or circumstance, like the Darwinian predator fixing its eye on the gazelle with the sprained leg, perfectly indifferent to the fact that another gazelle was lame two days ago, yet another will be lame tomorrow.

The Social Darwinist argument always arises to answer, or

to preclude, or in fact to beg, questions about social justice — during trade wars or in the midst of potato famines. We are not quite at ease with the chasm that may be opening in our society, and some of us seek out the comforts of resignation. And these comforts are considerable. Viewed in the light of science, or at least of something every bit as cold and solemn as science, we see manifest in this painful experience the invisible hand of spontaneous melioration, the tectonic convulsions meant to form the best of all possible worlds.

But, at the risk of a little discomfort, let us try another hypothesis, just to see if it has descriptive power as great or even greater than the one favored by sociobiology. Let us just test the idea that our problems reflect an inability to discover or prepare an adequate elite. Obviously the thought of deficiency at the top of society is more alarming than deficiency at the bottom, but that is all the more reason to pause and consider.

When we speak of an elite, do we mean people of high accomplishment, people who do valuable work with great skill, people who create standards and articulate values? Are we speaking of our brilliant journalists, our noble statesmen, the selfless heroes of our legal profession? To be brief, what part of the work of the culture that is properly the responsibility of an elite actually functions at the level even of our sadly chastened hopes? Are our colleges producing great humanists and linguists? Is spiritual grandeur incubating in our seminaries? How often do we wonder if the medical care we receive is really appropriate?

For the purposes of these sociobiologists, membership in the elite seems to be a matter of income. But doctors and professors and journalists are so much a part of the morphology of our civilization that they will be with us until goats are put to graze in our monuments, and will probably be pulling down a decent salary, too, by whatever standards apply. Their presence in roles that are ideally filled by competent people does not make them competent. "But IQ!" they will answer. Yes, and since our society is, statistically speaking, in the hands of people with high IQs, we have no trouble at all finding a good news magazine, and we can always go to a good movie, and we are never oppressed by a sense of vulgarity or stupidity hardening around us. "But that is condescension to the masses," they will say. "You have to do things that are very stupid to make enough income to qualify for a place in this elite of the bright and worthy." Yes. That accounts, I suppose, for the rosy contentment of the man in the street.

Or perhaps they would offer no such tortuous defense. Perhaps they would say that if an elite is defined as a group of highly competent, responsible people with a special gift for holding themselves to exacting standards, we have at present rather little in the way of an elite. Then perhaps a high IQ correlates strongly with sharpness of the elbows, and simply obtains for people advantages to which they have no true right. Qualities consistent with the flourishing of the individual can be highly inconsistent with the flourishing of the group. History makes this point relentlessly. We have forgotten that democracy was intended as a corrective to the disasters visited upon humanity by elites of one kind and another. Maybe the great drag on us all is not the welfare mother but the incompetent engineer, not the fatherless child but the writer of mean or slovenly books. When our great auto industry nearly collapsed, an elite of designers and marketing experts were surely to blame. But the thousands thrown out of work by their errors were seen as the real problem. No doubt many of these workers figure among the new lumpenproletariat, as the

Marxists used to call them, people who just are not bright enough.

These grand theories are themselves no proof of great intelligence in the people who formulate them. Obviously I am shaken by the reemergence of something so crude as Social Darwinism. But my point here is that regrettable changes in our economy may not simply express the will of the market gods, but may instead mean something so straightforward as that those whose decisions influence the economy might not be good at their work. If they were brighter, perhaps no pretext would ever have arisen for these ungracious speculations about the gifts of the powerless and the poor.

It seems to me that something has passed out of the culture, changing it invisibly and absolutely. Suddenly it seems there are too few uses for words like humor, pleasure, and charm; courage, dignity, and graciousness; learnedness, fairmindedness, openhandedness; loyalty, respect, and good faith. What bargain did we make? What could have appeared for a moment able to compensate us for the loss of these things? Perhaps I presume in saying they are lost. But if they were not, surely they would demand time and occasion — time because every one is an art or a discipline, and occasion because not one of them exists except as behavior. They are the graces of personal and private life, and they live in the cells of the great cultural reef, which takes its form and integrity from them, and will not survive them, if there is aptness in my metaphor.

Why does society exist, if not to accommodate our lives? Jefferson was a civilized man — clearly it was not his intention to send us on a fool's errand. Why do we never imagine that the happiness he mentioned might include a long supper with our children, a long talk with a friend, a long evening with a book? Given time, and certain fading habits and expectations, we could have comforts and luxuries for which no one need be deprived. We could nurture our families, sustain our heritages, and, in the pregnant old phrase, enjoy our*selves*. The self, that dear and brief acquaintance, we could entertain with a little of the ceremony it deserves.

It will be objected that we are constrained by the stern economics of widget manufacture. Perhaps. If that argument is otherwise persuasive, there is no real evidence that it is true. In either case, we should at least decide when such considerations should be determining. There is a terse, impatient remark in Paul's letter to the Galatians: "For freedom Christ has set us free." And why are *we*, by world and historical standards, and to the limit of our willingness to give meaning to the word — why are *we* free? To make hard laws out of doubtful theories, and impose them and obey them at any cost? Nothing good can come of this. Great harm has come of it already.

DIETRICH
BONHOEFFER

THE GERMAN LUTHERAN pastor and theologian Dietrich Bonhoeffer first put himself at risk in 1933 by resisting the so-called Aryan Clause, which prohibited Jewish Christians from serving as ministers in Protestant churches. In 1945 he was executed for "antiwar activity." This included involvement in a scheme to help a group of Jews escape to Switzerland in 1941, and a meeting in Sweden in 1942 with the British bishop George Bell at which he tried to secure Allied support for the planned coup against Hitler now known as the Officers' Plot. In the years between he helped to create and guide the Confessing Church, a movement of Protestant pastors and seminarians who left the official churches rather than accept their accommodation with Nazism.

Bonhoeffer was the son of a large, affectionate, wealthy, and influential family. He distinguished himself early, being accepted as a lecturer in theology at Berlin University in 1928, at the age of twenty-two. From the first, his lectures attracted students who shared his religious and political views. The divisions in the churches would also have the effect of surrounding him with committed and like-minded people, "the brothers" as he called them, who seem to have answered fairly well to the exalted vision of the church in the world which was always at the center of his theology. In some degree they must have inspired it, having accepted discipleship at such cost. Many of them would be arrested and imprisoned, or be drafted and die in combat.

Bonhoeffer's family were scholars, scientists, artists, and military officers. His own powerful attraction to "the church" — he might be said always to have used the term in a special sense — is apparent in his earliest writing, and also in his decision to be a pastor rather than an academic. He reacted to the introduction of racial doctrine into the polity of the Protestant churches as heresy and led a revolt against it based on the belief that the so-called German Christians had ceased to be the true church. He was active in European ecumenical circles, with the intention of informing the world about the struggle in Germany and of legitimizing and supporting the dissenters.

By "the church" Bonhoeffer means Christ in this world, not as influence or loyalty but as active presence, not as one consideration or motive but as the one source and principle of life of those who constitute the church. This was the resistance position prepared by the formidable work of the Calvinist theologian Karl Barth, Bonhoeffer's teacher and mentor and another early leader of the opposition to Nazism. Barth wrote the Barmen Declaration, which rejected the influence in the church of race nationalism together with all other "events and powers, forms and truths" on the grounds that "Jesus Christ, as He is attested to in Holy Scripture, is the one Word of God, whom we have to hear and whom we have to trust and obey in life and in death."

To make exclusive claim to the authority of Christ is the oldest temptation of Christianity, and full of difficulties no matter how sound the rationale behind it or how manifest its rightness in any particular instance. In his theology — that is, in thought and practice — Bonhoeffer corrects against these difficulties with a very strong bias toward grace. Falseness and error and even extremest viciousness are, for him, utterly within the reach of God's compassion, which is infinite. In Bonhoeffer's understanding, the otherness of God is precisely this boundless compassion. The failure of the church and the evil of the world are revealed in their perfect difference from this force of forgiveness, which they cannot weary or diminish or evade. Bonhoeffer's protest, after all, was against exclusivism in the official church, and the church of his contemplation is utterly broad, indefinite in its boundaries. But the basis of his ethics is that Christ wills that the weak and persecuted should be rescued, and he must be obeyed; that Christ is present in the weak and the persecuted, and he must be honored. Bonhoeffer's magnanimity and his inclusiveness — which governed his life and cost him his life — are profoundly Christ-centered. Characteristically, he wrote, "An expulsion of the Jews from the West must necessarily bring with it the expulsion of Christ. For Jesus Christ was a Jew."

Bonhoeffer's life and his thought inform each other deeply. To say this is to be reminded of the strangeness of the fact that this is not ordinarily true. Questions are raised about the consistency of his theology, with the implication that his political activity and his death give his writing a prominence it might not have enjoyed on its own merits. But clearly his experience is the subject of his theology. It is a study of the obedience he himself attempted, together with his students, colleagues, and friends. In 1932 he wrote, "[T]he primary confession of the

Christian before the world is the deed that interprets itself." An obedient act owes nothing to the logic or the expectations of the world as it is, but is affirmed in the fact of revealing the redeemed world. Action is revelation.

As a good Lutheran, Bonhoeffer would object on theological grounds to the suggestion that he earned the grace that seems so manifest in both his life and his writing, but the evidence of discipline, of rigorous reflection, is everywhere, most present in his most personal letters, those written nearest his death. Considering the circumstances of his life, so adversarial and then so besieged, and considering what was taking place in Germany and Europe, it is amazing how little notice he gives to sin or evil, how often he expresses gratitude. The church is described, but not its limits. Grace is described, but not its absence. He will not cease to love the world, or any part of it: "When the totality of history should stand before God, there Christ stands."

It is obvious from subsequent events that these brave and brilliant spirits did not teach Hitler to fear theology. Nor do they seem to have rescued the honor of the church, which, in popular memory, is at least as roundly blamed as any other institution for the disaster of Fascism. The disappearance of religion in Europe, which Bonhoeffer foresaw, is in fact far advanced — despite him, and, since he has been sentimentalized as a prophet, in some part because of him. The heresies he and Barth denounced now flourish independently of even the culture and forms of Christianity, beyond any criticism they might have implied. And we have not learned the heroic art of forgiveness, which may have been the one thing needful.

It seems to me that the harshest irony of Bonhoeffer's life and death lies in the use made of him by many who have claimed his influence. Looked at in the great light of his theol-

ogy, which is an ethics from beginning to end, he is always, and
first of all, a man devoted to the church, and to religious arts,
forms, and occasions, especially those associated with Lutheran
tradition. There can be no doubt that his clarity of purpose, his
steadfastness, his serenity, were owed to his very devout habits
of mind, and of life as well. Indeed, it is precisely in these habits
that his mind and life are least to be distinguished from one
another. He prayed and meditated and read and studied Scripture hours every day, looked forward joyfully to the events of
the liturgical year, and, in prison, joyfully remembered them.
He preached a sermon on the day he died.

Yet because he posed certain thoughts to his friend Eberhard Bethge about the relationship of sacred and secular, the
actual example of his life is lost to an interpretation that deval-
ues "religion" in the sense of religious art, discipline, and tradition, and the very comforts and resources of piety to which
Bonhoeffer in his life and writing never ceased to bear witness.
In a letter from prison in which he insists "my suspicion and
horror of religiosity are greater than ever," he says also, "I have
found great help in Luther's advice that we should start our
morning and evening prayers by making the sign of the cross."
The contradiction is not at all intractable. Commenting on his
aversion to religiosity he remarks, "I often think of how the
Israelites never uttered the name of God." Religiosity is a transgression against God's otherness.

"Religion," in the invidious sense common to Barth and
Bonhoeffer, exists when, in Barth's words, "the divine reality
offered and manifested to us in revelation is replaced by a
concept of God arbitrarily and wilfully evolved by man." For
Barth, though perhaps not for Bonhoeffer, falseness of some
kind is a universal phenomenon of religious consciousness. In
any case, the concept is not far from ideas such as hypocrisy or

Phariseeism. It is not difficult to understand why this stinging use of the word "religious" would seem appropriate when
most of the religious leaders of Germany were eager to embrace National Socialism. But using the word in this sense
is a great source of difficulty and confusion, for example in
the understanding of Bonhoeffer's famous phrase "religionless
Christianity."

The evolution of thinking associated with his name makes
Bonhoeffer himself seem an archaic figure, enthralled by that
very piety we in his "world come of age" have learned to find
strange and suspect. To the extent that his inspired obedience
to Christ, that is, his humane devotion to justice in this world,
drew from his piety, it is a resource lost to many who might
earnestly hope to be like him. And yet, while the abrupt ferocity of the modern world has, for now, been epitomized in Nazi
Germany, it certainly was not exhausted in it. If being modern
means having the understanding and will to oppose the passions of collective life that can at any time emerge to disgrace
us and, now, even to destroy us, then one great type of modern
man is surely Dietrich Bonhoeffer — more particularly, Pastor
Bonhoeffer in his pulpit, Pastor Bonhoeffer at his prayers.

While he never hesitated in his opposition to the National
Socialist and anti-Semitic influences in the official churches, at
times Bonhoeffer seems to have been uncertain how to respond to them. In April of 1933, he published an article titled
"The Church and the Jewish Question" in which he said, "the
church has an unconditional obligation to the victims of any
ordering of society, even if they do not belong to the Christian
community." This might mean "not just to bandage the victims under the wheel, but to jam a spoke in the wheel itself.
Such action would be direct political action." In June of 1933,
Karl Barth attacked Nazism in a stinging public address, and

sent Hitler a manifesto of protest. Bonhoeffer, with Pastor Martin Niemöller, a martyr in his own right, organized the Pastors' Emergency League to send uncorrupted ministers to serve in parishes whose ministers were influenced by Nazism. About two thousand pastors associated themselves with these initial acts of resistance. If these tempests among the churchmen seem marginal to the events of the time, it should be remembered how alone they were. Bonhoeffer's article was the *first* such defense of the Jewish people.

In October of 1933, Bonhoeffer went to England, where he had arranged to serve as pastor to two German congregations. He did not consult with Barth until he had arrived in London, though it had taken him some time to make the arrangements to leave Germany. When he did write to Barth, he very respectfully invited a rebuke, and he got one. Barth told him to return on the next ship, or the one after it. But Bonhoeffer stayed in England for two years. While he was there he made arrangements to go to India to be with Gandhi.

Only by the standards of his subsequent life do these choices seem doubtful. During his time in England he worked to establish support for the religious resistance in Germany, so he had not abandoned his homeland. And it is consistent with the openness of his views that he considered Gandhi's political actions Christ-like and wished to learn from him. He was a pacifist. He was newly ordained into a tradition he loved deeply and could hardly have wished to attack. His leaving Germany might also be partly explained by church treatment of the Bethel Confession, which he wrote with Martin Niemöller, and which declared, "It is the task of Christians who come from the Gentile world to expose themselves to persecution rather than to surrender, willingly or unwillingly, even in one single respect, their kinship with Jewish Christians in the Church, founded on Word and Sacrament." The paper had been watered down before it was circulated and signed by the dissenting pastors. He might reasonably have questioned the prospects of the religious resistance in Germany. And in fact, if it were not for Bonhoeffer, his writing, and especially his death, few would remember there had ever been any such resistance.

In 1935, the Confessing Church was founded, the church of the Protestant dissenters. Seminaries were established, and Bonhoeffer returned to Germany to head one of them. Later in the same year, Heinrich Himmler decreed that the church and its seminaries were both invalid and that those involved with them were liable to punishment. Finkenwalde, Bonhoeffer's seminary, was closed by the Gestapo in September 1937. Twenty-seven former students were arrested. In February of 1938, Bonhoeffer initiated contact with figures in the *political* resistance to Hitler.

Through all this, Bonhoeffer wrote theology — sermons, lectures, circular letters, and books. In a very great degree his writing is characterized by beautiful iterations of doctrine, a sort of visionary orthodoxy: "History lives between promise and fulfillment. It carries the promise within itself, to become full of God, the womb of the birth of God." To understand his method, one must remember his circumstances. He is asserting the claims of Christ in all their radicalism in order to encourage and reassure those drawn to what became the Confessing Church. At the same time, he is chastising those who use Christianity as an escape from the evils of the world and from the duties those evils imply, and he is chastising those who have accommodated their religion to the prevailing culture so thoroughly as to have made the prevailing culture their religion. His object is to make core beliefs immediate and compelling, to forbid the evasions of transcendence and of acculturation. He is using the scandal of the cross to discover the remnant church among the multitudes of the religious.

Because of the authority of his example, we look to Bonhoeffer for wisdom and guidance as to the right conduct of life, though he is perhaps more earnest in nothing than in insisting that there is no freestanding code through which goodness can be achieved. In his unfinished late work called *Ethics,* he says, "The will of God is not a system of rules which is established from the outset; it is something new and different in each situation in life, and for this reason a person must ever anew examine what the will of God may be. The heart, the understanding, observation, and experience must all collaborate in this task. It is no longer a matter of a person's knowledge of good and evil, but solely the living will of God; our knowledge of God's will is not something over which we ourselves dispose, but it depends solely upon the grace of God, and this grace is and requires to be new every morning."

This is an application of the classic Reformation teaching that no one can do the will of God on the strength of his or her own efforts. It is a statement of the faith that God is present and active in the whole of the world — if he were not he would not have a will to *be* newly expressed in every situation of life. It seems one should be able to extract a secular ethic from the thinking of a man so generous in his views and so positive in his treatment of the secular world as Bonhoeffer, yet to do so is to defeat his clear intention. "Situation ethics" as a form of relativism is obviously not the point, *because* it is what remains of this idea if the active will of God is factored out of it. Later in the same essay he says, "The world, like all created things, is created through Christ and with Christ as its end, and consists in Christ alone."

A scholar coming across such language in an ancient text would quite certainly identify it as a fragment of a hymn. Language of this kind pervades Bonhoeffer's work, which I think may be described as a meditation on it, and a celebration of it. Great theology is always a kind of giant and intricate poetry, like epic or saga. It is written for those who know the tale already, the urgent messages and the dying words, and who attend to its retelling with a special alertness, because the story has a claim on them and they on it. Theology is also close to the spoken voice. It evokes sermon, sacrament, and liturgy, and, of course, Scripture itself, with all its echoes of song and legend and prayer. It earns its authority by winning assent and recognition, in the manner of poetry but with the difference that the assent seems to be to ultimate truth, however oblique or fragmentary the suggestion of it. Theology is written for the small community of those who would think of reading it. So it need not define freighted words like "faith" or "grace" but may instead reveal what they contain. To the degree that it does them any justice, its community of readers will say yes, enjoying the insight as their own and affirming it in that way.

Theology may proceed in the manner of a philosophical treatise or a piece of textual criticism, but it always begins by assuming major terms. And all of them, being imbedded in Scripture and tradition, behave altogether differently from discursive language. To compound the problem, Christian thinkers since Jesus have valued paradox as if it were resolution. So theology is never finally anything but theology, words about God, proceeding from the assumptions that God exists and that we know about him in a way that allows us to speak about him. Bonhoeffer calls these truths of the church "a word of recognition among friends." He invokes this language of recognition and identification in attempting to make the church real and aware of itself, with all that implied when he wrote. For him, word is act. And, for him, it was.

In a very striking degree, Bonhoeffer's theology returns to

formulations which are virtually credal in their use of imagery taken from the narrative of the sacrifice of Christ. The effect is beautiful, musical. But the language functions not as ornament but as ontology. For him, it makes the most essential account that can be made of Being itself. For example, in a late letter famous for the statement that Christianity must be "demy- thologized" and biblical concepts reinterpreted in a "worldly" sense, he explains, "What is above this world is, in the gospel, intended to exist *for* this world; I mean that, not in the anthro- pocentric sense of liberal, mystic, pietistic, ethical theology, but in the biblical sense of the creation and of the incarnation, crucifixion, and resurrection of Jesus Christ." Clearly he does not consider such language mythological, and the case could be made that he does not consider it religious either. This fact expresses his belief in the preeminent reality of the cosmic narrative implied in the words Christ, incarnation, crucifixion, and resurrection. Myth and religion are at the margin. Christ is at the center.

Bonhoeffer invokes such language as the culminating ex- pression of any passionate argument, especially the great Nev- ertheless, that the world is to be loved and served and that God is present in it. The day after the failure of the attempt to assassinate Hitler, in which he and his brother and two of his brothers-in-law were deeply involved, Bonhoeffer wrote a let- ter to Bethge about "the profound this-worldliness of Christi- anity." He said, "By this-worldliness I mean living unreservedly in life's duties, problems, successes and failures, experiences and perplexities. In so doing we throw ourselves completely into the arms of God, taking seriously, not our own sufferings, but those of God in the world — watching with Christ in Gethse- mane . . . How can success make us arrogant, or failure lead us astray, when we share in God's suffering through a life of this kind?". These would seem to be words of consolation, from himself as pastor to himself as prisoner. But they are also an argument from the authority of one narrative moment. The painful world must be embraced altogether, because Christ went to Gethsemane.

In 1937, Bonhoeffer published *The Cost of Discipleship*. He attacked the "cheap grace" of prevailing Lutheran teaching, which seemed merely to make people comfortable with their sins. "Costly grace" (interestingly he does not call it "true" grace, though the implications of the distinction would almost justify the use of that word) carried with it the acknowledged obligation of discipleship, that is, obedience: "It is only through actual obedience that a person can become liberated to believe." He says that although, as Luther taught, faith is prior to obedience, in effect the two are simultaneous, "for faith is only real when there is obedience, never without it, and faith only becomes faith in the act of obedience." This argument does not cite Paul's Epistle to the Romans or otherwise ground itself in authority, though it means to overturn historical consensus about a crucial Reformation doctrine. The writing comes out of the time at Finkenwalde, from his teaching and his preaching to young men who were making a brave attempt at obedience. Their faith was "worldly," that is, active and costly, not theoretical or doctrinal. He is appealing over the head of conventional theology, to shared experience. This is another form of the "word of recognition among friends," an appeal to the experience of act as witness and as revelation. Bonhoeffer's theology is in its circumstance as much as on the page, and this must surely have been his intention. No other method would have been consistent with his theology.

Life Together, Bonhoeffer's book about Finkenwalde as a model of Christian community, came out two years later.

Again, the appeal is to experience, an intuition of how life might be, based on the kind of visionary memory that becomes more important in Bonhoeffer's writing as his life becomes more isolated and tenuous. The church — the eternal, present, felt being of Christ in the world which had always been at the center of his faith and his religious imagination — was or could be seen or apprehended in Finkenwalde or its like: "We have one another only through Christ, but through Christ we really do *have* one another. We have one another completely and for all eternity." The Gestapo, of course, had closed the seminary. His account of it is like mysticism barely concealed or restrained, though all that is being described is a community of the faithful. Visionary memory and anticipation are increasingly the "world" he will cling to until his death. To see divine immanence in the world is an act of faith, not a matter to be interpreted in other than its own terms, if one grants the reasonableness of the perceiver. And Dietrich Bonhoeffer thought and believed his way to a surpassing reasonableness.

In 1939, Bonhoeffer traveled to New York. He had studied there for a year, at Union Theological Seminary, as a young man of twenty-four. He contacted Reinhold Niebuhr, his former teacher, who was then in England, and asked him to arrange an invitation for him to return to the United States. He was at risk of being drafted into Hitler's army. The invitation was made, and he was offered a teaching post, but he returned to Germany after a month out of homesickness and a feeling that he would lose the right to influence Germany in the period after the war if he stayed in America. He was no longer allowed to teach in Berlin, and he would soon be prohibited from speaking in public and required to report regularly to the police. But his brother-in-law Hans von Dohnanyi was an officer in the Abwehr, the military intelligence, which was a center of covert resistance and which became the nucleus of the Officers' Plot. Dohnanyi took him on as an agent, an arrangement which kept him unmolested and allowed him to travel to Switzerland and Sweden in behalf of the resistance. In Switzerland he spoke with representatives of the Vatican and in Sweden he described to the English bishop George Bell a plan for simultaneous coups in Berlin and throughout occupied Europe, with support from unions, the military, and the Protestant and Catholic churches. This plan seems to have found no encouragement. During much of this time he lived as a guest in a Benedictine abbey near Munich and worked on the unfinished *Ethics.*

A few months before his arrest in April of 1943, Bonhoeffer became engaged to Maria von Wedemeyer, with whom, in keeping with the starchy customs of their class, and then with the conditions of his imprisonment, he was never to spend a single moment alone. He was thirty-seven and she was nineteen. Her family disapproved, and only announced the engagement when he was arrested, as a gesture of support. He wrote to her, as well as to Eberhard Bethge, imagining a sweetly ordinary domestic life even as bombs crashed into the prison buildings. His letters to her have long theological passages, too, gentler and more lyrical than those written to Bethge.

The fact that he wrote theology in these circumstances, in letters to dearly loved friends which he could not anticipate would ever be published, illuminates all his earlier work. These letters, too, are meant to actualize the sacred, that is, the relationship of love, the ground of shared understanding. Two ideas are essential to Bonhoeffer's thinking: first, that the sacred can be inferred from the world in the experience of goodness, beauty, and love; and second, that these things, and, more generally, the immanence of God, are a real presence, not a symbol or a foreshadowing. They are fulfillment as well as promise, like the sacrament, or the church. The mystery of the world for Bonhoeffer comes with the belief that immanence is pervasive, no less so where it cannot be discovered. The achieved rescue of creation brings the whole of it under grace. So moments that are manifestly sacred do not judge or shame the indifference of the world, or its misery or its wickedness. Instead, they imply a presence and an embrace sufficient to it all, without distinction. Bonhoeffer is certainly never more orthodox than in seeing the revealed nature of Christ as depending, one might say, on his making precisely this overreaching claim on recalcitrant humankind.

In *The Cost of Discipleship* he wrote: "Jesus does not promise that when we bless our enemies and do good to them they will not despitefully use and persecute us. They certainly will. But not even that can hurt or overcome us, so long as we pray for them. For if we pray for them, we are taking their distress and poverty, their guilt and perdition, upon ourselves, and pleading to God for them. We are doing vicariously for them what they cannot do for themselves. Every insult they utter only serves to bind us more closely to God and them. Their persecution of us only serves to bring them nearer to reconciliation with God and to further the triumphs of love." This is the power of Christ that is the weakness of Christ. He is present even where he is forgotten and efficacious even where he is despised. Such things could not be known about him except in a world like this one. So the secular and the "religionless" are an intrinsic part of divine self-revelation. As, in fact, they were central to the role of Jesus while he lived.

Watching with Christ in Gethsemane, Bonhoeffer worked at loving the world. In a letter to Bethge he wrote: "It is only when one loves life and the world so much that without them everything would be gone, that one can believe in the resurrection and a new world. It is only when one submits to the law that one can speak of grace, and only when one sees the anger and the wrath of God hanging like grim realities over the head of one's enemies that one can know something of what it means to love them and forgive them." But these exertions of forgiveness did not change his world. Bonhoeffer was in the hands of the SS. This cannot have been irrelevant to the drift of his thoughts about the future of Christendom, nor can the awareness of atrocities he must have had through Hans von Dohnanyi and others. When he says "the time of inwardness and conscience, which is to say the time of religion" is over, and "we are proceeding towards a time of no religion at all: men as they are now simply cannot be religious any more," it seems to me fatuous to imagine that he is simply postulating a cultural trend that is to be absorbed like others.

He might well have concluded that there is one thing worse than hypocrisy. Yet clearly he is using "religion" in his usual, Barthian sense, albeit with a certain nostalgia. He suggests that the conception of God among the generality of people, the "religious premise," might have been historical and temporary. Insofar as it was, he himself would never have hesitated to call it false. The God of revelation, of Barth and Bonhoeffer, is neither an "a priori" nor a creation of culture. These are the humanist views of God they both explicitly reject. But "the church" has always lived within religion, usually indistinguishable from it: "If religion is no more than the garment of Christianity — and even that garment has had very different aspects at different times — then what is a religionless Christianity?" In the course of the paragraph Bonhoeffer works his way back to his most characteristic assertion, that Christ is autonomously present, dependent on no human intention or belief or institution. He cannot answer his own question, but he can say, "God is the 'beyond' in the midst of our lives. The Church stands not where human powers give out, on the borders, but in the center of the village." That "religion" has made inappropriate claims, that God and "the church" should stand in opposition to it, is not a new idea for Bonhoeffer. Surely what is to be noted in all this is Bonhoeffer's steadfast refusal to condemn the "religionless" world, and his visionary certainty that it is comprehended in the divine presence.

This is Christ-like, only in the manner that the thoughts of a disciple might have been if one of them had watched with him on the night of his betrayal. It is striking how Bonhoeffer insists always on the role of disciple, of one among a company of equals, from which no one must be excluded. Though he was an aristocrat and aloof in his manner, he seems to have had no imagination of beatitude which is not a humanly understandable moment with a beloved friend. To Bethge, he wrote of his imprisonment, "One thing is that I do miss sitting down to table with others. The presents you send me acquire here a sacramental value; they remind me of the times we have sat down to table together. Perhaps the reason why we attach so much importance to sitting down to table together is that table fellowship is one of the realities of the Kingdom of God."

Neither has he any interest in himself as solitary martyr. He generalizes from his circumstance to the human condition with a consistency that leads commentators to forget how extreme his isolation really was, and how available the idea of martyrdom or abandonment would have been to him, if he had not always transformed his suffering into compassion for humankind, or for God. It is not hard to imagine what dark night might have preceded words like these: "The God who is with us is the God who forsakes us (Mark 15:34). The God who lets us live in the world without the working hypothesis of God is the God before whom we stand continually. Before God and with God we live without God. God lets the divine self be pushed out of the world onto the cross."

Bonhoeffer's family arranged to help him escape from prison, but he chose to remain because his brother Klaus, also in prison, might bear repercussions. He was executed in April of 1945, after nineteen months of imprisonment. His brother-in-law Hans von Dohnanyi died the next day, his brother Klaus and his brother-in-law Rudiger Schleicher within the month. A British prisoner wrote of Bonhoeffer in his last days that he "always seemed to diffuse an atmosphere of happiness, of joy in every smallest event in life, and a deep gratitude for the mere fact that he was alive." This same prisoner wrote that when he was taken away to his execution, Bonhoeffer said, "This is the end — for me, the beginning of life."

McGuffey and
the Abolitionists

THE ENGLISH LANGUAGE should provide us with a way of distinguishing among the very different things we call "history" — the temporal past, the past inherited as culture, the recorded past, the past interpreted. The true past is veiled in mystery, to the extent that it can be said to exist at all. Insofar as we receive it, it is liable to record itself in us culturally as assumption too fundamental to be reached by inquiry, or as memory so painful it must be rationalized, falsified, or suppressed. It is liable to being reconstrued to bear the blame for present vice or failure, or simplified and brutalized to allow a sense of relative progress. Records, of course, are biased toward the literate and the official and must always be assumed to be flawed by the methods and circumstances of record keeping, and the accidents of preservation and accessibility. The interpreted past incorporates all these difficulties and adds new distortions having to do with the motives, enthusiasms, sensibilities, talents, and scruples of interpreters. In dealing with a group like the abolitionists, who were profoundly self-aware and intent not only on making history but also on molding it, one finds all problems compounded.

The interested observer notes certain anomalies in the American use of American history. Here is an example. The *New England Primer* is fairly inevitably referred to as the great characteristic and formative expression of the New England mind. No one, in my experience, pauses over the fact that it was put together entirely from British materials by an English printer briefly resident in Boston, or that it was sold and used in England and Scotland into the nineteenth century. In other words, the *Primer* is offered as an instance of the cultural peculiarity and isolation of New England, when in fact it proves that New England was culturally and religiously very intimately connected with Britain. The *Primer* includes the Westminster Catechism, a finely honed document full of a long history of conflict and debate. The convention is to place the *Primer* as if at the beginning of our history, never alluding to the history with which it is so consciously burdened, and of which the New England settlers were so powerfully aware. I do not wish to say every historian has done this, simply that my own reading has not found an exception. Here again, the interested nonspecialist must linger over the great difference between information that is accessible but somehow inert and information or its like that actually affects thinking and writing. To say that certain work has been done is about equivalent to saying the South Pole has been visited. Another tribute to human diligence. On to other business.

I am the first to concede that much more work is produced in every field than anyone could hope to take in, but I suspect the real problem lies elsewhere, and is both stranger and more easily remedied. Where I have found the *New England Primer* mentioned, I have never found evidence that the writer has read it, no quotes or allusions except the inevitable "In Adam's Fall / We sinned all." It is a volume that can be read twice and pondered thoroughly in the space of ninety minutes, and since it is widely assumed to be the spirit in embryo of perhaps the most influential strain of American culture, one might expect simple curiosity to be motive enough to lead the occasional scholar to look into it. I am bold enough to suggest that somehow, as a culture, we disable simple curiosity, and that the history we write, allude to, repeat, and assume is profoundly conditioned by omissions of just this kind. To say that a certain text is essential to the development of American culture or consciousness is as if to say: Do not bother reading it. You know all you need to know. The book is crude or vexatious and in any case it is faithfully summarized in cliché and canard.

Generations of New Englanders read these lines in their *Primers:*

> Defraud not him who hired is,
> Your labour to sustain;
> And pay him still without delay,
> His wages for his pain,
> And as you would another man
> Against you should proceed,
> Do you the same to them again,
> If they should stand in need.
> Impart your portion to the Poor
> In money and in Meat
> And send the feeble fainting Soul
> Of that which you do eat.

This is a paraphrase of scriptural passages, for example Deuteronomy 24:14–15, "Thou shalt not oppress an hired servant that is poor and needy, whether he be of thy brethren or of thy strangers that are in thy land within thy gates. At his day thou shalt give him his hire, neither shall the sun go down upon it, for he is poor, and setteth his heart upon it, lest he cry against thee unto the Lord, and it be sin unto thee." Or Job 31:17, in which Job declares that he has never "eaten my morsel myself alone, and the fatherless has not eaten thereof." The bit of doggerel from the *Primer* is written in the language of social consciousness one finds in William Blake a hundred years later. Those familiar with English social history will recognize it as the language of the early left.

Modern assumptions about the Old Testament, now an unread classic, make it seem an improbable source for economic and social idealism. In fact, it is more insistent than Marx ever was in championing the poor and the oppressed. Its influence is thought to have made New Englanders severe, yet Jonathan Edwards (1703–1758), who is taken to personify their severity, preached an absolute obligation to assist the needy — before their need became urgent, before they were compelled to seek help, despite any question of their own worthiness or of the responsibility of relatives or others to assist them. Such assistance was to be given to them in addition to the support they received from the towns, since "it is too obvious to be denied, that there are in fact persons so in want, that it would be a charitable act in us to help them, notwithstanding all that is done by the town." Taking as text the passage in Deuteronomy 15 that says, among other things, "For the poor shall never cease out of the land: therefore I command thee, saying, Thou shalt open thy hand wide unto thy brother, to thy poor, and to thy needy, in thy land," Edwards says, "God gives us direction *how* we are to give in such a case, *viz. bountifully,* and *willingly* . . . We may also observe how peremptorily this duty is here enjoined, and how much it is insisted on. It is repeated over and over again, and enjoined in the strongest terms . . . The warning is very strict. God doth not only say, Beware that thou do not actually refuse to give him, but, Beware that thou have not one objecting thought against it, arising from a backwardness to liberality. God warns against the beginnings of uncharitableness in the heart, and against whatever tends to a forbearance to give . . . We are particularly required to be kind to the unthankful and to the evil; and therein to follow the example of our heavenly Father, who causes his sun to rise on the evil and the good, and sendeth rain on the just and on the unjust." No doubt Edwards would take a very fiery view indeed of present attitudes to the poor, of our "backwardness to liberality," so ignorantly based on a supposed reclaiming of traditional values. But his hearers would have known the words of Isaiah: "the liberal deviseth liberal things, and by liberal things shall he stand" (32:8).

Or consider these lines from another unread classic:

[W]hatever man you meet who needs your aid, you have no reason to refuse to help him. Say, "He is a stranger"; but the Lord has given him a mark that ought to be familiar to you, by virtue of the fact that he forbids you to despise your own flesh. Say, "He is contemptible and worthless"; but the Lord shows him to be one to whom he has deigned to give the beauty of his image. Say that you owe nothing for any service of his; but God, as it were, has put him in his own place in order that you may recognize toward him the many and great benefits with which God has bound you to himself. Say that he does not deserve even your least effort for his sake; but the image of God, which recommends him to you, is worthy of your giving yourself and all your possessions. Now if he has not only deserved no good at your hand, but has also provoked you by unjust acts and curses, not even this is just reason why you should cease to embrace him in love and to perform the duties of love on his behalf. You will say, "He has deserved something far different of me." Yet what has the Lord deserved? While he bids you forgive this man for all sins he has committed against you, he would truly have them charged against himself. Assuredly there is but one way in which to achieve what is not merely difficult but utterly against human nature: to love those who hate us, to repay their evil deeds with benefits, to return blessings for reproaches. It is that we remember not to consider men's evil intention but to look upon the image of God in them, which cancels and effaces their transgressions, and with its beauty and dignity allures us to love and embrace them.

That is from the *Institutes of the Christian Religion* (1559), the major theological work of John Calvin, not a man known among us for generosity of spirit. But then we do not do him or the many generations immersed in his thought the courtesy of reading him. No more do we hesitate to interpret their works and ways in light of assumptions that are smug and dismissive. Any reader of the *Institutes* must be struck by the great elegance, the gallantry, of its moral vision, which is more beautiful for the resolution with which its theology embraces sorrow and darkness. Again, if we looked at Calvin, we might perhaps understand why he engrossed so much of our culture for so long, and we might even have grounds for a new understanding of our tradition.

I raise these issues because they are important and because they are relatively straightforward. The *New England Primer* was or was not the product and expression of New England civilization. John Calvin did or did not encourage acquisitiveness, this-worldliness, intolerance, contempt for humankind, stoicism, and so on. Provision for the poor, by governments and by individuals, was or was not a feature of the ethic and practice of early America. Significantly misleading things are said and assumed about figures very accessible to scrutiny, whose reputations would greatly benefit from the slightest attention, and about texts that are never consulted though they are perfectly available.

All this is by way of preparation for a discussion of certain other texts which are always described as central to the development of American culture and which are very little read and little considered — the McGuffey readers. For those who have not looked into them, it may be useful to know that, as with the *New England Primer,* those who studied them were not assumed to be children. The fourth, fifth, and sixth readers were meant to be used in high school or college, but lessons that appear in the fourth reader in one edition will appear in the second reader in another. The content of the readers reflects the irregularity of education and the uneven spread of literacy as well as a great scarcity of books. As with Calvin, as with the *Primer,* it is as if we know so much about McGuffey's readers that we need know nothing at all about them. But in fact they are documents of remarkable interest, not least because they are an early and influential cultural product of the Middle West, a highly distinctive and crucial region which is very generally assumed to have neither culture nor history.

I am tracing a lineage here. McGuffey is the intellectual descendant of Calvin's *Institutes* and the *New England Primer,* an active Presbyterian minister and a professor of ancient languages and moral philosophy. He has not escaped the hereditary curse. He is believed to have created or codified a common American culture, and in doing so to have instilled shirtsleeve values of honesty and hard work in generations of children. Moral, cheerful, narrow, and harmless — insofar as such traits are consistent with harmlessness — his texts supposedly expressed and propagated the world view of the American middle class. The historian Henry Steele Commager, who edited a reprint edition of the Fifth Reader of 1879, says in his introduction, "For all its preoccupation with religion, the morality of the Readers was materialistic and worldly. It taught a simple system of rewards and punishments . . . Nothing was left to the imagination, nothing to chance, and nothing, one is tempted to say, to conscience . . . It was a middle-class, conventional, and equalitarian morality . . . Industry, sobriety, thrift, propriety, modesty, punctuality, conformity — these were the essential virtues, and those who practiced them were sure of success. Success, too, for all the patina of morality that was brushed over it, was clearly material." He concludes, mysteriously, "If [the Readers] did not themselves provide the stuff of culture and morality, they were one of the chief instruments for weaving this stuff into the fabric of American life." Commager discusses only William Holmes McGuffey, never mentioning that the fifth and sixth readers were always and only edited by his brother, Alexander Hamilton McGuffey.

I read a few of these books, and I came away persuaded that something else was going on with them. So I looked a little way into the matter and I found that William McGuffey was associated with a radical group in Cincinnati, and that the excerpts he collected and published for the most part anonymously are the work of writers he knew through this circle of radical reformers, or of writers sympathetic to them. According to Commager, "McGuffey, and his collaborators and successors, lived in the midst of the greatest reform era in our history . . . But the Readers show no awareness of this ferment of ideas, confess no temptation to challenge existing institutions, and reveal no inclination to enlarge the concept of social or political responsibility." But consider the following partial list of contributors to various editions of the fourth reader and the causes with which they were associated. If the reforms that engaged them do not seem radical now, it is because they succeeded. The high percentage of women among the writers McGuffey excerpted — it is significantly higher than in other readers of the period — is characteristic of the prominence of women in reform circles.

Dr. Daniel Drake, McGuffey's father-in-law, was an early public health and medical educator who supported universal compulsory education. Maria Edgeworth was an Anglo-Irish writer who championed education of women. Ann Taylor was a British writer who supported the Sunday school movement, an early major advance in popular education. Jacob Abbott was the founder of the Mount Vernon School, a girls' school which offered as rigorous education as any available to boys, and which was entirely governed by its students. James Thomas Fields was an abolitionist publisher and editor in Boston. Elihu Burritt was an American abolitionist and pacifist who founded the internationalist League of Human Brotherhood, based in London. Thomas Grimké, brother of the famous early anti-slavery writers and lecturers Sarah and Angelina Grimké, was founder of the American Peace Society, which advocated total nonresistance to violence. Rev. Lyman Beecher, father of Rev. Henry Ward Beecher and Harriet Beecher Stowe, was an early and crucial antislavery activist. Rev. Samuel Lewis worked with McGuffey for the creation of common schools in Ohio and founded with him the Western College for Teachers, a professional organization meant to support teaching standards. He was also the Anti-Slavery Party candidate for state senate, for congress, and for governor. Sarah Josepha Hale founded the first women's magazine and was an early women's rights activist. Rev. William Ellery Channing wrote a public letter of sympathy in 1836 to James G. Birney, an abolitionist printer in Cincinnati whose press was destroyed by a mob despite the efforts of Henry Ward Beecher to protect it. In 1837, Channing joined a public meeting in Boston to mark the killing in Alton, Illinois, of the abolitionist printer Rev. Elijah Lovejoy, whom Rev. Edward Beecher had attempted to protect. Channing became an active abolitionist, healing the breach between Unitarianism and theological traditionalists like Lyman Beecher, who had opposed it. John Greenleaf Whittier, a close associate of William Lloyd Garrison, was the secretary of the Abolition Society of Philadelphia. In 1839 the offices of his *Pennsylvania Freeman* were sacked and burned by a mob. From 1847 to 1859 he was an editor of the *National Era,* the antislavery periodical that first published *Uncle Tom's Cabin.* Caroline Norton was an English writer on the status of women. James Russell Lowell was associated with the *Anti-Slavery Standard,* edited by the great early abolitionist writer, Lydia Maria Child. Horace Greeley was an abolitionist, labor-reform advocate, and socialist. Harriet Martineau was a British writer on slavery and social reform, author of a little book titled *The Martyr Age in the United States* (1839), which celebrates by name and in detail the abolitionist community then centered in Cincinnati. Her title reflects the fact that the reforms they espoused — abolition first of all — were not popular. It should be noted that the writers associated with antislavery were involved from an early period, like Channing, or from the beginning of their careers, like Lowell, or both, like Whittier. Rufus Griswold's *Poets and Poetry of America* includes Southern writers in sufficient numbers to make their absence from the McGuffeys worthy of note. It is surely worthy of note, also, that when literary writers are included, they have activist credentials.

Abolitionism seems still to be somewhat tarnished by criticisms of it made 150 years ago. It was said then to be an enthusiasm of New Englanders who had no direct experience of slavery and who were not economically dependent on it. Abolitionists were said to exaggerate the horrors of the institution and to simplify the problems and consequences of putting an end to it. There is a tendency to exaggerate regional differences — New York freed the last of its slaves in 1827. It is true that New England outlawed slavery early, though perhaps this fact does not imply a lack of understanding of its nature. It is true that the North flourished without slavery, but there was much evidence from an early period that slavery in fact depressed the development of the South. That is to say, however entangled in slavery, the South was not, strictly speaking, dependent on it either. In any case, such criticisms overlook the degree to which abolitionism foresaw a reform of the whole of society, not simply the suppression of slavery in the states of the South. The impact of the movement is underestimated for this reason. It must be said also that the erosion of rights of black and white Northerners entailed in measures to protect slavery in the South, most notably in the Fugitive Slave Law, made many in the North intensely aware of the consequences of allowing slavery to continue. Yet it is true at the same time that the virulence of public reaction to antislavery activity in the East appears to have been a reason for the deployment of abolitionist resources and energies into the Middle West.

The salient of abolitionism I touch on here was largely the work of people from New England and New York who were Puritans by culture and descent and who saw their movement into the Middle West from the 1830s onward as a reenactment and in effect a vindication of the Puritan settlement in America in the seventeenth century. Notable among them were the numerous family of Rev. Lyman Beecher. They included also Rev. Josiah Grinnell and John Brown. One consequence of their mission was a revival of New England Congregationalism, centered in Iowa. Another consequence was the creation of schools and colleges throughout the Middle West which have greatly affected the cultural development of the region. A third, somewhat indirect, consequence was the publication of the McGuffey readers, the project of W. B. Smith, a publisher who came to Cincinnati from New Haven and who was a member of the congregation of Lyman Beecher.

The cultural colonization of the Middle West by abolitionists was a straightforward consequence of the Second Great Awakening. In 1821, in upstate New York, a Presbyterian minister named George Washington Gale converted (in the phrase of the period) and educated for the ministry a young lawyer named Charles Grandison Finney. Finney's gifts as a revivalist set off an outpouring of religious fervor throughout the Northeast, and gathered to him a band of converts of exceptional gifts and dedication, many of whom became passionate abolitionists. Among his converts was Arthur Tappan, a New York textile merchant and philanthropist who sheltered and guided the development of the antislavery movement through its long early years by dint of sheer openhandedness. The son of a Congregational minister in Northampton, Massachusetts, Tappan made a fortune importing British textiles, primarily silks, which were a product of the same industrial system that received the products of American slave labor. He poured this wealth into antislavery causes with a liberality that bankrupted him once and that led Southerners to put bounties on him. He was called "the most mobbed man in America."

George Washington Gale founded an experimental college

called the Oneida Institute (never to be confused with the Oneida Community), organized according to the Manual Labor System which would be characteristic of other schools founded under his influence, for example Knox College in Illinois and Mount Holyoke College in Massachusetts. Under this system, students and faculty did the work the college required, feeding hogs or planting vegetables or running the printing press. The system was intended to enhance the health and usefulness of educated people, and to remove economic barriers to education and class distinctions within it, by allowing and obliging students to pay their way by work. The Institute served to prepare Finney converts for divinity school. Its student body was racially integrated and deeply committed to abolition. Arthur Tappan supported the school financially and he sent his sons there.

When the first class of Oneida students were ready for divinity school, Tappan undertook to provide one for them. He sent a student, Theodore Weld, to find a good site for a school in the Middle West, and Weld chose Cincinnati, where Presbyterians had already started the Lane Theological Seminary. Tappan promised to support the school if Lyman Beecher would go to Ohio and serve as its president. He also undertook to pay Beecher's salary. Beecher moved his family from Connecticut to Cincinnati in 1832, where they remained for eighteen years. In the words of Harriet Beecher Stowe, "The Lane Theological Seminary was taken possession of as an anti-slavery fortification by a class of about twenty vigorous, radical young men, headed by that brilliant, eccentric genius Theodore D. Weld; who came and sustained themselves there ostensibly as theological students under Dr. Beecher and Professor Stowe, really that they might make of the Seminary an anti-slavery fort."

How all these powerful personalities interacted is not very clear. There was tension of a predictable kind between Beecher, a great intellectual of the period, and the populist Finney (though this difference is easily exaggerated — Beecher, a Yale graduate, was the son of a blacksmith, and a revivalist himself. Finney, a lawyer, lacked formal training for the ministry, but his writings were published and studied in Britain and Germany). It was after contact with Finney that Beecher agreed to leave the East and the eminence he enjoyed there to shepherd Finney's converts through divinity school. In the event, most of the students left Lane Theological Seminary in a body, to protest attempts by the trustees to forbid abolitionist activities and discussion — Weld and the Oneida graduates had converted all their fellow students to antislavery, using Finney's revivalist methods, and they had given themselves over to setting up schools for the black population of Cincinnati and teaching in them, printing tracts and mailing them into the South, lending their horses to fugitives from Kentucky, and, worst of all, simply socializing with local black families. Cincinnati was already a big city with a painful racial history and a penchant for mob violence, and the seminary was threatened. Beecher is blamed for failing to intervene to prevent the trustees from acting, but the situation might well have been truly untenable. Only a few years earlier, the city had attempted to deport its entire black population to Canada. It was usual there, as elsewhere, for resentment to find targets of opportunity.

Beecher eventually had the trustees' rules rescinded, and his school and his circle remained an important center of abolitionism. The so-called Lane Rebels lived in Cincinnati, teaching one another and continuing their antislavery activity, supported by Arthur Tappan, till Tappan discovered Oberlin

College, then in the planning stages. He moved the students to Oberlin, funded the school, and brought in Charles Grandison Finney as professor of theology. "In a great forest, in a mud hole" as Finney described it, the college could institutionalize the radicalism of the Lane Rebels without giving unbearable offense. Oberlin students, most notably the great Theodore Weld, taught and evangelized all over the Middle West, turning public opinion against slavery.

Rev. George Washington Gale came west, too, and founded Knox College, a school so Puritan it did not observe Christmas and so radical that it did celebrate the anniversary of emancipation in the British West Indies. Colleges with strong religious affiliations and reformist social agendas proliferated through the Middle West, little intellectual communities that put into practice their belief in educating women, in forbidding the use of alcohol, in expediting the escape of fugitives from slavery, in enlarging the influence of religious revivalism. This last brought educated people into intense contact with the scattered and transient population of the region, and made them feel moral responsibility for national policies, in a setting where history had not yet hardened around them.

In the manner of colonists, these people came west to do what they could not do at home. Arthur Tappan had tried to assist the founding of a school for young black girls in Canterbury, Connecticut, and a college for black men in New Haven, and both attempts had ended in mob violence. Theodore Weld preached abolition all over Ohio, and absorbed threats and abuse, and made converts. But in Troy, New York, crowds injured him so badly that he never recovered his health. In the East, major institutions encouraged opposition to abolition. But the abolitionists' educating and institution-building, their preaching and publishing and propagandizing, were unrivaled in the Middle West, virtually unanswered, except by mobs, whose excesses they had learned to exploit to excite public sympathy. When Henry Ward Beecher, Lyman's son, went back to accept a pulpit in Brooklyn, New York, he brought the experience of an Ohio abolitionist, educated in the skills of political evangelization, who had worn guns to protect an anti-slavery publisher, who raised money in Northern churches to arm New England colonies in Kansas. His sister Harriet clearly knew the skills of evangelization as well as he did. Both of them undertook to shape public opinion, in one degree or another to make history by interpreting present and collective experience. By any reckoning, they succeeded.

Thus I arrive at last at my starting place, William Holmes McGuffey and his readers. It is hard to know much about McGuffey. He was a westerner by the standards of the time, born in western Pennsylvania in 1800, rescued from childhood poverty by a benevolent schoolmaster, a teacher himself at age fourteen. He became a college professor and then a Presbyterian minister, and lectured and preached for decades, leaving neither lecture nor sermon behind him because he did not write them down. He came to Cincinnati from Miami University in Oxford, Ohio, and served for several years as president of Cincinnati College. He was influential in the creation of a public school system in Ohio, the first such system in the country.

William B. Smith approached Catherine Beecher, who ran a school for girls, with his plan for a series of readers. She declined and suggested McGuffey. Catherine may have been the most conservative of Lyman Beecher's children. She was an abolitionist, however, like her father, Smith's pastor. So far as I have discovered, there is no actual evidence to indicate the kind and degree of affinity that existed between McGuffey and the Beecher circle, beyond a commitment to establishing and strengthening public education. Catherine Beecher went on to establish the National Board of Popular Education to send women teachers into the western territories, an undertaking complementary to McGuffey's. Calvin Stowe, husband of Harriet Beecher and professor at Lane, traveled to Prussia to report on education there, for the purposes of McGuffey's design of a system for Ohio. Clearly this circle did not make clean distinctions between preaching, teaching, and reform, and among them education was a political and visionary enterprise, designed to establish new norms of thought and behavior. Of course the laws that forbade the education of slaves were a great proof of the liberating force of education.

Certainly McGuffey's most remarkable achievement was to have put together texts that were enormously popular in both the Middle West and the South before, during, and after the Civil War. When supplies of the books were cut off by the war, bootleg editions were printed in the South. There was little in the way of cultural consensus in this period. It was by no means clear in the early 1830s, when the McGuffeys first appeared, what kind of economy would develop in the Middle West. Forms of slavery were legal in Illinois. And of course the struggle for Kansas and the lower Middle West was precisely a struggle about which economic system would prevail there. Harriet Beecher Stowe wrote that "Cincinnati was herself to a large extent a slaveholding city. Her property was in slaveholding states. Negroes were negotiable currency; they were collateral security on half the contracts that were at the time being made between the thriving men of Cincinnati and the planters of the adjoining slave states." The rhetorical battles that preceded the Civil War were waged in the language of Scripture, splitting the churches, so even those bonds between interests and loyalties and regions were strained or severed. In the circumstances, the McGuffey readers must be considered a work of considerable tact.

Yet they can be interpreted in the polemical terms of the period. To the extent that it is fair to say McGuffey's texts establish modest well-being as a norm of life, they are positioning themselves on the side of the controversy also associated with the spread of literacy and the establishing of schools. To the extent that these texts portray wealth and standing as the reward of individual effort and character, they are promoting values that are the clear antithesis of the values invoked to justify slavery, whose apologists found norms in what are called aristocratic cultures and precedents in feudalism. Americans are terribly imprecise in their use of economic terms, perhaps because fragments of old polemic have outlived their occasion. So they see McGuffey's smallholder republic as early capitalism, and the colonial economy of the South — a spectacular instance of the expropriation of the worker which existed to supply raw materials for the British and American industrial systems — as something else, something a little more poetical. McGuffey's readers are assumed to be the sweetest statement of mean and minor aspirations, and no one reflects on them further.

In any case, it is easy to overstate the degree to which the books emphasize thrift and industry and so on. To the extent that they do, a context for these virtues is created by more numerous lessons urging kindness and generosity. In a story titled "Emulation" (Fourth Reader, 1866) a rich boy and a poor boy compete for first place in their school. When the poor boy cannot pay for his books, the rich boy buys them for him, then loses the competition. The story has no other moral than that generosity is to be admired. Far from proposing an ethical regime of minor worldly virtue, of self-interest enlightened by piety or benevolence or at least contained by limited aspiration, the lessons are rather ethereal. Their insistence on generosity and kindness is in turn given context by frequent references to death, and to the Bible, which, in the words of one poem, "in teaching me the way to live / Teaches how to die." In other words, the things of this world are very much overshadowed by ultimate things in McGuffey's readers — not surprisingly, since the man was a minister active in a culture where piety and evangelization were so routinely associated with education. It is surprising over against the modern reputation of the readers, however.

The great issue of the status of African-Americans during and after slavery is never alluded to in the readers, nor for that matter are African-Americans, or slavery itself, except in an adulatory essay titled "The Character of Wilberforce," which appeared in the 1837 edition and was removed in 1844. Wilberforce, the British emancipationist, was a hero of the antislavery movement in America. This is not a mere failure to notice the existence of non-Europeans. Indians are represented rather frequently and sympathetically, and their dispossession and destruction are lamented, though they were then ongoing. If the readers neither reflected nor formed public opinion as it is manifested in the history of the period, this only reinforces the argument that they were the product of a special view of society, comparatively candid, humane, moral, and critical.

McGuffey's readers are consistently contemptuous of war, before and after the Civil War. What may look to us like an evasive and calculating handling of explosive issues may have seemed to McGuffey conciliatory, as well as expedient, and therefore consistent with a belief in nonviolence shared by William Lloyd Garrison and his followers, and not inconsistent with abolitionism. After a payment by W. B. Smith of twenty-five dollars, when he agreed to assemble the readers, McGuffey never received another penny for them, though he supervised numerous revisions. So cynicism seems not to have been a factor in the silences that made the texts acceptable in the South, and for that matter in the Middle West.

I have noted before that the South did not respond to the prolonged abolitionist onslaught of publication, evangelization, and institution-building in the Middle West with similar efforts of its own. Oddly enough, in the circumstances, there was not even a publisher of schoolbooks in the South itself. People so education-minded as McGuffey and his circle in Cincinnati might very well consider how such a vacuum should be filled. For them, education was the method as well as the substance of reform, yet education in the Middle West, as well as in the South, would have to take account of intense hostility to the antislavery movement.

It is interesting to consider what else besides slavery is missing from McGuffey's readers. Factories and cities come to mind, an interesting omission for a man living in the so-called London of the West, also known as Porkopolis. Foreign countries, especially Germany, are given respectful notice, but there seem to be no immigrants — and this despite the large and growing German presence in the Middle West. No one in the readers seems to be transient, though the books were distributed into an unsettled frontier. As Mrs. Stowe wrote, "The little western villages of those days had none of the attractions of New England rural life. They were more like the back suburbs of a great city, a street of houses without yards or gardens, run up for the most part in a cheap and flimsy manner, and the whole air of society marked with the impress of a population who have no local attachments, and are making a mere temporary sojourn for money-getting purposes." In fact, the world of the readers suggests rural New England in its fondest memories of itself. This is a consequence of the fact that, under cover of his own westernness, perhaps, McGuffey was publishing New England writers for whom primitive New England served as a norm or an ideal.

Abolitionists set great store by the fact that slavery is not mentioned by name in any of the country's founding documents. To them this meant that these documents anticipate the end of slavery and refuse it the implication of acceptability and permanence that would come with acknowledging it by name. The McGuffey readers acknowledge neither slavery nor the factory system outright, but they teach an ethic so consistently opposed to both of them that they are arguably the subject of the books, in the same way that life in nineteenth-century society is the subject of *Walden,* and the preoccupation of Brook Farm and of Oberlin College. Just as the intention of individual stories in these collections is exemplary, so the intention of the readers altogether is also exemplary.

For years, reasoning about our cultural origins seems to have gone this way: We are a capitalist civilization, therefore the influences that formed us must have encouraged capitalism. From which it follows that these influences, to be understood aright, must be seen as protocapitalist. Putting aside the doubtful language, the simplicity of this approach to history is bald and barbarous and tendentious. We begin with our conclusion, then dismiss as aberrant or insignificant whatever does not support it, including, as it happens, those same formative influences, which are often invoked and never quoted, and, coincidentally, do not yield themselves to this kind of reading. I have no conclusion to offer in place of the old one, except that history is very strange and beautiful and instructive in the absence of all conclusion. The reform movement I mention

here was centered around people who were theologically conservative even in the terms of their time, many of whom took
their theology jot and tittle from Jonathan Edwards. While
teaching at Lane, Lyman Beecher was tried for heresy, in part
because he taught that Edwards's was the only theology worthy of attention. Precisely the same energies that produced
the revival that swept Mount Holyoke College during Emily
Dickinson's time there produced Mount Holyoke College itself,
and the unprejudiced admission of women to Oberlin College,
and the unprejudiced admission of blacks to Oberlin College,
and the proliferation of schools, especially in the Middle West,
meant to promote and to normalize just such reforms.

All this runs contrary to expectation. Yet if one reads
Calvin, the *New England Primer,* and Edwards, as these reformers
did, it all seems logical enough. Our historiography is too rid-
den with expectation, which in its workings is like bias or parti-
sanism, incurious and self-protective. That expectations change
or vary a little hardly matters, since they are crude in their
nature. I wish it could be as if we knew nothing. Then we
would be freer to wonder where those audiences came from
whose intelligence and patience and humanity taught and encouraged Abraham Lincoln to speak as he did, and why national leadership — Lincoln, Grant, Sherman, and so many
others — emerged from the Middle West during the crisis of
the Civil War, and where the Middle West acquired its special
tradition of intellectualism and populism, moral seriousness
and cultural progressivism.

The McGuffeys undertake to correct the provincialisms of
pronunciation of frontier America, and are therefore a sort of
compendium of dialect of their period and region — "Do not
say *geth-uz* for *gath-ers; un-heerd* for *un-heard.*" The readers in fact
seem at least as intent on teaching those who use them to

speak as to read. In 1834, Daniel Drake delivered a once famous address at Miami University in Ohio titled "A Discourse on the History, Character and Prospects of the West," which suggests a relationship between the content of the readers and their great emphasis on spoken language, and with the style and method of the Beechers and others in the reform community. Drake asked, "Ought not the literature of a free people to be declamatory? Should it not exhort and animate? If cold, literal and passionless, how could it act as the handmaid of improvement? . . . In despotisms, it is of little use to awaken the feelings or warm the imagination of the people — here an excited state of both, is indispensable to those popular movements, by which society is to be advanced. Would you rouse men to voluntary action, on great public objects, you must make their fancy and feelings glow under your presentations; you must not carry forward their reason, but their desires and their will . . . Whenever the literature of a new country loses its metaphorical and declamatory character, the institutions that depend on public sentiment will languish and decline." This address was published by W. B. Smith in Cincinnati in 1835, the year before he began the publication of the readers.

We now would no doubt worry over demagogues and mob rule, in the face of so much declaiming. The religious revivals of the time looked to many contemporaries like mass hysteria, dangerous to those caught up in them, and to religion, and to the whole structure of democracy. Yet these passions fueled what was indeed the greatest period of reform in American history. Perhaps reform was effectual, and no doubt it seemed desirable, because people at large could be moved to such extremes of generosity and hope. And what did they hope for? The universalization of literacy and of modest prosperity, to judge from the readers. And the normalization of democratic attitudes and manners, which were a novelty in the world at that time. We have not ourselves achieved these things, nor do we hope for them.

Democracy is profoundly collaborative. It implies a community. It seems to me we have almost stopped using the word in a positive sense, preferring "capitalism," which by no means implies community, and for which, so far as I have seen, our forebears found no use at all. It is possible to imagine that, in a society where democracy was the thing valued and longed for, there could be a reasonable presumption that people would wish to act toward one another in good faith, to promote, as they used to say, the general welfare. That would no doubt go far toward ensuring the wholesomeness of collective passions. Our new ethic is retrojected into the past, onto poor Reverend McGuffey's readers, which were themselves a generous, democratizing work, like McGuffey's other great project, the creation of a public school system. There is no reason to expect the survival of institutions which were the products of an ethos we have effaced and lost. But history is a little forgiving. We need only be ready to put aside what we think we know, and it will start to speak to us again.

Puritans

and Prigs

PURITANISM was a highly elaborated moral, religious, intellectual, and political tradition which had its origins in the writing and social experimentation of John Calvin and those he influenced. While it flourished on this continent — it appears to me to have died early in this century — it established great universities and cultural institutions and an enlightened political order. It encouraged simplicity in dress and manner and an aesthetic interest in the functional which became bone and marrow of what we consider modern. Certainly the idea that a distaste for the mannered and elaborated should be taken to indicate joylessness or an indifference to beauty is an artifact of an old polemic. No acquaintance with New England portrait or decorative art encourages the idea that Puritan tastes were somber. Even their famous headstones display a marked equanimity beside headstones in Church of England graveyards in Britain, with their naturalistic skulls with bones in their teeth and so on. Puritan civilization in North America quickly achieved unprecedented levels of literacy, longevity, and mass prosperity, or happiness, as it was called in those days. To isolate its special character we need only compare colonial New England and Pennsylvania — Quakers as well as Congregationalists and Presbyterians were Puritans — with the colonial South.

Or let us compare them with ourselves. When crops failed in Northampton, Massachusetts, in 1743, Jonathan Edwards of course told his congregation that they had their own wickedness to blame for it. They had failed to do justice (his word) to the poor. He said, "Christian people are to give to others not only so as to lift him above extremity but liberally to furnish him." No one bothers us now with the notion that our own failures in this line might be called sinful, though we fall far short of the standard that in Edwards's view invited divine wrath. Nor does anyone suggest that punishment might follow such failures, though the case could easily be made that our whole community is punished for them every day. In one respect at least we have rid ourselves entirely of Puritanism.

My reading of Puritan texts is neither inconsiderable nor exhaustive, so while I cannot say they yield no evidence of Puritanism as we understand the word, I can say they are by no means characterized by, for example, fear or hatred of the body, anxiety about sex, or denigration of women. This cannot be said of Christian tradition in general, yet for some reason Puritanism is uniquely regarded as synonymous with these preoccupations. Puritans are thought to have taken a lurid pleasure in the notion of hell, and certainly hell seems to have been much in their thoughts, though not more than it was in the thoughts of Dante, for example. We speak as though John Calvin invented the Fall of Man, when that was an article of faith universal in Christian culture.

For Europeans, our Puritans showed remarkably little tendency to hunt witches, yet one lapse, repented of by those who had a part in it, has stigmatized them as uniquely inclined to this practice. They are condemned for their dealings with the Indians, quite justly, and yet it is important to point out that contact between native people anywhere and Europeans of whatever sort was disastrous, through the whole colonial period and after. It is pointless to speak as if Puritanism were the factor that caused the disasters in New England, when Anglicans and Catholics elsewhere made no better account of themselves. Cortés was no Puritan, but William Penn was one. By the standards of the period in which they flourished, American Puritans were not harsh or intolerant in the ordering of their own societies. Look a little way into contemporary British law — Jonathan Swift would never have seen a woman flayed in New England, yet it is Old England we think of as having avoided repressive extremes. If a Puritan writer had made Swift's little joke — that it altered her appearance for the worse — I wonder how it would sound to us. As for religious intolerance, one must again consider the standards of the period. The Inquisition was not officially ended until 1837. Quakers living in Britain were deprived of their civil rights well into the nineteenth century, as were Catholics and Jews. It seems fair to note that such tolerance as there was in Europe was to be found in Calvinist enclaves such as Holland.

What does it matter if a tradition no one identifies with any longer is unjustly disparaged? If history does not precisely authorize the use we make of the word "Puritanism," we all know what we mean by it, so what harm is done? Well, for one thing we make ourselves ignorant and contemptuous of the first two or three hundred years of one major strain of our own civilization. I am eager to concede that in our cataclysmic world this is a little misfortune, arousing even in me only the kind of indignation that could be thoroughly vented in a long footnote somewhere. In fact it is by no means proved to my satisfaction that a society is happier or safer or more humane for having an intense interest in its own past.

Yet the way we speak and think of the Puritans seems to me a serviceable model for important aspects of the phenomenon we call Puritanism. Very simply, it is a great example of our collective eagerness to disparage without knowledge or information about the thing disparaged, when the reward is the pleasure of sharing an attitude one knows is socially approved. And it demonstrates how effectively such consensus can close off a subject from inquiry. I know from experience that if one says the Puritans were a more impressive and ingratiating culture than they are assumed to have been, one will be heard to say that one finds repressiveness and intolerance ingratiating. Unauthorized views are in effect punished by incomprehension, not intentionally and not to anyone's benefit, but simply as a consequence of a hypertrophic instinct for consensus. This instinct is so powerful that I would suspect it had survival value, if history or current events gave me the least encouragement to believe we are equipped to survive.

To spare myself the discomfort of reinforcing the same negative associations I have just deplored, and for weightier reasons, I will introduce another name in the place of "Puritanism" to indicate the phenomenon we are here to discuss. I choose the word "priggishness." This fine old English word, of no known etymology and therefore fetched from the deep anonymous heart of English generations, is a virtual poem in the precision with which it expresses pent irritation. One imagines the word being spat, never shouted, which suggests it is a trait most commonly found among people who are at some kind of advantage. *Webster's Third New International Dictionary* defines "priggish" as "marked by overvaluing oneself or one's ideas, habits, notions, by precise or inhibited adherence to them, and by small disparagement of others." In adopting this word I hope to make the point that the very important phenomenon it describes transcends culture and history. I believe we have all heard accounts of unbridled priggishness during the Cultural Revolution in China, for example, or in Spain under the dictatorship of Franco.

Americans never think of themselves as sharing fully in the human condition, and therefore beset as all humankind is beset. Rather they imagine that their defects result from their being uniquely the products of a crude system of social engineering. They believe this is a quirk of their brief and peculiar history, a contraption knocked together out of ramshackle utilitarianism and fueled by devotion to the main chance. This engineering is performed by them and upon them negligently or brutally, or with shrewd cynicism or mindless acquiescence, all tending to the same result: shallowness, materialism, a merely ersatz humanity.

Clearly there is an element of truth in this. The error comes in the belief that they are in any degree exceptional, that there is a more human world in which they may earn a place if only they can rid themselves of the deficiencies induced by life in an invented nation and a manufactured culture. They have one story they tell themselves over and over, which is: *once we were crude and benighted, and in fact the vast majority of us remain so, but I and perhaps certain of my friends have escaped this brute condition by turning our backs on our origins with contempt, with contempt and derision.* When anything goes wrong, the thinkers among us turn once again to the old conversion narrative: *This is a resurgence of former brutishness, which we will spurn and scorn till we have exorcised it, or at least until those whose approval we covet know this old spirit no longer has power over us, personally — though we cannot, of course, speak for all our friends.* In great things as in small, we are forever in a process of recovery from a past that is always being reinterpreted to account for present pathologies. When things went wrong in Calvinist America, the minister or mayor or governor or president, including of course Lincoln, would declare a Day of Fasting and Humiliation, during which businesses and offices closed and the population went to their various churches to figure out what they were doing wrong and how to repent of it.

The assumption of present responsibility for the present state of things was a ritual feature of life in this culture for two and a half centuries, and is entirely forgotten by us now. Though I cannot take time to make the argument for it here, it is my belief that a civilization can trivialize itself to death, that we have set our foot in that path, and that our relation to the issue of responsibility is one measure of our progress. No matter, it is a self-limiting misfortune — by the time the end comes, the loss to the world will be very small. My point here is simply that there is a reflex in this culture of generalized disapproval, of small or great disparagement, of eagerness to be perceived as better than one's kind, which is itself priggish, and which creates the atmosphere in which these exotic new varieties of priggishness can flower.

The Calvinist doctrine of total depravity — "depravity" means "warping or distortion" — was directed against casuistical enumerations of sins, against the attempt to assign them different degrees of seriousness. For Calvinism, we are all absolutely, that is equally, unworthy of, and dependent upon, the free intervention of grace. This is a harsh doctrine, but no harsher than others, since Christian tradition has always assumed that rather few would be saved, and has differed only in describing the form election would take. It might be said in defense of Christianity that it is unusual in a religion to agonize much over these issues of ultimate justice, though in one form or another every religion seems to have an elect. The Calvinist model at least allows for the mysteriousness of life. For in fact life makes goodness much easier for some people than for others, and it is rich with varieties of cautious or bland or malign goodness, in the Bible referred to generally as self-righteousness, and inveighed against as grievous offenses in their own right. The belief that we are all sinners gives us excellent grounds for forgiveness and self-forgiveness, and is kindlier than any expectation that we might be saints, even while it affirms the standards all of us fail to attain.

A Puritan confronted by failure and ambivalence could find his faith justified by the experience, could feel that the world had answered his expectations. We have replaced this and other religious visions with an unsystematic, uncritical and in fact unconscious perfectionism, which may have taken root among us while Stalinism still seemed full of promise, and to have been refreshed by the palmy days of National Socialism in Germany, by Castro and by Mao — the idea that society can and should produce good people, that is, people suited to life in whatever imagined optimum society, who then stabilize the society in its goodness so that it produces more good people, and so on. First the bad ideas must be weeded out and socially useful ones put in their place. Then the bad people must be identified, especially those that are carriers of bad ideas. Societies have done exactly the same thing from motives they considered religious, of course. But people of advanced views believe they are beyond that kind of error, because they have not paused to worry about the provenance or history of these advanced views. Gross error survives every attempt at perfection, and flourishes. No Calvinist could be surprised. No reader of history could be surprised.

Disallowing factors of disruption and recalcitrance called by names like "sin," what conclusion can be drawn? If human beings are wholly the products of societies, and societies are accessible to reform, what other recourse is there than to attempt to reform one and the other? The question seems pressing now that the community increasingly fails its individual members, and as it is more and more feared, abused, or abandoned by them.

I depend here on the general sense that we are suffering a radical moral decline which is destroying the fabric of society, seriously threatening our sense of safety as well as of mutual respect and shared interest. Such anxieties can be dangerous and irrational — perhaps they are in most cases. But the evidence is impressive that we are now looking at real decay, so I will accept the notion for the purposes of this discussion. I take on faith Tocqueville's lapidary remark that we were great because we were good, when he knew us. Let us say, as history would encourage us to do, that one great difference between then and now is the sense of sin which then flourished, the belief that mortals are born in a state of sin, that no one is or is likely to be perfected. One implication of that belief is certainly that neither social engineering nor intellectual eugenics could produce a good society full of good people. Americans studied the example of biblical Israel, for whom God himself had legislated, and who sinned and strayed very much in the manner of people less favored. The teaching that surrounded the biblical history of Israel suggested that to do justice and love mercy made the community good, but never that the community could be so ordered as to create a population conditioned always to do justice and love mercy. The community never ceased to struggle against contrary impulses, which it did not induce in itself and from which it could not free itself. Christian individualism enforced the awareness that exactly the same impulses are always at work in one's own soul.

The Stalinist vision is much more optimistic. It can propose a solution. Society is simply other people, useful or not, capable of contributing to the general good, or not. Creatures of society, they are also the reasons for the continuing failure and suffering of society. At the same time, since society is the only possible agent of its own transformation, the victim stands revealed as the enemy, the obstacle to reform, the problem to be eliminated. Freed of those it has maimed, it might at last be perfect. This is a great solipsism, a tautology, based on a model of human being-in-the-world which, curiously, has long seemed scientific to people because it is so extremely narrow and simple and has no basis in history or experience.

This social vision has also an attraction that Puritanism never had, Puritanism with its grand assertion and concession, In Adam's Fall / We sinned all. It creates clear distinctions among people, and not only justifies the disparagement of others but positively requires it. Its adherents are overwhelmingly those who feel secure in their own reasonableness, worth, and goodness, and are filled with a generous zeal to establish their virtues through the whole of society, and with an inspiring hope that this transformation can be accomplished. It would seem to me unfair and extreme to liken our new zealots to Stalinists, if I did not do so with the understanding that the whole of the culture is very much influenced by these assumptions, and that in this as in other ways the zealots differ from the rest of us only as an epitome differs from a norm.

Optimists of any kind are rare among us now. Rather than entertaining visions, we think in terms of stopgaps and improvisations. A great many of us, in the face of recent experience, have arrived with a jolt at the archaic-sounding conclusion that morality was the glue holding society together, just when we were in the middle of proving that it was a repressive system to be blamed for all our ills. It is not easy at this point for us to decide just what morality is or how to apply it to our circumstances. But we have priggishness at hand, up-to-date and eager to go to work, and it does a fine imitation of morality, as self-persuaded as a Method actor. It looks like morality and feels like it, both to those who wield it and to those who taste its lash.

(Since I am already dependent on one, I will attempt a definition of authentic morality, based on common usage. When we say someone is moral, we mean that she is loyal in her life and behavior to an understanding of what is right and good, and will honor it even at considerable cost to herself. We would never say she was not moral because she did not urge or enforce her own standards on other people. Nor would we say she was more moral for attempting to impose her standards than she would be if she made no such attempt. Similarly, we say someone is immoral because she does not govern her behavior to answer to any standard of right or good. That being true of her, we would never say she was not immoral because she tried to enforce a standard of virtue on the people around her, nor even that she was less immoral for making such an attempt. Nor would we say someone was moral because her society had in one way or another so restricted her behavior that she could not, in its terms, do anything wrong.)

Though etymologically "morality" means something like social custom, as we use it it means the desire to govern oneself, expressed as behavior. People who attempt this fail, and learn in the course of failing that to act well, even to know what it is to act well, is a great struggle and a mystery. Rather than trying to reform others, moral people seem to me especially eager to offer pardon in the hope of receiving pardon, to forego judgment in the hope of escaping judgment.

So perhaps what I have called priggishness is useful in the absence of true morality, which requires years of development, perhaps thousands of years, and cannot simply be summoned as needed. Its inwardness and quietism make its presence difficult to sense, let alone quantify, and they make its expression often idiosyncratic and hard to control. But priggishness makes its presence felt. And it is highly predictable because it is nothing else than a consuming loyalty to ideals and beliefs which are in general so widely shared that the spectacle of zealous adherence to them is reassuring. The prig's formidable leverage comes from the fact that his or her ideas, notions, or habits are always fine variations on the commonplace. A prig with original ideas is a contradiction in terms, because he or she is a creature of consensus who can usually appeal to one's better nature, if only in order to embarrass dissent. A prig in good form can make one ashamed to hold a conviction so lightly, and, at the same time, ashamed to hold it at all.

I will offer an example of the kind of thing I mean. Our modern zealots have dietary laws. Puritans did not, Calvin having merely urged moderation. For him, many things were "things indifferent," that is, he considered it wrong to attach importance to them. This is a concept alien to the new zealotry.

There has been much attention in recent years to diet as a factor in determining the length and quality of life. That is, the idea together with all sorts of supporting information and speculation has been more than commonplace for a very long time. So here priggishness has a natural stronghold. One codicil of these dietary laws: It is good to eat fish. It is good to eat fish because it is bad to eat beef, an inefficient way to package protein, as Ralph Nader told us years ago, and a destructive presence in the world ecology, and a source of fat and cholesterol. It is good to eat fish because breast cancer is relatively rare in Japanese women and the Japanese life expectancy is imposing and beef was associated somewhere by someone with aggressive behavior in men. Also, steers are warm and breathy and have melting eyes, while fish are merely fish.

A shift in American tastes is a shift in global ecology. The sea has been raided and ransacked to oblige our new scruple, till even some species of shark are threatened with extinction. I myself am inclined to believe that no ecology is so crucial as the sea, or so impossible to monitor or to repair. Until we have some evidence that that great icon the whale can learn to live on municipal refuse and petroleum spills, we might try a little to respect the intricate and delicate system of dependencies necessary to its survival and already profoundly disturbed. Fish is a terribly inefficient way to package protein, if it is provided on a scale that diminishes the productivity of the sea. And consider: the sea is traditionally the great resource of the poor. We are ashamed to eat beef because only a very wealthy country could sustain such a food source. And it makes us fat, parodies of ourselves. So what is any self-respecting people to do? Why, take away the food of the poor. Then at last we will be virtuous, as they are.

As for the matter of the health benefits of eating fish, I think that person is a poor excuse for an ecologist who would tax a crucial and faltering natural system to extend her life a few years, assuming so much can be hoped. People in poor countries whose coasts and fishing grounds have been ruined will give up many years for the sake of the few she will gain, losing children to lengthen her old age. But certain of us have persuaded ourselves that a life lived in accordance with sound principles will be long, so longevity is as solemnly aspired to as goodness would have been in another time.

It is not hard to raise questions about the virtue of eating fish, or about the ecological consequences of mining quartz for those crystals that make us feel so at one with the earth. And is it really worth the petroleum, the pollution, the environmental wear and tear, to import drinking water? Such questions would be inevitable, if these were not the tastes of people who are strongly identified in their own minds as virtuous, and if these were not in fact signs by which they make themselves recognizable to others and to themselves as virtuous. For a very long time this country has figured in the world as a great appetite, suddenly voracious, as suddenly sated, disastrous in either case. The second worst thing that can be said about these virtuous people is, they have not at all escaped the sins of their kind. The worst thing that can be said is they believe they have escaped them.

People who are blind to the consequences of their own behavior no doubt feel for that reason particularly suited to the work of reforming other people. To them morality seems almost as easy as breathing. Fish-eating water-drinkers who confront their geriatric disorders in long anticipation — we could all be like them. But if there is, as I wish to suggest, little to choose between the best of us and the worst of us in terms of our ecological impact, how do the zealots command the attention they do? Why do they have no real critics?

First of all, as I have said, they are archdefenders of the obvious, for example, of the proposition that the planet needs looking after, and that one's health needs looking after — and while their diligence may in fact be as destructive as the general lethargy, it is reassuring to all of us to think that there is a radical vanguard, girded with purpose, armed with fact, etc.

Second, there is simple snobbery. Here I am, reaching yet again into the lexicon of British dialect — no language of flatterers, in fact a reservoir of painful truth. Our zealots adopt what are in effect class markers. Recently I saw a woman correct a man in public — an older man whom she did not know well — for a remark of his she chose to interpret as ethnocentric. What he said could easily have been defended, but he accepted the rebuke and was saddened and embarrassed. This was not a scene from some guerrilla war against unenlightened thinking. The woman had simply made a demonstration of the fact that her education was more recent, more fashionable, and more extensive than his, with the implication, which he seemed to accept, that right thinking was a property or attainment of hers in a way it never could be of his. To be able to defend magnanimity while asserting class advantage! And with an audience already entirely persuaded of the evils of ethnocentricity, therefore more than ready to admire! This is why the true prig so often has a spring in his step. Morality could never offer such heady satisfactions.

The woman's objection was a quibble, of course. In six months, the language she provided in place of his will no doubt be objectionable — no doubt in certain quarters it is already. And that is the genius of it. In six months she will know the new language, while he is still reminding himself to use the words she told him he must prefer. To insist that thinking worthy of respect can be transmitted in a special verbal code only is to claim it for the class that can concern itself with inventing and acquiring these codes and is so situated in life as to be able, or compelled, to learn them. The more tortuous our locutions the more blood in our streets. I do not think these phenomena are unrelated, or that they are related in the sense that the thought reforms we attempt are not extensive enough or have not taken hold. I think they are related as two manifestations of one phenomenon of social polarization.

There is more to this little incident. In fact, I must back up a considerable distance, widen the scene a little, if I am to do it any sort of justice. First of all, where did the idea come from that society should be without strain and conflict, that it could be satisfying, stable, and harmonious? This is the assumption that has made most of the barbarity of our century seem to a great many people a higher philanthropy. The idea came from Plato, I suppose. Our social thought has been profoundly influenced by a categorical rejection of Periclean Athens. No point brooding over that.

Let us look at the matter scientifically. The best evidence must lead us to conclude that we are one remote and marginal consequence of a cosmic explosion. Out of this long cataclysm arose certain elements and atmospheres, which in combination and over time produced, shall we say, New York City, with all it embraces and implies. Well, all right. Imagine accident upon coincidence upon freak, heightened by mysterious phenomena of order and replication, and there you have it. That natural process should have produced complicated animals who exist in vast aggregations is conceivable. But, I submit, that they should be suited to living happily — in vast aggregations or in farming villages or as hermits on the tops of mountains — is a stroke of thinking so remarkable in a supposedly nontheological context that it takes my breath away. Scientifically speaking, we are weird, soft, bigheaded things because we adapted to the mutable world by keeping a great many options open. Biologically speaking, we are without loyalties, as ready to claim an isthmus as a steppe. In our bodies we are utterly more ancient than Hittites and Scythians, survivors of the last swarm of locusts, nerved for the next glaciation. We have left how many cities standing empty? That any condition of life should be natural and satisfactory to us is an idea obviously at odds with our nature as a species, and as clearly at odds with our history. Would not mass contentment be maladaptive? Yet so much of modern life has been taken up with this nightmare project of fitting people to society, in extreme cases hewing and lopping away whole classes and categories. Humankind has adopted and discarded civilization after civilization and remained itself. We have done the worst harm we have ever suffered by acting as if society can or should be stable and fixed, and humankind transformed by whatever means to assure that it will be.

I am making this argument in terms not natural to me. My heart is with the Puritans. I would never suggest that history, whatever that is, should be left to take its natural course, whatever that is. I accept what Jonathan Edwards might have called the "arbitrary constitution" of behests and obligations. I draw conclusions from the fact that we cannot reason our way to a code of behavior that is consistent with our survival, not to mention our dignity or our self-love. But, even in the terms of this argument, what could have been more brutal than these schemes to create happy and virtuous societies? Might we not all have been kinder and saner if we had said that discontent is our natural condition, that we are the Ishmael of species, that, while we belong in the world, we have no place in the world? And that this is true not because something went wrong, but because of the peculiar terms of our rescue from extinction? Our *angst* and our *anomie* have meant to us that society has gone wrong, which means that other people have harmed us. The corollary of this notion, that our unhappiness is caused by society, is that society can make us happy, or remove the conditions that prevent us from being happy. And if the obstacle to collective happiness is believed to be other people, terrible things seem justified.

When the woman in the episode I described rebuked and embarrassed someone for using the wrong language, she was acting on an assumption that is now very common and respectable, which is that vice, shall we call it, is perpetuated in society in words, images, narratives, and so on; that when these things are weeded out vice is attacked; that where they still appear vice is flourishing. The cruelest words and the most disturbing images have normally been discountenanced in this society, and have been cherished by those who love forbidden things, just as they are now. Formerly the society was more tolerant of racial slurs and vastly less tolerant of depictions of violence, especially against women. It was also more racist and less violent. I cannot speculate which is cause and which effect, or even if it is meaningful to describe the phenomena in those terms. In any case, the "vice" in this instance was on the order of saying Mohammedan for Muslim, Oriental for Asian. Neither of the forbidden words has a hint of aspersion in it. They are simply associated with old attitudes, which they are taken to contain and reveal. No matter that the man who misspoke is known to be a very generous-spirited man, who would never intend an aspersion against anyone. Social methods that have been used to restrict the expression of obscenity or aggression — shaming, for example — are now slurring over to control many other forms of language (and therefore, on the short-blanket principle that is always a factor in moral progress, no longer restrict obscenity and aggression). This is done on the grounds that certain words are socially destructive, as indeed in varying degrees and circumstances they may sometimes be. This would be no fit subject for an analysis of priggishness if it did not have at least one foot in safe moral territory.

But, needless to say, there are problems. One is in the binary assumption that ideas equal words and that words carry ideas in them. If the relationship between words and ideas were indeed that close, no one would be paid for writing. Words would not be transformed by use. New ideas would depend on new coinages. This is thinking of the kind I call Stalinist, because it derives moral confidence and authority from its incredible simplicity. Now, if anything in the world is complex, language is complex. But the point is not really to characterize language but to characterize society by implying that certain things are true about language. A great mythic world rests on the back of this small conceptual turtle.

Very early on I proposed that priggishness is so available to us, and that where we do not subscribe to it we are nevertheless so helpless against it, because we cherish a myth of conversion in which we throw off the character our society gives us and put on a new one in all ways vastly superior. Normally this great change is achieved by education, enhanced by travel, refined by reading certain publications, manifested in the approved array of scruples and concerns, observed ritually in the drinking of water, the eating of fish, the driving of Volvos, and otherwise. (I think to myself, if we must be so very imitative, why can we never imitate a grace or an elegance? But that is outside the range of the present discussion. Though I do note that priggishness has never shown any aptitude for such things, any more than elegance or grace have claimed an affinity with priggishness.) Among us salvation is proved by a certain fluency of disparagement and disavowal. The prig in us could not enjoy all this, or believe in it, if the distinctions made were only economic and social. They must also, first of all, be moral.

Here I will divulge a bitter thought. I will say, by way of preparation, that much of the behavior I observe in these people looks like the operations of simple fashion. Phrases and sensitivities change continuously, perhaps as a function of evolving consciousness, perhaps as a feature of intense and active peer group identification. Clearly, as economic subset, our zealots experience the same frissons of consumer optimism we all do, though they might be focused on fetish bears rather than video cameras, one desideratum supplanting another in the ordinary way. Traffic in moral relics is an ancient practice, and while it is not harmless, neither is much else.

But I think there might be another impetus behind all this mutation. I think because our zealots subscribe to the conversion myth, they can only experience virtuousness as difference. They do not really want to enlist or persuade — they want to maintain difference. I am not the first to note their contempt for the art of suasion. Certainly they are not open to other points of view. If it is true that the shaping impulse behind all this stylized language and all this pietistic behavior is the desire to maintain social distinctions, then the moral high ground that in other generations was held by actual reformers, activists, and organizers trying to provoke debate and build consensus, is now held by people with no such intentions, no notion of what progress would be, no impulse to test their ideas against public reaction as people do who want to accomplish reform. It is my bitter thought that they may have made a fetish of responsibility, a fetish of concern, of criticism, of indignation.

More bitter still is the thought that those who are, in Edwards's terms, in need of justice, are, in contemporary terms, damaged, imperfectly humanized, across the divide. The fact is that in this generation, change in the lives of the poor and the undefended is change for the worse, again for the worse, always for the worse.

If serious efforts at rectification were being made, would this be true? If serious solutions were being attempted, would not someone hold them to the standard of their effect, and suggest a reconsideration?

While Calvinists spoke of an elect, Leninists and suchlike have spoken of an elite. The two words come from the same root and mean the same thing. Their elect were unknowable, chosen by God in a manner assumed to be consistent with his tendency to scorn the hierarchies and overturn the judgments of this world. Our elites are simply, one way or another, advantaged. Those of us who have shared advantage know how little it assures, or that it assures nothing, or that it is a positive threat to one's moral soundness, attended as it is with so many encouragements to complacency and insensitivity. I have not yet found a Puritan whose Calvinism was so decayed or so poorly comprehended that he or she would say to another soul, I am within the circle of the elect and you are outside it. But translated into the terms of contemporary understanding, and into the terms of my narrative, that is what that woman said to that man.

A small thing, foolishness, bad manners. I run the risk of being ungenerous in taking this woman so much to task, and there is a whiff of snobbery in my own scorn for her pretensions. I accept the justice of all this, yet I persist.

The American salvation myth and the Stalinist salvation myth have in common the idea that the great body of the culture is a vast repository of destructive notions and impulses, that certain people rise out of the mass in the process of understanding and rejecting all that is retrograde, and that, for those people, there is never any use for, nor even any possibility of, conversation on equal terms with those who remain behind. The history of elites is brutal and terrible. When the impact of scientific and industrial and political elites finally becomes clear — and it has been devastating in every part of the world — it will become clear also that people picked at random off the street would probably have made better decisions. It would be wonderful if there were a visible elect, a true elite, who could lead us out of our bondage, out of our wilderness. But we are not so favored. Our zealots seem to assume they do provide such leadership — that if one cannot embrace their solutions it is surely because one is indifferent to great problems, or complicit in them. This is a manifestation of their presumption of legitimacy that I find especially disturbing, not least because their solutions then become the issue while the reality of the problems is forgotten, except by the police, the courts, the coroners.

If there is any descriptive value in the definition of morality I offered above, its great feature is autonomy. Tacitus admired the morality of the Germans, Calvin admired the morality of Seneca and Cicero — anyone who considers the question knows that morality can take any number of forms, that it can exist in many degrees of refinement and so on. We all distinguish instantly between a moral lapse and a difference of standards. Whatever else it is, morality is a covenant with oneself, which can only be imposed and enforced by oneself. Society can honor these covenants or not. Historically, it seems that repression often encourages them. The great antidote to morality is cynicism, which is nothing more than an understanding of how arbitrary morality is, how unpredictable and unenforceable, how insecurely grounded in self-interest. It appears to me that even very thoughtful people discover what terms they have made with themselves only as they live, which prohibitions are conditional, which absolute, and so on. So in this great matter of moral soundness or rigor or whatever, we are as great mysteries to ourselves as we are to one another. It should not be that way, of course. The human condition has an amazing wrongness about it. But if it is agreed that we are in this respect mysterious, then we should certainly abandon easy formulas of judgment. If it is true that morality is a form of autonomy, then social conditioning is more likely to discourage than to enhance it.

If, putting out of consideration the inwardness of people, and putting aside the uniqueness of the terms in which everyone's relations with the world are negotiated, and excluding the very prevalent desire of people to align themselves with what they take to be right, and ignoring the fact that people have ideas and convictions for which they cannot find words, we choose to believe all the errors of our past are stored in the minds of those who use language we have declared to embody those errors, then we make the less sophisticated tiers of the society the problem and the enemy, and effectively exonerate ourselves. We know what they mean better than they do, so we only listen to hear them condemn themselves. In the name of justice we commit a very crude injustice. We alienate a majority of our people, and exclude them from a conversation of the most pressing importance to them, having nothing but our smugness to justify the presumption.

We must find a better model to proceed from.

This is John Calvin glossing the text "Love thy neighbor":

Here, therefore, let us stand fast: our life shall best conform to God's will and the prescriptions of the law when it is in every respect most fruitful for our brethren . . . It is very clear that we keep the commandments not by loving ourselves but by loving God and neighbor; that he lives the best and holiest life who lives and strives for himself as little as he can, and that no one lives in a worse or more evil manner than he who lives and strives for himself alone, and thinks about and seeks only his own advantage.

Here is John Calvin answering the question "Who is our neighbor?"

It is the common habit of mankind that the more closely men are bound together by the ties of kinship, of acquaintanceship, or of neighborhood, the more responsibilities for one another they share. This does not offend God; for his providence, as it were, leads us to it. But I say: we ought to embrace the whole human race without exception in a single feeling of love; here there is no distinction between barbarian and Greek, worthy and unworthy, friend and enemy, since all should be contemplated in God, not in themselves. When we turn aside from such contemplation, it is no wonder we become entangled in many errors. Therefore, if we rightly direct our love, we must first turn our eyes not to man, the sight of whom would more often engender hate than love, but to God, who bids us extend to all men the love we bear to him, that this may be an unchanging principle: Whatever the character of the man, we must yet love him because we love God.

No one is so contemptible or worthless "but the Lord shows him to be one to whom he has deigned to give the beauty of his image." This is the theological basis for Jonathan Edwards's wonderful definition of "justice."

Whatever confronts us, it is not a resurgence of Puritanism. If we must look to our past to account for our present circumstances, perhaps we might ponder the impulse long established in it to disparage, to cheapen and deface, and to falsify, which has made a valuable inheritance worthless. Anyone who considers the profound wealth and continuing good fortune of this country must wonder, how do we make so little of so much? Now, I think, we are making little of the language of social conscience and of the traditions of activism and reform. We are losing and destroying what means we have had to do justice to one another, to confer benefit upon one another, to assure one another a worthy condition of life. If Jonathan Edwards were here, he would certainly call that a sin. I am hard pressed to think of a better word.

Marguerite
de Navarre

T HE TITLE OF THIS ESSAY is somewhat misleading.
My intention, my hope, is to revive interest in Jean
Cauvin, the sixteenth-century French humanist and
theologian — he died in 1564, the year Shakespeare was born
— known to us by the name John Calvin. If I had been forthright about my subject, I doubt that the average reader would
have read this far. Anyone interested in American history
knows that Calvin exerted as important an influence on it as
anyone — John Locke was deeply in his debt, and this is hardly
surprising, since Locke's political thinking was formed during
the great Calvinist experiment of the English Revolution and
Commonwealth. Yet when we talk about our history, Calvin
does not figure in the conversation, or when he does, it is as
Adam Smith's censorious cousin. People know to disapprove of
him, though not precisely why they should, and they know he
afflicted us with certain traits the world might well wish we
were in fact afflicted with, like asceticism and an excess of
ethical rigor. His misdeeds are somehow of a kind to forbid

attention. Coincidentally, they are not great, by the standards of his century or of ours.

And if his misdeeds were very great, and we are marked by a grim paternity, then we should certainly know the particulars of our inheritance. Finding the etiologies of our crimes and vices has given purpose to much writing of history. Surely if Calvin is as bleak an influence as we ordinarily assume, he presents an opportunity not to be missed. A more flamboyant life than his would have attracted attack and then inevitable defense, or celebration and then ferocious debunking. Calvin was a sickly, diligent pastor, scholar, diplomat, and polemicist, who wrote theology of breathtaking beauty and tough-mindedness as well as line-by-line commentary on most books of the Bible. When he died he was buried, as he had asked to be, in an unmarked grave.

(I use the name Jean Cauvin in this essay to free the discussion of the almost comically negative associations of "John Calvin," which anglicizes the Latin name under which he wrote, Ioannes Calvinus. Even scholarship in French uses the surname Calvin. Still, it is so burdened that I choose to depart from custom.)

To argue that Marguerite de Navarre, sister of the French king François I, was a decisive influence on the literary and religious imagination of Jean Cauvin is to do her no service at all until Calvin is recovered and rehabilitated. On the other hand, the fact of her influence does place Cauvin in his true context, as an elegantly educated Frenchman with aristocratic connections, very much the creature of Renaissance humanism. Marguerite herself is a writer of great interest. She was ambitiously educated, very learned in philosophy and an early exponent of the revival of Platonism in Renaissance Europe. Although Platonism had been deeply influential in the writings of Augustine and others, at the time of Marguerite interest in it amounted to an attack on the Aristotelianism that dominated the schools, and was sometimes punished as heresy. She was also a patroness of writers and especially of religious reformers. Scholars debate the degree to which she was influenced by Cauvin, and not the degree to which he might have been influenced by her, though she was almost a generation older than he and interested in reform ideas years before he was, and though, in her lifetime, she enjoyed great prestige. So she deserves as much as he does to be summoned out of obscurity. It gives me no little pleasure to find a woman at the head of this formidable stream of tradition, the last place I would have expected to find one.

Putting Cauvin into the context appropriate to him should draw attention to the fact that New England political and intellectual culture was more Continental than British in its origins, or Continental by way of Britain, not only through the influence of Cauvin on the early settlers, and on Cromwell, Milton, and the whole of English Puritanism. New England was Continental (and Calvinist) in its tendency toward relatively popular government. New England church polity and the distinctive political order associated with it had emerged generations earlier, in Europe. In 1528 Geneva became an autonomous city governed by elected councils as the result of an insurrection against the ruling house of Savoy. Though the causes of the rebellion seem to have had little to do with the religious controversies of the period, in the course of it two preachers, Guillaume Farel and Pierre Viret, persuaded the city to align itself with the Reformation, then recruited Cauvin to guide the experiment of establishing a new religious culture in the newly emancipated city. That is to say, Calvinism developed with and within a civil regime of elections and town meetings.

In 1572, the northern Dutch fought themselves free of control by Spain and established their federation, which they called the United Provinces, under strong Calvinist, therefore Genevan, influence. Persecution and exile made Calvinism at once international and strongly identified with Geneva, its capital and city of refuge, and therefore greatly magnified the influence of the Genevan example. So the association of Calvinism with government that was popular by the standards of the time (and of our time) was established long before the settlement of New England, and endorsed by the uncanny power and prosperity of its two tiny republics.

Seventeenth-century New Englanders were called the Dutch of the British Empire. The American South was not Calvinist, not settled as New England was by Puritans who felt oppressed by the religious and political order of England before Cromwell's Puritan revolution, or who fled the country after it. It did not send its young men to fight on the side of Cromwell against the king. The South was instead a direct and characteristic offshoot of British colonial policy. It compared to New England as England compared to Holland: despite far more considerable resources, its population was relatively poor and illiterate (English agricultural workers did not thrive better than American slaves) and very sharply stratified. In other words, the similarity of New England to other Calvinist societies, despite differences of culture and language, and its difference from the South, despite shared origins and language, argue that powerful political models and values can be transmitted actively as ideas, through writing and example.

We tend to imagine that political culture must in effect be inherited, passively received. This assumption has as a corollary the notion that the social order will sustain itself if we do not think and theorize about it, and in any case will not benefit if we do. More disturbingly, it implies that populations not already acculturated to orderly representative government will not become capable of it. To say that ideas now have no place in our own political conversation is to understate the matter. It would be truer to say that we no longer have a political conversation. We grope for "traditions" (except for such honorable old customs as substantive debate) as if safety lay in them, and we indulge a somber fear of the outside world, and more particularly of the outsiders among us, in part because we suppose these are the conditions for preserving democracy.

Insofar as these assumptions are articulated as ideas, we are told that representative government found a sheltering niche in liberal aristocracy and blossomed there, and that its flourishing had awaited certain fortuitous erosions in the structure to which its existence finally was owed. This notion allows us to derive our institutions from England, obvious dissimilarities — rights established in law, for example — not at all withstanding. Besides flattering a kind of nativism, this lightens the work of historians. For example, to treat the balance of powers as Enlightenment theory first put to the test in our cheerfully mechanistic Constitution is much more congenial labor than to ponder the murky struggles of the three councils that governed Geneva 250 years before our Constitution was written.

Our great experiment did not spring from the brain of John Locke. It had been tried successfully elsewhere, as our ancestors were well aware. In 1717, the American Puritan John Wise described democracy as follows:

This is a form of government which the light of nature does highly value, and often directs to, as most agreeable to the just and natural prerogatives of human beings. This was of great account in the early times of the world; and not only so, but upon the experience of several thousand years, after the world had been tumbled and tossed from one species of government to another at a great expense of blood and treasure, many of the wise nations of the world have sheltered themselves under it again, or at least have blendished and balanced their government with it.

Wise is defending New England Congregationalism and "its ancient constitution of church order, it being a democracy."

Significantly, Wise argues from the antiquity and wisdom of democratic political order to justify church polity, and not the other way around. Again, the republican institutions of Geneva were in place before Calvin set foot in that city; the Northern Netherlands freed itself and governed itself under Calvinist influence, which was strong but never exclusive; the New Englanders embraced a revolutionary order whose greatest exponents were Southerners. John Wise describes democracy as tried, practical, and stable, and suited to "the natural prerogatives of human beings." The fact of the association of relative political democracy — it is always relative, now as then — with centers of Calvinism clearly does not imply to him any dependency of either upon the other.

The affinity of Calvinism for one characteristic type of modern government does suggest that the theology and the civil polity arose from an impulse, or a history, that was common to them, and that they elaborated and legitimized each other. The outlaw status of both of them no doubt heightened their affinity. There was an ancient tradition of relative republicanism and autonomy in the great urban civilization of southern France and northern Italy, and also of popular, anti-hierarchical religious radicalism, epitomized in Catharism, a powerful old heresy with which Calvinism has always been

associated by its detractors. A great exertion of papal and monarchical power, the Albigensian Crusades (1209–1226) and the
first Inquisition (1233–1350), had suppressed the heresy together
with the autonomy of the cities. Historians tend to treat this as
a successful cultural extirpation. But Calvin alludes several
times to Catharism in his commentaries, in contexts which
make it clear that its beliefs were still abroad and still influential, though the culture had been destroyed generations before
he wrote. Geneva with its Calvinists looks very like a resurgence of that old martyred civilization.

Yet many innovations of great historical importance are
assigned to the influence of John Calvin, including modern
marriage, modern capitalism, the modern, "disciplined" self. In
precisely the sense that these aspects of life may have deserved
to be called Calvinist, if only by affinity, we have closed the
historical parentheses, and passed beyond the modern. The
idealization of marriage; an economics based on asceticism and
a sense of vocation, that is, of sanctified calling; a kind of per-
sonality formed around self-scrutiny and concern for the state
of one's soul — these are not things for which we need any
longer chide ourselves. Stable, lawful representative government, "modern" government, is no longer an ethos, and is
always less a habit.

This is not to say that Calvinism did indeed undergird modern civilization, except as other moral systems did also. Calvinists were always a reviled minority, who therefore enjoyed the
ominous tribute of having their influence found everywhere.
The German sociologist Max Weber, in *The Protestant Ethic and the
Spirit of Capitalism* (1906), associates them with late capitalism by
way of expressing his distaste for it and for them. The polemical intent of this ostensibly scholarly argument is as striking
as the imprecision of its terms, but the book — or perhaps its

title, since that is much more widely read — has been taken terribly seriously, and has greatly influenced the historical reputation of Protestantism and especially of Calvinism, and has perhaps encouraged us to feel that an ethic is itself a doubtful thing, an anxiety, a neurosis.

In the summer of 1922, Karl Barth, Calvin's great modern exponent, gave a series of lectures on Calvin's theology. He described its famous ethical dynamic this way: "Knowledge of God engenders a desire to act. A desire to act engenders a new seeking of God. A new quest for God engenders new knowledge of God. That is the way Reformed thinking goes." Cauvin himself said, "The only true knowledge of God is born of obedience." Weber's thought is not of a kind to grant significance to "knowledge of God," either as motive or as experience. These two contemporaries, Barth and Weber, are writing from entirely different conceptual models. If there is any merit in Weber's thesis, if there is truth in the belief that Calvinism was in fact a cultural watershed, perhaps it is fair to distinguish between these two conceptions as the one from which the modern came, and the one in which it ended.

For at least a century we have diverted ourselves with the fact that it is possible to translate whole constellations of ideas into terms inappropriate to them. And when, thus transformed, they seem odd or foolish, we have acted as if we had exposed their true nature — in its essence, the alligator was always a handbag. We have alienated ourselves from our history by systematically refusing it the kind of understanding that would make it intelligible to us, until we are no longer capable of understanding. Barth says, about theology, "[W]e need to ask ourselves how it has come about that something that did speak once will no longer speak to us. We certainly should not suppress the historical truth that it did speak once."

There are objections to Calvin and to the enterprise of classical theology which it would be well to address at the outset. This great project, theology, which for so many centuries was the epitome of thought and learning, the brilliant conceptual architecture of western religious passion, entirely worthy of comparison with any art which arose from the same impulse, has been forgotten, or remembered only to be looted for charms and relics and curiosities. We are forever drawing up indictments against the past, then refusing to let it testify in its own behalf — it is so very guilty, after all. Such attention as we give to it is usually vindictive and incurious and therefore incompetent. I will touch on certain subjects as they are dealt with in the writing of old John Calvin, with no wish to suggest that in one instance or another he is typical, or exceptional, or even that he is always clearly faithful to his own best insights — though extreme consistency is a thing of which he has often been accused.

Theology of the period of Cauvin employs a characteristic language which discredits it in the eyes of modern readers, including extreme disparagements of the physical body, and more generally of humankind under the aspect of sin or fallenness. The first thing that must be borne in mind is that those who wrote in such terms, whether Cauvin or Luther or John of the Cross, did it in the service of an extraordinarily exalted vision of the human soul. It is a form of hyperbole — purity is corruption, pleasure is illusion, wisdom is folly, virtue is depravity, by comparison with the holiness that can be imagined, not as the nature of God only, but as the nature of humankind also, whom — in the translation of Psalm 8 in the Geneva Bible, a sixteenth-century English Bible assembled, annotated, and printed by English Calvinist exiles in Geneva — God has made "a little lower than God, and crowned him with glory and worship."

The self-abnegation that is always the condition of a true perception of the self or of God can only be understood as the rigorous imagination of a higher self. This is more complex than it sounds. Cauvin has an unsettling habit of referring to himself or to any human being as a "worm." His readers would have known that the speaker of Psalm 22 uses this word to describe himself. That is the psalm Jesus recites from the cross, and Christian interpreters have always identified the speaker of the psalm with Christ. So the use of the word describes temporal estrangement from God and at the same time ultimate identity with Christ. In context it is the farthest thing from a term of contempt. In Book I of his *Institutes of the Christian Religion,* Cauvin says, "Indeed, if there is no need to go outside ourselves to comprehend God, what pardon will the indolence of that man deserve who is loath to descend within himself to find God?" He argues passionately that humankind is itself a sufficient revelation of the divine presence:

How detestable, I ask you, is this madness: that man, finding God in his body and soul a hundred times, on this very pretense of excellence denies that there is a God? They will not say it is by chance that they are distinct from brute creatures. Yet they set God aside, the while using "nature," which for them is the artificer of all things, as a cloak. They see such exquisite workmanship in their individual members, from mouth and eyes to their very toenails. Here also they substitute nature for God. But such agile motions of the soul, such excellent faculties, such rare gifts, especially bear upon the face of them a divinity that does not allow itself readily to be hidden.

This is humankind in its *fallen* state. We have today no comparable language for celebrating human gifts and graces, and no comparable awareness of them, or pleasure in them. The disparagement of "the flesh" is one half, an intrinsic part, of an assertion about human nature which exalts it above all perceivable reality. Modern scholars point to the language of extreme disparagement as if it were exactly what it is not, inhumane and world-hating. It is true that Christian tradition has sometimes approved extreme asceticism in service of the "mortification of the flesh." Cauvin forbade such practices, because in his view sinfulness is not associated with the physical body more than with the whole of the mortal state, and no effort of ours can free us from it. Still, he retained the language of self-disparagement, and the discipline of self-perception implied in it is as essential to his understanding of religious experience as it is to the vision of any mystic.

Since Calvinism is associated with a brooding preoccupation with fallenness, it is worth pointing out that Cauvin considered the Fall of Man to be, on balance, a good thing. As a result of it, God's grace "is more abundantly poured forth, through Christ, upon the world, than it was imparted to Adam in the beginning." His commentary on Genesis, completed the year before his death, is a joyful and effusive work, in which he relaxes the discipline of brevity which so strongly marks his earlier exegetical writing. It is touching to find this sick and weary man so eager to call Creation good.

Nor does he find in the Fall any grounds for antipathy toward women. He sees it as a grave sin in Adam that he tried to blame Eve: "Adam, not otherwise than knowingly and willingly, had set himself, as a rebel, against God. Yet, just as if conscious of no evil, he puts his wife as the guilty party in his place." He says that Eve, equally with Adam, was made in the image of God "respecting that glory of God which peculiarly shines forth in human nature, where the mind, the will and all the senses, represent the Divine order." Of her creation from Adam's rib he says, "He lost, therefore, one of his ribs; but, instead of it, a far richer reward was granted him, since he gained a faithful associate of life; for he now saw himself, who had before been imperfect, rendered complete in his wife . . . Moses also designedly used the word *built,* to teach us that in the person of the woman the human race was at length complete, which had before been like a building just begun." He is at special pains to dissociate human propagation from sin. Commenting on Genesis 1:28, in which God blesses Adam and Eve and tells them to "be fruitful and multiply," he says, "This blessing of God may be regarded as the source from which the human race has flowed . . . here Moses would simply declare that Adam with his wife was formed for the production of offspring, in order that men might replenish the earth. God could himself indeed have covered the earth with a multitude of men; but it was his will that we should proceed from one fountain, in order that our desire of mutual concord might be the greater, and that each might the more freely embrace the other as his own flesh." Marriage is "the bond which God has preferred to all others."

In this Calvin entirely rejects Augustine, whom he follows in many other things, and embraces Chrysostom, who also influenced his theology profoundly. Augustine says, "A good Christian is found in one and the same woman to love the creature of God, whom he desires to be transformed and renewed; but to hate the corruptible and mortal conjugal connection and sexual intercourse: *i.e.* to love in her what is characteristic of a human being, to hate what belongs to her as a wife . . . This is to be understood of father and mother and the other ties of blood, that we hate in them what has fallen to the lot of the human race in being born and dying, but that we love what can be carried along with us to those realms where no one says, My Father; but all say to the one God, 'Our Father.'"

But Chrysostom writes, "For why do we not all spring out of the earth? . . . In order that both the birth and the bringing up of children, and the being born of one another, might bind us mutually together . . . Whence also many kinds of affection arise. For one we love as a father, another as a grandfather; one as a mother, another as a nurse . . . And He devised also another foundation of affection. For having forbidden the marriage of kindred, he led us out unto strangers and drew them to us again . . . uniting together whole families by the single person of the bride, and mingling entire races with races." On one hand Cauvin rarely innovates, and never claims to. On the other hand, his singular devotion to the literature of theology prepared him to exploit its great richness.

In the matter of human dominion over the earth, Cauvin remarks Calvinistically that in giving man the earth to cultivate, God "condemned, in his person, all indolent repose." Then he says:

Let him who possesses a field, so partake of its yearly fruits, that he may not suffer the ground to be injured by his negligence; but let him endeavor to hand it down to posterity as he received it, or even better cultivated. Let him so feed on its fruits, that he neither dissipates it by luxury, nor permits it to be marred or ruined by neglect. Moreover, that this economy, and this diligence, with respect to those good things God has given us to enjoy, may flourish among us; let every one regard himself as the steward of God in all things which he possesses. Then he will neither conduct himself dissolutely, nor corrupt by abuse those things which God requires to be preserved.

If subsequent generations found in Cauvin a pretext for misogyny or rapacity or contempt for humankind, as historians sometimes claim, it is surely because they were determined to find one. They could easily have found pretexts in his theology for acting well, if they had wanted them.

Finally, those who know anything about Calvinism know that Cauvin asserted and defended a doctrine of election or predestination: we are lost or saved as God wills and our destiny has always been known to him. In this he parts with Chrysostom and embraces Augustine. His position is a consequence of his refusal to allow any limit to the power or knowledge of God or to the efficacy of his grace. Cauvin's apparent isolation with the burden of this thorny doctrine is an artifact of the history of polemic rather than of controversy. His great contemporary and nemesis, Ignatius of Loyola, says in his treatise, *Spiritual Exercises,* "Whilst it is absolutely true that no man can be saved without being predestined and without faith and grace, great care is called for in the way we talk and argue about these matters." Furthermore, he warns, "Nor should we talk so much about grace and with such insistence on it as to give rise to the poisonous view that destroys freedom . . . our language and way of speaking should not be such that the value of our activities and the reality of human freedom might be in any way impaired or disregarded, especially in times like these which are full of dangers."

Ignatius was writing for an elite of highly committed men; Cauvin, for anyone who could read him. Cauvin's theology does not permit the esotericism that allows Ignatius to nuance this doctrine by advising "great care" in the manner in which it is discussed, though in the *Institutes* he also warns that the subject be approached with caution. Certainly neither Cauvin nor Loyola lived the life of a fatalist, nor does either show the least reluctance to urge others to act decisively. Anomalies must be expected along the conceptual frontier between the temporal and the eternal. Clearly it is not at all Ignatius's purpose in writing to find logical solutions to theological problems — "I will believe that the white object I see is black if that should be the decision of the hierarchical church." Nor is it Cauvin's, who does not "contrive a necessity out of the perpetual connection and intimately related series of causes, which is contained in nature." He is as committed to the freedom and mystery of God as Ignatius is to the divine authority of the Church. The logical difficulties of their positions matter only if the question is understood in terms both explicitly reject.

A great part of Cauvin's authority, in his lifetime and for as long as he was read, came from his gifts as a writer. He was splendidly educated in classical literature, and his Latin was concise and elegant. His translations of his own work into French were early classics in the use of French as a literary language. What is most remarkable about his work is that it seems to have been treated almost from the beginning as an "orthodoxy," when, as such things were measured when he wrote, it was grandly, systematically heterodox. This would have been true in part because of his extraordinary mastery of Scripture and of the writing of the Early Fathers. His theology is compelled and enthralled by an overwhelming awareness of the grandeur of God, and this is the source of the distinctive aesthetic coherency of his religious vision, which is neither mysticism nor metaphysics, but mysticism as a method of rigorous inquiry, and metaphysics as an impassioned flight of the soul. This vision is still very present in writers like Melville and Dickinson. It is the consequence of a poetic or imaginative stance which, I will argue, Cauvin learned from the religious poetry of Marguerite de Navarre.

Still, I would like to consider a little longer the strange

figure of Jean Cauvin himself, because he is a true historical singularity. The theologian Karl Barth called him "a cataract, a primeval forest, something demonic, directly descending from the Himalayas, absolutely Chinese, marvelous, mythological." And in fact, the more deeply one reads in him the more thoroughly his thinking baffles paraphrase. Then, too, his personal life is so featureless it seems to have been lived to make reticence redundant. In matters of unavoidable interest, for example the circumstances under which he left Catholicism and embraced the Reformation, he is silent. He served for decades as a pastor in Geneva, but no one knows when or whether he was ordained. His contemporaries would have had the example of Luther in mind, who literally personified the struggles of conscience from which such epochal decisions arose. Cauvin seems to have chosen so far as possible to avoid all personalization, a choice his temperament made very available to him. But the power he derived from this remarkable self-negation suggests that he understood its effects. Only he among the Reformers enjoyed equal status with Luther while they lived, and over the centuries his influence has eclipsed that of Luther, though Cauvin never hesitated to acknowledge that he was deeply in Luther's debt.

Luther was a monk, the son of prosperous peasants. He was brilliant, learned, coarse, robust, emotional. Cauvin, seventeen years younger than he, was the son of a lawyer, and was himself trained as a lawyer. As a child Cauvin was sent, after the death of his mother, to be reared and educated in an aristocratic family, and as a young man he studied classical literature and languages with some of the finest teachers in Europe. Scripture and theology he taught himself. In portraits made in his youth, Cauvin looks refined and gentle. In portraits made toward the end of his life, he looks crabbed and depleted. There is an assumption abroad among historians that the ravages of time spare those who live their lives well, that a harsh portrait is as absolute an exposure of the soul as one finds this side of Judgment. Perhaps this is not true in every case. It is worth remembering that a fair part of anyone's life would be required to read what Cauvin read, and then to read what he wrote, even someone in good health, with decent light to work by and a comfortable chair. His commentaries on the Psalms and on Jeremiah are each about twenty-five hundred pages long in English translation, and he wrote commentary on almost the whole Bible, besides personal, pastoral, polemical, and diplomatic letters, treatises on points of doctrine, a catechism, and continuous revisions of his *Institutes of the Christian Religion,* the first, greatest, and most influential work of systematic theology the Reformation produced. At the same time, he preached and lectured several times each week, and married, buried, and baptized people like any other pastor. He was endlessly caught up in the religious and political controversies that swept through Geneva and Europe, and he was frequently the city's emissary to councils and disputations. Yet he considered himself temperamentally unsuited for anything but scholarship. His shortness of temper and his headaches and sickliness, and those late portraits, seem to bear him out. There is only his singular religious, political, and cultural influence to contradict him.

Cauvin did not claim that the theology he articulated was in any sense original with him. His first theological work, the first form of the *Institutes,* was written, he says, to give an account to the king of France, and to the world, of the beliefs of people then being burned in France in a persecution that had forced Cauvin (no one really knows why) to flee Paris for Nérac in Angoulême and then for Basel. Nor did he figure in the insurrection that established the autonomy of Geneva, nor did he influence the form of its government, which was in place when he arrived. He did not establish the reform church at Geneva, but instead carried forward work already begun there by pastors Pierre Viret and Guillaume Farel. Cauvin, who says so little about himself, is careful to make these things clear. He never held any office in Geneva except pastor and lecturer, and he hesitated some months before agreeing to serve as a pastor. He did not accept Genevan citizenship until five years before his death. His famous preeminence, or dominance, in Geneva emerged gradually, over years. He loomed as he did in large part because the civil government produced no figures striking enough to rank with him. Through years of turmoil and fractiousness, he appears to have upheld, by steady, lawyerly deference, a magistracy his personal authority was for a very long time great enough to overwhelm. His insistence that honor be given to magistrates should be understood in this light.

In his commentaries on Scripture, he scarcely slights a verse, or fails to pause over any issue of interpretation of the Hebrew or Greek. By dint of unimaginable labor he creates a body of interpretation that is not allegorical, not analogical, and not offered by him as certainly true. Where he is uncertain, he offers alternative interpretations and tells the reader to decide among them. He tries to avoid forced readings, and he is carefully attentive to the immediate context of a phrase or passage. He is sometimes called the father of modern exegesis.

Cauvin emphasizes the literary character of the books of the Bible and their human authorship — while at the same time claiming for them unique sacredness and authority. Like all controversial writing of the period, his commentaries are marred by bursts of polemic. But even these are not entirely without interest. He frequently vents outrage and exasperation at Jewish interpretations of Old Testament passages, as well as at Catholic interpretations. In the second instance he clearly wishes to refute traditional understandings he might assume were in the minds of his readers. But he would have no grounds for assuming that his readers would be aware of Jewish interpretations or attracted by them. All the complaining means that Cauvin, for the purposes of exegesis, made a habit of consulting the Jewish interpreters. His attention to them is not surprising. He considered the covenant of God with Israel in effect identical with the covenant of Christ, and the Old and New Testaments one continuous revelation — "all men adopted by God into the company of his people since the beginning of the world were covenanted to him by the same law and by the bond of the same doctrine as obtains among us." His exasperation with Jewish scholars is not surprising either, since their methods of interpretation are very remote from his. Still, they seem to have helped him toward a certain objectivity. For example, though the doctrine of the Trinity was a sensitive point with him, Cauvin refused to follow other Christian writers in finding evidence for it in the use in Genesis of the plural form Elohim to refer to God, insisting instead on the Hebrew use of the plural to emphasize or intensify.

Cauvin is sometimes called the father of the modern university, because he designed an academy at Geneva to prepare Reform clergy, training them in languages and literature and in scholarship and criticism, to anchor the biblicism of the movement in humanist learning. Clearly such training would liberate those who followed him from dependency on his commentaries, and would diminish the authority of his own great learning. Evidence of his success may lie in the fact that one can read very far into the voluble literature of his tradition — not a tradition inclined to spare citations or balk at footnotes

—and never find him quoted or even alluded to. I offer our own Jonathan Edwards as a case in point. His revivalism has no basis in Cauvin, who would surely have denounced these efforts to precipitate salvation as Catabaptist or worse. But his philosophical essays are grounded in Cauvin absolutely. Clearly Edwards feels no need to account for his departure in the first instance or to declare his indebtedness in the second, and no need to invoke authority in any case whatever.

Marguerite de Navarre was the sister of the king of France, and they were devoted to each other. She frustrated, so far as she could, her brother's attempts to destroy the Reform movement by persecution, and he tolerated her efforts to encourage it by her patronage and influence and by her own writing. Perhaps for her sake he protected Protestants in other countries even while he oppressed them at home. Navarre, of which she was titular queen, lay in a region of northern Spain once beyond full control of either Spain or France, in the old land of the Cathars. Whatever significance the title still held seems to have been customary, a courtesy to the king's relatives. Nevertheless it became a great rallying point of Protestant resistance to royal power, which was led by these same relatives. Marguerite's daughter, Jeanne d'Albret, was to make a gift of all her jewelry to the Protestant cause, and of her son as well, Henri de Navarre, who became Henri IV.

Jean Cauvin had contact with the influence of Marguerite (then Marguerite d'Angoulême) in many forms. It is speculated that he fled Paris because he had written a defense of a book of her poetry, which was under scrutiny for "Lutheran" sympathies. It is known that he went to her court at Nérac in Angoulême, where she sheltered Reform preachers and writers who were suffering persecution. He went from there to the house of the aristocratic du Tillet family, also in Angoulême, where he studied theology in their vast private library, and then to Basel, where he lived under a pseudonym while he wrote the first version of the *Institutes.* He prefaced his book with an address — not an appeal or a dedication — to François I, the king himself, in which he declares that the intention of his book is to prove that the movement being persecuted in France is neither heretical nor seditious. This second point was crucial, since the persecutions had stirred sympathy for the French dissenters in Germany, and the French had justified themselves by claiming that the dissenters were a threat to public order. In the circumstances, Cauvin's "address" seems itself oddly seditious. This reading of it is very much reinforced by the chapter on civil government with which his treatise ends. Through all his revisions, and even after the death of François I, Cauvin left the address and the chapter on civil government unchanged.

In the address, the obscure young man tells the great king that it is in fact the Established Church which is heretical, using the drastic examples of Elijah and Noah to make the point that the True Church is sometimes very small indeed. This is not the soft answer which turneth away wrath. Elijah can hardly be imagined working out a compromise with King Ahab and Queen Jezebel, or Noah reaching an understanding with his neighbors. It certainly does not suggest that kings are in all cases (or in this case) to be deferred to. The obscure young man warns the great king not to "connive" with those who oppress the dissenters, that "the strong hand of the Lord" will "come forth armed to deliver the poor from their affliction and also to punish their despisers." What must Marguerite have thought of this production? After the publication of the *Institutes,* Cauvin was invited to the court of her cousin, Renée de France, duchess of Ferrara, also a Reform sympathizer and a protector of Protestant exiles and refugees. It appears Marguerite took it in good part, and feared her brother might not.

Cauvin begins his chapter on civil government by saying that authority must be obeyed even when it is corrupt or tyrannous, because it is established by God. Indeed, a tyrant is a punishment ordained by God. Yet, in biblical history, one whose calling it was to overthrow a tyrant, was "armed from heaven [and] subdued the lesser power with the greater, just as it is lawful for kings to punish their subordinates." Even wicked rebels did God's work "unwittingly" — accommodation to events is the genius of providential history. Cauvin's conclusion tells us what is salient for him in this argument: "Let princes hear and be afraid."

The last section of the chapter is titled "Obedience to Man Must Not Become Disobedience to God," an allusion to Acts 5:29, in which Peter says, "We must obey God rather than men." Cauvin published his commentary on Acts in 1560, and it was published in English in 1585. The gloss on 5:29 says "So soon as rulers do lead us away from obedience to God, because they strive against God with sacrilegious boldness, their pride must be abated, that God may be above all in authority. Then all smokes of honour vanish away . . . If a king, or ruler, or magistrate, do become so lofty that he diminisheth the honour and authority of God, he is but a man." The same, adds Cauvin, is true of pastors. Furthermore, he says, "any magistrates of the people, appointed to restrain the willfulness of kings," if they should tolerate kings "who fall upon and assault the lowly common folk . . . they [the magistrates] dishonestly betray the freedom of the people, of which they know that they have been appointed protectors by God's ordinance." This view of revolution as the work of parliaments would have profound consequences in England and America.

In 1647, Charles I of England, all smokes of honour vanished, would be brought to trial as plain Charles Stuart, accused of crimes including complicity in the death of his father and found guilty of treason and murder for persisting in warfare against the parliamentary government established by Oliver Cromwell. As king, in the view of the court, Charles had been "trusted with a limited power to govern by and according to the laws of the land, and not otherwise; and by his trust, oath and office [had been] obliged to use the power committed to him, for the good and benefit of the people, and for the preservation of their rights and liberties" and, with his failure to abide by this trust, his legitimacy and authority had passed into the hands of Parliament, and his resistance was therefore insurrection. Evidence against him included depositions by common soldiers who had seen him or his banner at the scene of a battle. (Cromwell is always named among the commissioners in attendance, though no special prominence seems to have been given him. Nor is there evidence in the record that he spoke.)

Surely Jefferson and his lawyer friends knew the transcript of this famous trial, and were familiar with the kind of language the parliamentary commission employed: "Resolved, That the people are (under God) the original of all just powers . . ." The Declaration of Independence, with its lengthy indictment of George III, is clearly as much a Calvinist as an Enlightenment document. If monarchy were simply wrong in itself, the character of any particular king would be irrelevant, unless as an instance of the general tendency of power to corrupt. For the American as well as the English revolutionaries, the provocation of tyranny was required to sanctify the claims of those who would act in the name of the people.

The Geneva Bible, first published in 1560, was a very great

influence on political thought in England and America. It was the Bible of Shakespeare and Milton, the Bible one hears referred to sometimes as the "breeches" Bible, because its Adam and Eve, unlike the Adam and Eve of the King James Bible, did not have the presence of mind to fashion their fig leaves into "aprons." The implication is that it was a crude or naive translation, but in fact it is largely identical with the King James Bible, which was published in 1611. Both of them are based on still earlier translations, most notably the work of William Tyndale, who published a New Testament in 1526 and a Pentateuch in 1530. Tyndale was burned at the apparent behest of Henry VIII, who would not approve any translation of the Bible into English.

The great difference is that the copious interpretive notes that fill the margins of the Geneva Bible are gone from the King's Authorized Version. At Acts 5:29, the Geneva Bible comments, "We ought to obey no man, but so farre foorth as obeying him, we may obey God." The notes are compiled from commentary by Reform writers including Cauvin, and they are full of seditious sentiments, from a monarchical point of view. They are also scholarly and informative, enormously interesting as background for English and American history and literature into the eighteenth century. Printing of this Bible in England was forbidden, and it was gradually driven out of circulation in England and America by the King James Version, which basks in the legend that it is a masterpiece created by a committee, and enjoys the reputation of having been the great watershed of English-language literature. Now even highly educated people have never seen a Geneva Bible, and, interestingly, it does not occur to them that they have not seen one.

Neither John Calvin nor his Geneva is associated in the collective mind with revolution or with zeal for the rights of the downtrodden, but rather with severity, repression, and persecution. Such were the passions of the times, and so cataclysmic and transforming their consequences, that every major figure on every side was demonized and also sainted, which greatly complicates the problems of history. Characterizations of Calvinist Geneva are only meaningful relative to the standards of the time, and relative to reasonable expectation. Pluralism was not a value of late medieval and early Renaissance Europe, the period of the Inquisitions, of the expulsion of the Moors and the Jews from Spain, of the destruction of the Hussites in Bohemia — these centuries were one long, fierce purge. I know of no reason to consider Geneva severe at all by the norms that prevailed around it.

Judicial violence — torture and barbarous punishment — was commonplace everywhere; if this is not borne in mind, it is easy to mistake the normal workings of civil law for bizarre manifestations of local pathology. The atmosphere of Geneva was said to be somber, but elsewhere *autos-da-fé* were gaudy public spectacles. Clearly such judgments reflect individual preferences. Johan Huizinga, in his classic history, *The Autumn of the Middle Ages* (1919), describes France and Europe in the fifteenth century this way: "It is an evil world. The fires of hatred and violence burn fiercely. Evil is powerful, the devil covers a darkened world with his black wings." If there is truth in this, then Geneva in the early sixteenth century can hardly be expected to have put off entirely the dire traits of the larger civilization. Of course Geneva was repressive. The questions to be asked are what the origins of repressiveness were, and whether the influences of republicanism and Calvinism intensified or moderated the harshness of European life as it was lived in Geneva. On one hand, Cauvin, with Farel and Viret and others, did attempt to have all Genevans sign a statement of belief, with the proclaimed but unenforced penalty of banishment from the city for those who refused. On the other hand, when the people of Geneva decided this demand was unacceptable, even though most of them did sign the statement, they could and did banish Cauvin and his friends from the city. Severity so liable to correction hardly deserves the name.

After three years Geneva called Cauvin back again, greeting his return with a public festival. But his relationship with the city never became entirely harmonious. His presence attracted exiles from all over Europe, especially from France, overwhelming the local population with zealous foreigners, many of whom were naturalized as citizens. Cauvin and his supporters seem to have been intent on consolidating a revolution, one in which religion was as central to the imagination of the project as political liberty would be in the eighteenth and nineteenth centuries and economics and nationalism in the nineteenth and twentieth. Traditionally European societies instructed their members in approved beliefs through rituals, processions, feasts, fasts, pilgrimages, and iconography. Geneva replaced all that with hour upon hour of sermons and lectures, and a system of education that was compulsory for all children and free for the poor. Cauvin rejected the "old saw that images are the books of the uneducated" remarking, "I confess, as the matter stands, that today there are not a few who are unable to do without such 'books' . . . those in authority in the church turned over to idols the office of teaching for no other reason than that they themselves were mute." If all these lectures and sermons seem a poor exchange for pageants and altarpieces, it is well to remember the Renaissance passion for books, and for the languages and literatures of antiquity, first of all the Bible. Cauvin's virtuosic scholarship could be thought of as monumental public art, by analogy with the work of contemporaries like Michelangelo.

The revolutionary impulse to try to change the way people think is inevitably more or less coercive, as is the counterrevolutionary impulse to prevent or suppress new thinking. This is a fallen world. Geneva became the model or laboratory of Reform civilization, which otherwise could not have discovered its own implications or its own coherency or viability as a social ethos, nor developed its own institutions. This same experiment, the creation of a new social order, has been tried repeatedly in our century, usually with horrific consequences, beside which Genevan rigors and excesses are surely very mild indeed.

Cauvin's special reputation for severity was established by the burning of Michael Servetus for heresy. Cauvin did not serve on the tribunal which condemned Servetus, but he did approve of the sentence of death, even in anticipation of Servetus's arrival in Geneva. He is associated with only this one such death, though he did use his influence to have an enemy of his banished and another forced to walk around the city twice in his bare feet and shirttails. Of course, the assent to the killing of Servetus is absolutely deplorable, but precious few who have figured in religious and political history as significantly as Cauvin did, in his time or in ours, have only one life to answer for. This is not exculpation — he of all people should have had advanced views about tolerance toward heresy, he being a great promulgator of heresy by the lights of those who traditionally made such judgments. It is fair to remember, however, that his association with the killing of Servetus was an anomaly in his career.

A friend of Servetus, Sebastiano Castellio, attacked Cauvin very powerfully for approving and then defending in principle the punishment of heresy as a crime. So far as I can discover,

Cauvin's defense has not been published in English, except for the excerpts which are quoted by Castellio for the purposes of rebuttal. This is no doubt a thing for which Cauvin should be grateful. The consequence of the whole affair was that the practice of religious and intellectual repression was vigorously attacked, and was not effectively defended. Nothing better could have come of it.

But the issue of repression, or of freedom, is obliquely illuminated by Castellio. His rhetoric implies that Cauvin invented the idea that heretics should be persecuted. Yet he argues that for the sake of consistency Cauvin ought to have been punishing Catholics as heretics — which reminds us that he did not — or at least "he ought to have apprehended the Cardinal Tournon when shortly before the death of Servetus he went through Geneva, on his way, as all know, to burn the godly men who lay in chains at Lyons, and whom not long after he did burn." This event was clearly graver than the death of Servetus by the factor of the undisclosed number of godly men, but Castellio wishes to isolate Cauvin with the scandal of persecution, so he does not pause over this fact. The success of Castellio in making Cauvin seem peculiarly and monstrously bent on persecution lingers as the darkest element in the modern reputation of John Calvin.

Another attack on Cauvin's inconsistent practice of repression — a rhetorically interesting use of the fact that it was not characteristic of him — casts further light on the subject of the repressiveness of Geneva. Castellio asks, "Why does he not prohibit the printing and sale of other pernicious books at Geneva? Aristotle is allowed, though he denies the foremost article of the creed, the creation of the world. The Koran is permitted and Apuleius, Martial, Plautus, Terence, Horace, Catullus, Tibullus, Propertius, and other nefarious corrupters of morals. Ovid's *Art of Love* — that is, of Adultery — is allowed, as well as the words of his imitator Clément Marot . . . What shall I say of the trash that is printed there?" We can say that it is Renaissance and humanist and not evidence of a generally repressive atmosphere.

Why was Servetus executed in Geneva? His writings were so perfectly calculated to offend prevailing Christian opinion that if the authorities had simply sent him on his way he would surely have met the same end somewhere else. As was customary, at the time of his trial the Genevans solicited the views of the magistrates of neighboring cities, all of whom concurred in their judgment. They even sent queries to the Inquisition in Vienna. Though Cauvin appealed for a more humane method of execution, Servetus was burned, and so were his books. His famous, fatal book was an attack on the doctrine of the Trinity. To the end, Servetus could have saved his life by repeating a phrase to the effect that Christ was a person of the Trinity, but with touching courage he refused to do it.

Heresy implies orthodoxy. The trial and execution of Servetus defined important limits to Calvinist departure from Catholic teaching. Such limits were necessary if his movement was to be regarded as a reform of Christian practice and tradition rather than as an abandonment of them. If Cauvin were not simply to release the centrifugal energies contained by mystery and complexity and paradox, he had to make clear which things were to be kept as well as which were to be rejected. The doctrine of the Trinity, reconciling belief in the divinity of Christ to belief in the unity of God, was vulnerable because it does not have an unambiguous basis in Scripture — in Reform theory Scripture was the standard to be applied to everything. Then, too, Manicheanism was a virtual synonym for heresy because it had been attacked as such by Augustine, so nonconformists were usually accused of it. And parts of Europe very receptive to Calvinism had, centuries before, been

very receptive to Catharism, which resembled the older Manichean heresy in that it asserted the existence of a "true God"
and an evil god, the latter being the creator of the physical
world, which was therefore essentially evil as well. So this kind
of dualism is what Cauvin might have expected his followers to
be accused of, and also, perhaps, to be predisposed to. He had
had to defend himself, early in his stay in Geneva, against a
charge that *he* denied the Trinity.

So the trial and death of Servetus would have clarified Cauvin's position on that point, once and for all, for his detractors
and for his supporters as well. This is no extenuation. Nor is
Cauvin justified by the fact that his attacks on Servetus in the
Institutes coincide with, or are the occasion for, the distinctive
understanding of the Old Testament which allowed Jews and
Judaism to flourish in safety in Calvinist societies as they could
not anywhere else in European Christendom. (I know it is
customary to remark that these societies were rewarded for
such "tolerance" — why have we never found a better word?
— with prosperity, the implication being that the motives behind it were grasping, which would in turn imply that persecutors of Jews acted from loftier motives. It is customary also
to trace this decency to a source in Cauvin's theology. But
cynics and mercantilists are not notoriously inclined to turn to
systematic theology for guidance. So it seems reasonable to
consider it a benign consequence of the singular reverence
with which he regarded the covenant relationship between
God and the Jewish people.) Servetus, like the Cathars before
him, insisted that the God of the New Testament did not reveal himself to the ancient Hebrews. The God of the Old Testament was for the Cathars the evil creator. For Servetus — here
I am following Cauvin's account — he was an angel they mis-
took for God, and his covenant with the Jews was entirely
this-worldly. Cauvin makes the argument at great length that

justification by faith is as central to the Old Testament as to the New: "For the same reason it follows that the Old Testament was established upon the free mercy of God, and was confirmed by Christ's intercession . . . Who, then, dares to separate the Jews from Christ, since with them, we hear, was made the covenant of the gospel, the whole foundation of which is Christ? Who dares to estrange from the gift of free salvation those to whom we hear the doctrine of the righteousness of faith was imparted?" Again, he says, in Corinthians Paul "makes the Israelites equal to us not only in the grace of the covenant but also in the signification of the sacraments . . . For Paul here means to disabuse Christians of thinking they are superior to the Jews through the privilege of baptism." (In fairness to the Cathars, who have had little enough fairness — despite what is said to have been their view of the Old Testament, the culture in which they flourished seems to have had amicable relations with Jews. An important center of Talmud studies in the south of France, in which Sephardic and Ashkenazic influences were both active, was destroyed together with the Cathars, and a condition of surrender for nobility who had defended Cathars was that they must no longer employ Jews.)

In arguing for the effective presence of Christ in the Old Testament, Cauvin's rebuttal of Servetus's teachings follows certain of Augustine's writings against the Manicheans, except that he carries the argument farther, finding Christ himself where Augustine found the prefiguration of him. But he could have claimed the authority of Augustine's gloss of Psalm 105, which anticipates his argument closely. As usual, his apparent innovations really amount to selection and emphasis within a tradition made available to him by great learning. This is the posture of orthodoxy over against which he attacked heresy, the same one which allowed him to consider himself engaged in the basically conservative enterprise of reform, however radical and distinctive his teachings might be in effect.

If one may judge by Cauvin's refutations, Servetus did not believe in baptism of infants or children, but he did believe in the damnation of those who died unbaptized, even children. Cauvin did believe in the baptism of infants as a sign of God's care for them, though he did not believe that baptism was unconditionally necessary for salvation. Of infants, Cauvin says, "anyone Christ blesses is freed from the curse of Adam and the wrath of God. Since, therefore, it is known that infants were blessed by him, it follows that they were freed from death." Altogether, in the death of Servetus, it seems that a mean doctrine was meanly suppressed, with the result that meanness won out.

Cauvin's detractors have always condemned him for his severity on account of Michael Servetus. Worse, within his tradition he himself has been so stigmatized with intolerance that when certain of his loyalists have defended severities he himself explicitly discouraged — the strictures on church membership and communion enforced by Jonathan Edwards and others being one example — this is taken as a pure manifestation of Calvinism. It is no accident that the most liberal branch of American Protestantism descends from Calvinism, or that New England and upstate New York, in their Calvinist era, were great centers of social and educational reform and experimentation. (And gloomy, like Geneva, we are always told — compared with the slave states, presumably. Again, people differ in where they find cause for gloom.)

But where this side of Cauvin's heritage has survived it has done so by denying his paternity, or by supposing it has in fact rejected or defied his heritage precisely in carrying forward its most distinctive elements. There are things for which we in this culture clearly are indebted to him, including relatively popular government, the relatively high status of women, the separation of church and state, what remains of universal schooling, and, while it lasted, liberal higher education, education in "the humanities." All this, for our purposes, emanated from Geneva — in imperfect form, of course, but tending then toward improvement as it is now tending toward decline. That mysterious energy, Calvinism, appears to be spent. It seems, in retrospect, utterly specific to its origins and circumstances, to the excitements of the Renaissance and of revolution and defiance and martyrdom, and to the vast stimulus of the availability of printed books, especially the Bible in modern languages. It is hard to imagine our recovering a sense of it. Certainly we cannot recover the thing itself.

Yet, lacking curiosity and the habit of study and any general grasp of history, we have entered a period of nostalgia and reaction. We want the past back, though we have no idea what it was. Things do not go so well for us as they once did. We feel we have lost our way. Most of us know that religion was once very important to our national life, and believe, whether we ourselves are religious or not, that we were much the better for its influence. Many of us know that Calvinism was a very important tradition among us. Yet all we know about John Calvin was that he was an eighteenth-century Scotsman, a prude and obscurantist with a buckle on his hat, possibly a burner of witches, certainly the very spirit of capitalism. Our ignorant parody of history affirms our ignorant parody of religious or "traditional" values. This matters, because history is precedent and permission, and in this important instance, as in many others, we have lost plain accuracy, not to speak of complexity, substance, and human inflection. We want to return to the past, and we have made our past a demonology and not a human narrative.

Marguerite
de Navarre,
PART II

MARGUERITE DE NAVARRE is entirely as striking a
presence in history, and absence from history, as
Jean Cauvin. When she is mentioned at all it is
usually as the great patroness of letters and learning in the
early French Renaissance, and the great protector of the early
Reformation in France. These things by themselves should be
more than sufficient to merit interest and respectful attention,
one would think. She also wrote, poetry, plays, and fiction,
all of them in French, which was only then emerging as a
literary language. The *Encyclopaedia Britannica,* in its 1910 edition,
speculates that her reputation fell victim to the prejudice
against women of letters. Presumably her fame would have
been greater if she had done less to deserve it.

(Her name is problematic also. Historians and reference
books often call her Marguerite d'Angoulême, her name by
birth, rather than Marguerite de Navarre, her name from her
second marriage, to the titular king of Navarre. Navarre is and
was in northern Spain, and while Marguerite was queen of

Navarre her court was at Pau, in southern France. Her status seems to have been notional, almost fanciful, though because of her royal birth, her power was very real. I think she may have found a sort of metaphysical humor in her situation. The speaker in her poetry often refers to herself as Rien, Nothing, which I take to be a play on the title Royne, as they spelled it in those days. She chose the king of Navarre over far more advantageous offers of marriage. She is a witty-looking woman, to whom Rabelais dedicated the fourth book of *Pantagruel* with an absurd little poem.)

With the distinguished exception of the doctors of the Sorbonne, who paid her first book of poetry the compliment of scrutinizing it for heretical ideas, theologians seem never to consider that her writings might have theological content, let alone that her influence on theology could have extended beyond her interventions on behalf of imperiled dissenting preachers. Her religious poems and plays, when they are discussed at all, have been regarded as mere mystical pietism. She lived in the great age of mystical piety, the age of Teresa of Ávila and John of the Cross among so many others. But her poems are treated as mere effusions, or as Catholicism or Protestantism set to rhyme, statements of possibly momentary allegiance to doctrines formulated by others, containing nothing of her own religious thought or religious experience.

So far as I have discovered, available information about her involvement with the Reformation in France is sketchy and oblique, but not inconsistent with her having played a very decisive role in its emergence. At the time of the publication of her first book of poems, in 1530, Protestants were still called "Lutherans." Cauvin had published only a commentary on Seneca's *De Clementia*, a fine piece of scholarship in which he presumed to differ with the great Erasmus, but which showed no indication of the course his life was to take. At the time of the persecutions in Paris — set off by the so-called Affair of the Placards, when leaflets derogating the Mass appeared all over Paris, one even in the king's bedchamber — Cauvin made his way to Nérac in Angoulême, to the court of Marguerite, already the first recourse of dissenters needing shelter.

I have never read that they were acquaintances, nor even found speculation about whether or not they were, nothing except a comment in an old French encyclopedia that the two had met frequently in Paris before he came to Nérac. Cauvin was the brilliant student of humanists like the German Lutheran Melchior Wollmar, whom Marguerite brought to the university at Bourges and who taught him Greek there. It seems impossible that she could have been unaware of him. Cauvin's close friend in Paris, Nicolas Cop, was the son of her brother's physician. Her *valet de chambre,* the poet Clément Marot, was forced to leave Paris when Cop and Cauvin were, apparently made suspect by the same associations. It is hard to imagine how these lives were lived. But it is clearly true that Marguerite surrounded herself with intellectual and literary people whom Cauvin also would have known, and that she was devoted to encouraging just such gifts as he had displayed. He has been without honor in his own country for a long time now, and perhaps it has seemed ungallant to historians to associate him with this amiable queen. But in fact the world she created around herself created him. And perhaps it is true to say *she* created him.

It seems to be assumed that Cauvin became acquainted at Nérac with Jacques Lefèvre d'Étaples, the old priest and humanist who had been Marguerite's tutor in her childhood, and that he may have "converted" Cauvin to the Reform cause, though he himself never underwent any such conversion.

There is no reason to look for one decisive influence. Cauvin's friend and cousin, Pierre Robert — called Olivetan, which means Midnight Oil — had by this time made a translation of the Bible into French, and was involved in the movement. Cauvin does seem to have been strongly affected by his stay at Nérac, given direction by it, but this need not be interpreted as meaning he underwent a conversion there, especially since he says nothing to encourage the idea that he did. He went from there to the du Tillet household, where he availed himself of their library, and from there to Basel, where he wrote the first version of the *Institutes of the Christian Religion*, giving distinctive form and expression to a Protestant movement that was French and non-Lutheran. None of this is inconsistent with Marguerite's having recruited this promising and sympathetic young humanist to be the formulator of a distinctive French Protestantism, nor is the fact that after the publication of the *Institutes* he went to the court of her niece in Italy, Renée de Ferrara.

At about the same time, Marguerite sent her protégé Clément Marot to shelter with her niece. Although Marot had been arrested twice for heresy (and abjured it once) he was popular and influential as a secular poet, until 1539, when he published rhymed and metrical translations of the first thirty psalms. These were set to music, and swept France, and became the hymns of the churches in Geneva, greatly enriching and advancing Reform worship, and music itself, or so I have read, because it developed to accommodate the great expressiveness of congregational singing. (Such passion surrounds this history that more than usual caution is called for in accepting such judgments — one French authority has said that no matter what contemporaries may have thought, these translations of the psalms were "one of the most lamentable abortions to have been recorded in literary history.")

Music to be sung by the congregation had already become important among the Lutherans. Marguerite tried her hand at religious lyrics set to popular tunes, which were published in a little book titled *Chansons Spirituelles,* an allusion to Paul's encouraging the Christians at Ephesus to sing "hymns and psalms and spiritual songs." Cauvin himself attempted translations of the psalms that would be suitable for singing. Marot's translations were immediately embraced by Cauvin in preference to his own, and became as definitive of Calvinism in their way as the *Institutes.* Marot went to Geneva for refuge when his book of psalms was condemned as heretical by the Sorbonne, but stayed there only briefly and died the next year in Turin.

Marguerite's importance as a literary patroness cannot have been accidental. Either she chose very gifted writers to be her protégés, or her influence was considerable enough to establish those she favored as the dominant writers of the period. The first seems more probable, since her choices were in no sense obvious or safe, the most famous of them being the heretical defrocked monk and general scapegrace François Rabelais. She could not prevent another of them, Étienne Dolet, from being burned at the stake. She favored those who wrote in French, Rabelais being an early master of the language. Marot, in his later poetry and his psalms, is said to have turned French poetry toward a "modern" vernacular simplicity, relative to prevailing conventions. She encouraged Lefèvre d'Étaples to make a translation of the New Testament into French from the Latin of Jerome. And, of course, she also wrote poetry in French, in a style that might well be seen as modern, like Marot's, though in anticipation of him, if it were not read as lady's poetry and therefore as all she asked of herself, or the best she could do. Emily Dickinson comes to mind.

Marguerite wrote poems and plays, almost all on religious subjects, and she wrote *The Heptameron,* a collection of short stories modeled on Boccaccio's *Decameron*. The seventy stories of her collection, like the one hundred of his, are narratives of profane love, many of them crude and anticlerical. To a modern reader, *The Heptameron* seems rather startling beside the rest of her work. But Boccaccio produced rarefied religious writing also. It seems to have been true of medieval Europe that these two poles of experience could coexist in one sensibility, as a cycle of sin and repentance, perhaps. Then, too, marriage among the aristocracy was made to suit calculations of power and diplomatic advantage, and to produce heirs. It is no great surprise that they regarded it casually or cynically or as a kind of captivity, or that infidelity was acceptable in the circles *The Heptameron* represents.

Cauvin invented modern marriage, if that is what he did, by basing his vision of it on the Old Testament use of the metaphor of married love to describe the covenant relationship between God and Israel, in which adultery is idolatry and apostasy, and faithfulness is joy and salvation. He was married for nine years, very happily, to Idelette de Bure, a widow with two children. His only child died within days of its birth, and he outlived Idelette by twenty-five years. Throughout his life the idea of marriage seems only to have been more cherished by him. In the enormous positive significance he attached to it, he set himself apart from the religious tradition which idealized virginity and celibacy, and also from the humanist embrace of the sensuality of courtly and pagan literature (which was, nevertheless, published in Geneva, during Cauvin's prominence there). Perhaps he was fascinated with marriage in part because it integrated these extremes. It is the strongest impulse of his thought to reject polarities. This enshrining of marriage is seen as narrowness in Cauvin, as Puritanism. But perhaps it should be seen as the solution to a problem Marguerite would have acknowledged. In *The Heptameron,* a fictional party of stranded aristocratic travelers tell stories to pass the time. The ladies in the company are better and brighter than the men, but the tales are so often brutal and charmless, to the detriment of women, that the world they describe seems like a world well lost. The book was not published until nine years after the queen's death.

In imitating Boccaccio, Marguerite was turning to a writer who died more than 120 years before she was born. And she was identifying herself with the old vernacular literary culture of southern France and northern Spain and Italy. From childhood, she was instructed in Spanish and Italian, as well as Latin and some Greek and Hebrew, so this literature would have been very available to her. Before Boccaccio, there was Petrarch, and before him, Dante, who makes a place in hell for the pope who called down Crusader armies from the north to extirpate the culture of the Cathar heretics and the troubadour poets, centered in the region of France which came to be called Languedoc. Religious dissent and vernacular literature were powerfully associated in French history, and extraordinary piety was associated with the celebration of courtly life and profane love. If one may judge from Marguerite's writing, and from the writing she encouraged, it was the disrupted culture of southern Europe, not the forgotten culture of antiquity, that she most hoped to see renascent. This includes the translation of the New Testament she commissioned from Lefèvre d'Étaples — vernacular New Testaments (the language of the region, Occitan, was closer to Spanish than to French) were at the center of Cathar piety.

If France was feeling the stimulus of the Lutheran movement, as the disorders and persecutions make clear, and elements of Catharism were still abroad, as Cauvin's mention of them proves, then problems might be anticipated from the fact that the Cathars really were heretics. That word must have been used very loosely — Ignatius of Loyola was a student in Paris when Cauvin was, having come there to escape repeated arrest for heresy in Spain, and Teresa of Ávila and John of the Cross also underwent painful scrutiny. French Waldensians, English Lollards, Bohemian Hussites were all condemned and suppressed as heretics, and, when one looks at whatever remains in the way of evidence about their beliefs, they are precursors of the Reformation, neither more nor less. But there was an exotic element in Cathar doctrine, a departure much more profound than disputes about the authority of the institutional church or the nature of the priesthood or even about the Eucharist. They believed in a good or "true" God, and in a false and evil god, who created the world. They believed that those who belonged to the true God could be perfect, and that those who were initiated into their clergy *must* be perfect, or their administration of the Cathar sacraments was of no effect.

Catharism is traceable to a Bulgarian named Bogomil, whose teachings spread to Bosnia and were carried by missionaries across the Adriatic to France and Italy. Its adherents are said to have believed, like Servetus, that the Old Testament was essentially the chronicle of the evil god, though their texts quote the Old Testament frequently and respectfully. They are said also to have believed in the reincarnation of souls, leading finally to the perfection and salvation of all of them. This seems actually to obviate the dualism of the orthodox understanding, which would leave Satan everlastingly in possession of some fair part, at least, of humankind. (Interestingly, Cauvin's account of hell does not mention Satan. But this is a merely technical solution to the problem.) To propose an alternative scheme of salvation, however, as both the Bogomils and Cathars did, is to depart very essentially from the broadest Christian tradition. In a daunting, and rare, display of like-mindedness, the Eastern church destroyed the Bogomils in its territories at the same time and by the same means that the Cathars were destroyed in western Europe.

Catharism seems to have flourished for about two centuries, and to have enjoyed the respect of those it did not convert, who were always the great majority. Its clergy, male and female equally and indifferently, were chosen out of the general Cathar population as people who lived godly lives, and were instructed and initiated as "good people" or "good Christians." History and their detractors call them "Perfecti." These people lived in the world, but as ascetics, refusing meat and wine and other comforts and luxuries. They wandered and preached, barefoot and simply clothed, always carrying their Bibles. When Rome first began to try to deal with the heresy, delegations were sent to preach to the people and to debate with the Perfecti, but without success because of their opponents' great mastery of Scripture. They had no churches, no images or symbols of any kind, no hierarchy. They were completely nonviolent, laying great stress on the love of enemies. They absolutely refused to take oaths. For a long time they were resolutely defended, and rarely betrayed, by people who were not themselves Cathars.

If one were to compare Calvinism to Lutheranism, one would note its absence of hierarchy, the abandonment of the idea of apostolic succession, and the fact that its clergy are, in effect, elected by the congregations they serve. Certainly Calvinism positively refused the use of images and symbols, which Lutheranism retained, though with the understanding that they were not to be objects of veneration. Its understanding of the sacraments tended to grant them a spiritual reality as opposed to the objective reality implied in Catholic transubstantiation or Lutheran consubstantiation. Calvinism emphasized preaching and almost eliminated liturgy, which remained important in Lutheranism. It had no clearly formalized relation with civil authority. It rejected the idea of free will. In all this, it departs from Lutheranism and resembles Catharism. Even the strange this-worldly asceticism always associated with Calvinists, which Cauvin seems to have epitomized but which in fact his theology does not at all require, has a Cathar feeling about it. This would perhaps account for the affinity, in fact the deep attachment, of worldly people like Marguerite de Navarre and Clément Marot to a religious movement that seems, superficially, at least, to have been of another spirit entirely.

Let us say that the grafting of certain essential Lutheran doctrines to the stock of Catharism was Marguerite's idea. She was of Luther's generation and attentive to his writing from the beginning. Let us say she set out to ensure that there would be a reformation in France, one that would stay within the bounds of orthodoxy, and would be aesthetically and temperamentally pleasing to the French. So she wrote and published anonymously a book of poems, *Miroir de l'Âme Pécheresse* — *The Mirror of the Sinful Soul*. (The only translation of the book into English seems to have been the prose one made in 1548 by the young princess Elizabeth Tudor as a gift for Catherine Parr, titled *A Godly Medytacion of the Christen sowle concerning a love towards God and Hys Christe* . . .) The full title of Marguerite's first poem is "The Mirror of the Sinful Soul in which she recognizes her faults and sins — also the graces and kindnesses done her by Jesus Christ her spouse" (my translation). Of course it was entirely conventional to speak of the soul as female, as the bride of Christ — John of the Cross did, Jean Cauvin did — so there is no reason to assume that the first readers of these poems thought of the writer or even the speaker of the poems as female.

As the book first appeared, passages of Scripture which the poem interpreted were printed in French in the margins, so that the poem was in effect an interpretive gloss on texts which assert human sinfulness («*Rom. vii. Peché habite en moy*»), and texts which assert divine grace («*Jehan iii. Car Dieu a tant aymé le monde, qu'il a donné son seul filz*»). The poem is ingeniously constructed so that a series of narratives of God's faithfulness and the soul's infidelity — its failure as mother, paraphrasing the narrative of the judgment of Solomon; as child, paraphrasing the parable of the prodigal son — reads like the experience of a single soul, always failing and always meeting new and constant grace. The metaphor of the book as mirror was well worn by the time Marguerite took it up, but her use of it is, again, ingenious. The mirror of the soul is Scripture, the poem says, and the narratives in it are its living image, straying and restored, offending and forgiven, so that these two states are in effect simultaneous, integral. And the mirror is Christ, whose fidelity is the measure of the soul's inevitable failure, and also of its undiminished worth. In either case, the metaphor is an allusion to the figure of the mirror in the Epistle of James, a text full of implied dualism which Marguerite seems to be reinterpreting here. The Christian soul is perfect in the sense that its imperfections are made good by God's faithfulness and grace — and perfect in no other sense.

Cauvin will use the image of the mirror almost obsessively, in this same way, to describe a state of being that is experiential, fluid, momentary and relational, and which reveals, without in any sense limiting or becoming identical with the thing revealed. In this sense the natural world mirrors God, a human being mirrors God. The vision of the unworthy soul in an unmediated encounter with Christ, for all the world as if there were no other souls in the universe whether more or less worthy, as if there were no time, no history, certainly neither merit nor extenuation — this is the classic Calvinist posture, though it should be called Margueritist, clearly, since she described it before he did.

The voices of the first two poems in Marguerite's little volume sound not so much like confession as shocked self-recognition. Both begin abruptly, sudden cries of frustration at the subjective burden of human self-defeat. This is like the despair of the self that prepares the mystic for his or her encounter with the divine, with the important difference that this self-recognition is not the preparation, but is in fact the encounter. She says, in the words of Elizabeth Tudor's translation, "He doth see the evil that I have, what and how much it is . . . And this the same unknown sight doth bring me a new desire, shewing the good that I have lost by my sin, and given me again through his grace and bounty, that which hath overcome all sin." In the *Institutes,* Cauvin will likewise say, "It is certain that man never achieves a clear knowledge of himself unless he has first looked upon God's face, and then descends from contemplating him to scrutinize himself." The first poem differs from other mysticism also in the fact that in place of the vision of the Spouse one finds in John of the Cross, for example, there is Scripture, which for Marguerite, as later for Cauvin, is itself a visionary experience. She says, "Now, my lord, if thou be my father, may I think that I can be thy mother? Indeed I cannot well perceive how I should conceive thee that createdst me . . . I believe then, that hearing and reading thy words which thou hast taught and uttered by thy holy prophets, the same also which through thy true preachers, thou dost daily declare unto men, in believing it and stead-fastly desiring to fulfill, I conceive thee and bear thee by love." As Cauvin will do, Marguerite makes a great point of staying close to the text, actually setting it beside her poems. At the same time, as he will do, she evokes a sense of astonished realization, of a constant, overwhelming present moment.

The second, shorter poem in the book is titled "Discord existing in mankind on account of the contrariety of the spirit and the flesh and his peace through spiritual life, which is an annotation of the end of the seventh chapter and the begin-ning of the eighth, of the Epistle of Saint Paul to the Romans." It is hard, though clearly possible, to overlook the theological seriousness of the writer's intentions. In this poem, the speaker, again a universalized soul, confesses its mingled nature, the simultaneity of faith and disbelief, of love and hatred of the law, of serenity and turmoil, in an intricately rhymed para-phrase of the passage from Romans in which Paul laments: "For I allow not that whiche I do: for what I would, that do I not: but what I hate, that doe I. If I doe then that which I would not, I consent to the Law, that it is good. Now then, it is no more I, that doe it, but sinne that dwelleth in me . . . I finde then that when I would do good, I am thus yoked, that evill is present with me . . . O wretched man that I am, who shall deliver me from the body of this death!" (Geneva Bible, Ro-mans 7:15–17, 21, 24). This same passage is a point of departure for the first poem. Its significance for Marguerite is clearly very great indeed.

The second poem concludes that we must try to avoid sin or error, and when we fail we must turn to God's unfailing clemency. This is the Lutheran doctrine of salvation by faith alone. The insistence on the experience of persisting sinfulness in the soul, even as the soul is the object of grace, can be considered as reinterpreting Paul's passage to remove the implication that sin resides in the literal flesh or body, as distinct from the soul. But it also makes the point that perfection is not possible to anyone. The poem recovers the psychological, dramatic quality of Paul's outcry, making it feel more like grief and frustration, less like philosophy or doctrine; more like a realization of inextricable complexity, less like a formula for creating ontological categories of good and evil, pure and impure. Perhaps this is the emergence of the modern self.

Cauvin's first commentary, published in 1539, was on the Epistle to the Romans, although, as he notes in the preface, a number of commentaries had been written on it already, including a notable one by Luther. Clearly he is eager to give his own inflection to Protestant interpretation of this key text. In his gloss of the end of the seventh chapter, which he interprets as Marguerite had done years before, he concludes, "This is a suitable passage to disprove the most pernicious dogma of the Purists, (*Catharorum,*) which some turbulent spirits attempt to revive at the present day." In every context in which he mentions Catharism, it is to refute its teachings about perfection. Cauvin is known not only for the doctrine of predestination but also for the doctrine of "total depravity," a phrase so forbidding one hesitates to ponder it. In Genevan French *dépraver* is clearly still near its Latin root, which means "to warp" or "to distort." The word does not have the lurid overtones it has for us. Jérôme Bolsec was banished for, among other things, having *dépravé plusieurs passages de l'Éscriture pour soustenir ceste faulse et perverse doctrine* — the doctrine that predestination would make God a tyrant like Jupiter. This is Cauvin's characteristic use of the word, to refer to distortion of the meaning of a text. *Corruption,* in the French of the period, can mean "exhaustion" or "brokenness," or it can be used just as we use it now when we speak of the corruption of a text.

In Cauvin's mind, the mirror is by far the dominant metaphor for perception and also for Creation, so distortion would be a natural extension of the metaphor, especially in a time when the art of making glass mirrors was newly recovered and flaws and distortions would have been inevitable. Yet it is also true that, in its essence, experience is a text he reads. That is why the very textuality of Scripture gives it such authority, and why his scholarly struggles with the flaws in the text, the mistranslations and scribal errors and forced interpretations, are identical in his understanding with the problem of discovering and establishing truth — a thing which he is too good a scholar to imagine can ever really be achieved. It is strikingly true of Cauvin that his sense of things is overwhelmingly visual and cerebral, that the other senses do not interest him. Ignatius, in his meditation on hell, wishes "with the sense of smell to perceive the smoke, the sulphur, the filth, and corruption." Cauvin says, "[B]ecause no description can deal adequately with the gravity of God's vengeance against the wicked, their torments and tortures are figuratively expressed to us by physical things, that is, by darkness, weeping and gnashing of teeth." Hell is "to be cut off from all fellowship with God." Making perception and understanding the primary locus of reality rescues the world and the flesh from dualism, whether Cathar or Augustinian. They are rescued from the opprobrium of existing in a state of opposition to the soul because they are addressed to and exist for the soul, for perception and understanding. Marguerite anticipates him in this. Her modern self has no grounds for rejecting or despising what is, therefore, the modern world.

The consequences of the sharp correction against dualism in these two poems of Marguerite's are notable. Luther seems to have been entirely at ease with the devil, allowing him a very great place in theology and in life. But in Marguerite's poems, though they are both about sin and fallenness, there is no Satan, no tempter, no adversary, no external source of evil at all. In the first lines of the title poem, the soul cries out for a hell infernal enough to punish a tenth of its sins, a startling assertion of the primacy of subjective experience, over against the claims of the actual terrors of an objectively existing hell. By contrast, Ignatius of Loyola begs for "a deep sense of the pain which the lost suffer, that if because of my faults I forget the love of the eternal Lord, at least the fear of these punishments will keep me from falling into sin." There is frustration, astonishment, and grief in the voices of Marguerite's poems, but no fear or suspense, because there is nothing external to the soul but the Lord, whose grace need not be doubted. There is, in effect, only one narrative, always complete, irrespective of any particular sin or error. In this, Marguerite anticipates Cauvin, who believes in eternal reprobation, but who never seems to allow himself to imagine it. She may also anticipate the sect called the Libertines, who taught, according to Cauvin, that devils are "nothing but evil inspirations," a view he denounced. Nevertheless he mentions Satan rarely, preferring, as Marguerite does, to ponder discords within the soul, and he gives short shrift to hell — one long paragraph in the fifteen hundred pages of the final version of the *Institutes*. This is not how he is thought of. Whether his tradition parted with him in these matters or whether it also has been misinterpreted or misrepresented, he did not encourage any special interest in damnation.

Finally, in her book about the sinful soul, Marguerite mentions Eve twice, once in passing and once because her name occurs in the prayer Salve Regina, which she translates into French, with Christ as mediator in place of Mary, conforming the prayer to Lutheran or Protestant teaching. Eve has no special role in the Fall, no special weakness to predispose her to it, no special liabilities as a consequence of it — fallenness as a parable of gender is not in any way touched upon. The soul who speaks could be, humanly speaking, male or female, Adam or Eve. In the whole of the *Institutes,* Cauvin will not mention Eve once, even in passing. As a consequence, the thought that women carry any special burden of guilt or sinfulness cannot even arise, nor can the thought that sin bears any special relation to sexuality. This permits Cauvin to speak as he does of marriage, and it is one reason for the high status women have traditionally enjoyed in Calvinist cultures.

The profound isolation of the soul, which seems so fearful to those to whom it does not seem true, so daunting to those for whom it is not exhilarating, is fully present in Marguerite's poems years before the word "Calvinism" would be uttered. It is an aspect of the doctrine attributed to John Calvin which is supposed to reflect the contemptible harshness of his disposition. But what if he learned it from the earthy, worldly, indulgent sister of the king? One need imagine no more than that some Paris acquaintance lent him her book. Considering her prominence among literary and intellectual people, the life-and-death importance to the Reform movement of her active sympathy, the boldness of the publication then of poetry based on translation of Scripture into French, the startling response of the Sorbonne — surely *The Sinful Soul* would have been read with great interest. One account of the events that forced Cauvin to leave Paris was that he may have helped Nicolas Cop write a lecture which defended the book.

When the soul in Marguerite's poems calls itself Rien, it must be remembered that the imagination behind it is that of someone who enjoyed extraordinary privilege. Marguerite's mother, Louise de Savoie, was *régente* of France during the childhood of her son François, and one of the great women of Europe who met in 1529 to negotiate the Paix des Dames, which brought to an end years of intractable warfare. After her brother the king was captured in a failed military venture in Italy, Marguerite herself went to Madrid to negotiate his release from prison. She spent her adult life steadily and tactfully forming the French Renaissance. That is to say, when, in the person of the soul, she renounces every claim to estimation, she is renouncing a very great deal, and that is the point. The soul participates in the nature of the eternal by putting aside the temporal, that is, everything it can know of itself. Power and erudition are of no more account than ignorance and weakness. It is only as nothing that the soul can be without limitation. Its true or essential being is in relation to God, toward whom it exists in the roles God affords to it — in Marguerite's poem "Mirror of the Sinful Soul," the very lofty roles of sister, mother, son, spouse. The soul is a perceiver upon whom perception is visited — "the gift whereof the virtue is unknown to my little power." What is described is not the diminishing of the self, but an imagination of it enlarged and exalted far beyond what is within its power to imagine or to desire.

In his commentary on Genesis, Cauvin will describe heaven (which he almost never does) in these terms: "[T]he earth, with its supply of fruits for our daily nourishment, is not there set before us; but Christ offers himself unto life eternal. Nor does heaven, by the shining of the sun and the stars, enlighten our bodily eyes, but the same Christ, the Light of the World and the Sun of Righteousness, shines into our souls; neither does the air stretch out its empty space for us to breathe in, but the Spirit of God quickens us and causes us to live. There, in short, the invisible kingdom of Christ fills all things, and his spiritual grace is diffused through all." Heaven's essence for him is that it is inconceivable in the world's terms, another order of experience. This is true even though his conception of this world is utterly visionary. He says that while God is not to be seen "in his unveiled essence" he "clothes himself, so to speak, in the image of the world, in which he would present himself to our contemplation . . . arrayed in the incomparable vesture of the heavens and the earth . . ." Every understanding of the self is meaningless where the whole of existence is changed beyond our ability to conceive of it, where all understanding is of the nature of revelation, that is, of perception overwhelmed. This being true, there is no meaningful distinction to be made between one soul and the next — each one is simple, absolute soul, and as if the only soul. This is heaven without hierarchy, a very revolutionary idea. It privileges anyone's relationship with God above any other loyalty or duty.

Christ, in Marguerite's "Mirror of the Sinful Soul," is brother (or sister), never king: "[W]e seeing him to be called man, we are bold to call him sister and brother. Now the soul which may say of herself, that she is the sister of God, ought to have her heart assured." She makes the perspective of the whole of humankind, without condition or distinction, one of privileged intimacy with God. Her insistence on the sinfulness of the soul as a condition of its humanity — Cauvin's "total depravity" — and on the sins it sees in itself as archetypal rather than personal and singular, implies the equality of all souls. Cauvin could have found encouragement in her to address the king so bluntly, and to assert the divine right of the common folk to be protected against the abuses of kings.

John Calvin is said to have made the first extended use of French as a language of systematic thought, and to have impressed it with the restraint and lucidity of his style. He is said to have made French an international language because of the wide influence of his writing. What little is said of him tends almost always to ascribe to him truly epochal significance, for weal or woe, which he could not deserve if his thought and work were not more original by far than he ever claimed they were. So it is no disrespect to him to look elsewhere for the sources of his originality. If, as is often said, he was the greatest theologian of the Reformation, it is because he was not primarily a theologian, but a humanist, a man of letters, an admiring student of this world. His theology was so influential in part because he understood its implications in such broad terms. He reimagined civilization, as his spiritual progeny would do again and again. In her own way, Marguerite was at the same work sooner, through her patronage and her own writing, using books and languages to open other worlds, including the potent world of the modern vernacular.

Marguerite was born to Louise de Savoie when Louise was a girl of sixteen. At twenty, Louise was a widow with another child, a two-year-old boy, François. Learned herself, she was devoted to the education of her children. In the year of Marguerite's birth, 1492, Spain expelled its Moors and Jews, scattering its strangest riches over Europe. There had been a great many Moors and Jews in the old kingdom of Navarre. In the time of the Albigensian crusades, troubadours had gone there for refuge. Some scholars say their art of sung poetry had first been learned from the Moors. Marguerite, as a child, learned Spanish, and a little Hebrew. Who can imagine how the things we call ideas live in the world, or how they change, or how they perish, or how they can be renewed?

Psalm Eight

O ne Easter I went with my grandfather to a small
Presbyterian church in northern Idaho, where I
heard a sermon on the discrepancies in the gospel
accounts of the resurrection. I was a young child with neither
the habit nor the expectation of understanding, as the word is
normally used, most of what went on around me. Yet I remember that sermon, and I believe in some degree I took its
meaning.

As an older child in another church and town, on no special occasion, I heard the Eighth Psalm read, and kept for myself a few words from it, because they heartened certain intuitions of mine — "When I consider thy heavens, the work of
thy fingers, the moon and the stars . . . What is man, that thou
art mindful of him? and the son of man, that thou visitest him?
For thou hast made him a little lower than the angels . . ." I
quote the King James Version because those were the words I
heard and remembered. The thought never entered my mind
that the language could be taken to exclude me, perhaps be-

cause my experience of it was the religious one, of words in some exceptional sense addressed precisely to me.

I can imagine myself that primal Easter, restive at my grandfather's elbow, pushing my nickels and dimes of collection money into the tips of my gloves to make toad fingers, struggling with the urge to swing my legs, memorably forbidden to remove my hat, aware that I should not sigh. In those days boredom for me was a misery and a passion, and anticipation a pleasure so sharp I could not tell it from dread. So of course I hated holidays. For these and other reasons my entire experience of being in the world was slightly galled and antagonized. Quotidian events, dawn and evening for example, I found almost unbearable. I remember exasperating the kindly intentions of elders with moodiness and weepiness I could not explain. I do not remember childhood as happy but as filled and overfilled with an intensity of experience that made happiness a matter of little interest. I can only imagine that other versions of me, realer than that poor present self forever being discarded in their favor, larger than me and impatient with my immaturity and my awkwardness, simply wanted out. Metamorphosis is an unsentimental business, and I was a long time in the thick of it, knees scraped, clothes awry, nerves strained and wearied.

I doubt I concealed my restlessness, or much of it, and I doubt my grandfather knew the hour was anything but tedium for me. He would not have known, because no one knew, that I was becoming a pious child, seriously eager to hear whatever I might be told. What this meant precisely, and why it was true, I can only speculate. But it seems to me I felt God as a presence before I had a name for him, and long before I knew words like "faith" or "belief." I was aware to the point of alarm of a vast energy of intention, all around me, barely re-

strained, and I thought everyone else must be aware of it. For
that reason I found the majestic terrains of my childhood, to
which my ancestors had brought their ornate Victorian appre-
ciation at daunting cost in life and limb, very disturbing, and I
averted my gaze as I could from all those luminist splendors. I
was coaxed to admire, and I would not, admiration seeming so
poor a thing in the circumstances. Only in church did I hear
experience like mine acknowledged, in all those strange narratives, read and expounded and, for all that, opaque as figures of
angels painted on gold.

This is of course to employ language a child would never
use. Then again, I describe experience outside the constraints of
understanding that asserted themselves in me as I grew into
this strange culture and century, and which oblige me to use
language as little mine as mine is the language of that child. I
describe the distantly remembered emotions of a girl long vanished — I am sure if I met her on the street I would not recognize her. In another time and place she and I might have
grown up together, and she would have been able to speak for
herself. Asked if I romanticize or exaggerate the world she saw
and felt, she would reply, She does not touch the hem of it.

All the old writers on the subject remark that in every age
and nation people have had the idea of a god of some sort. So
my archaic self might have been nothing other than a latter-
day pagan whose intuitions were not altogether at odds with,
as it happened, Presbyterianism, and so were simply polished to
that shape. Or it might have been that I was a mystic by vocation and, despite Presbyterianism, suffered atrophy of my gift in
a life where I found little use for it. For all I know I am a mystic
now, and simply too close to the phenomenon to have a clear
view of it. In any case I began as a pagan and have ended as one,
though only in the sense that I have never felt secure in the

...on of the ideas and loyalties that are dearest to me. I am ... in a basilica, refusing to admire so that anyone can see ..., thrown back on impassivity as my only notion of deco-...I am surely wrong if I blame history for this sense I have ...tuous claim, wrong to invoke the notion of blame at all. ...loper though I may be, I enjoy the thief's privilege of pleasure in the simple preciousness of things that are not my own. I enjoy it far too much to attempt to regularize my situation. In my childhood, when the presence of God seemed everywhere and I seemed to myself a mote of exception, improbable as a flaw in the sun, the very sweetness of the experience lay in that stinging thought — not me, not like me, not mine.

By the standards of my generation, all my life I have gone to church with a kind of persistence, as I do to this day. Once recently I found myself traveling all night to be home in time for church, and it occurred to me to consider in what spirit or out of what need I would do such a thing. My tradition does not encourage the idea that God would find any merit in it. I go to church for my own gratification, which is intense, though it had never occurred to me before to try to describe it to myself.

The essence of it, certainly, is the Bible, toward which I do not feel in any degree proprietary, with which after long and sometimes assiduous attention I am not familiar. I believe the entire hypertrophic bookishness of my life arose directly out of my exposure, among modest Protestant solemnities of music and flowers, to the language of Scripture. Therefore, I know many other books very well and I flatter myself that I understand them — even books by people like Augustine and Calvin. But I do not understand the Bible. I study theology as one would watch a solar eclipse in a shadow. In church, the devout old custom persists of merely repeating verses, one or another luminous fragment, a hymn before and a hymn afterward. By grace of my abiding ignorance, it is always new to me. I am never not instructed.

I have shifted allegiances the doctrinal and demographic inch that separates Presbyterians from Congregationalists, but for all purposes I am where I ought to be, as sociologists calculate, and I should feel right at home. I will concede only that the sensation of exclusion is more poignant to me in these precincts than in others, being after all these years so very familiar. The people around me every Sunday are as reserved and attentive as I am, like very respectful guests, in a church they own, sustain, and entirely govern.

From time to time, on the strength of the text, the minister will conclude something brave and absolute — You *must* forgive, or, If you think you have anything because you deserve it, you have forgotten the grace of God, or, No history or prospect of failure can excuse you from the obligation to try to do good. These are moments that do not occur in other settings, and I am so far unregenerate that they never cease to impress me deeply. And it touches me that this honorable art of preaching is carried forward when there is so little regard for it among us now. But the most persuasive and forthright explication of that text is still theology. For me, at least, the text itself always remains almost entirely elusive. So I must come back to hear it again; in the old phrase, to have it opened for me again.

The four gospels do not agree in their accounts of the discovery of the empty tomb on the morning of the resurrection. The sermon I heard with my grandfather established that fact with the forensic concern for textual detail some ministers reserve for grand occasions. This would account for the great restlessness which, as I recall, nearly overthrew my better self.

As it happens, Matthew reports that, apparently "with

Mary Magdalene and the other Mary" watching, "behold, there was a great earthquake: for the angel of the lord descended from heaven, and came and rolled back the stone from the door, and sat upon it. His countenance was like lightning, and his raiment white as snow: And for fear of him the keepers did shake, and became as dead men. And the angel answered and said unto the women, Fear not ye: for I know that ye seek Jesus, which was crucified. He is not here: for he is risen, as he said. Come, see the place where the Lord lay."

In Mark's account, "Mary Magdalene and Mary the mother of James, and Salome" came to the tomb at the rising of the sun with spices to anoint the body. "And they said among themselves, Who shall roll us the stone away from the door of the sepulchre? And when they looked, they saw that the stone was rolled away: for it was very great. And entering into the sepulchre, they saw a young man sitting on the right side, clothed in a long white garment; and they were affrighted. And he saith unto them, Be not affrighted: Ye seek Jesus of Nazareth, which was crucified: he is risen; he is not here: behold the place where they laid him."

According to Luke, women who had come with Jesus from Galilee prepared spices and ointments and came to the tomb to find the stone rolled back. "And they entered in, and found not the body of the Lord Jesus. And it came to pass, as they were much perplexed thereabout, behold, two men stood next to them in shining garments: And as they were afraid, and bowed down their faces to the earth, they said unto them, Why seek ye the living among the dead?" The disciples with whom, unrecognized, Jesus walks to Emmaus, tell him the women described "a vision of angels."

In the Gospel of John, Mary Magdalene goes to the tomb early in the morning, sees the stone rolled back, and runs to tell the disciples that the body of Jesus has been removed. Peter and another disciple, presumably John himself, run to the sepulchre, and Simon Peter "went into the sepulchre, and seeth the linen clothes lie, and the napkin, that was about his head, not lying with the linen clothes, but wrapped together in a place by itself . . . But Mary stood at the sepulchre weeping: and as she wept, she stooped down, and looked into the sepulchre, and seeth two angels in white sitting, the one at the head and the other at the feet, where the body of Jesus had lain. And they say unto her, Woman, why weepest thou?"

The minister who drew my attention to this mystery, a plump old man in a white vestment as I remember him, must have asked how it came about or what it could mean that this essential moment was described differently in every report of it. What I recall of the sermon would have been offered as an answer to that question. He dwelt on the other figures at the tomb, not the women or the disciples but the figures described as angels in three accounts and, in one, as a young man in a long white garment. He asked what it would mean if all the descriptions were in fact of one or two young men, followers of Jesus who had simply stayed the night by the tomb or arrived there before the women in the morning. Or if the one young man was in fact an angel. The Bible, he said, was full of proof that angels could pass for men, which must certainly mean that men could pass for angels. He concluded that, insofar as a young man is seen under the aspect of joy and kindness and holiness, he is properly seen as an angel, because that is a vision of his immortal nature. And that insofar as the joy and kindness and holiness of angels are addressed to human beings, angels are like us and at one with us, at their most beautiful when they express attributes most beautiful in us. That such a confusion could have occurred is central to the meaning of the resurrection, because it reminds us what we are. Amen, he said, having blessed my life with a lovely thing to ponder.

The families of both my parents settled and established themselves in the northern mountains, where there is a special sweetness in the light and grace in the vegetation, and as well a particular tenderness in the contact of light and vegetation. We used to hunt for wild strawberries in places in the woods where there had once been fires. These meadows, which for decades or centuries would hardly have felt more sunlight than the floor of the sea, were avid for it. Because of the altitude, or the damp, or the kind of grass that grew in such places, they were radiant, smoldering, gold with transparency, accepting light altogether. Thousands of florets for which I would never learn names, so tiny even a child had to kneel to see them at all, squandered intricacy and opulence on avid little bees, the bees cherished, the flowers cherished, the light cherished, visibly, audibly, palpably.

John Calvin says that when a seed falls into the ground it is cherished there, by which he means that everything the seed contains by way of expectation is foreseen and honored. One might as well say the earth invades the seed, seizes it as occasion to compose itself in some brief shape. Groundwater in a sleeve of tissue, flaunting improbable fragrances and iridescences as the things of this strange world are so inclined to do. So a thriving place is full of intention, a sufficiency awaiting expectation, teasing hope beyond itself.

To find in the sober woods these little Orients of delectation was like hearing a tale of opulent grace poured out on modest need or of miracle astonishing despair, a parable brilliant with strangeness, cryptic with wisdom, disturbing as a tender intention full of the frightening mercy of foreknowledge. God will wipe away all tears, the dead will rise, meant to me then, Little girl, you will mourn and you will die. Perhaps that was some great part of the difference I felt between the world and myself, that while it was a thousand ways true that it knew me as I could not know myself — my old relatives remembered people with my voice or my eyes and how they lived and how their lives ended — I hoarded the notion of this singular self in this singular moment, as if such things could exist, and shrugged away intention and anticipation and cherishing, knowing they meant that even I never was my own.

I knew my grandfather for many years, but I am not sure I ever knew him well. He seemed stern to me and I was very shy of him. I had heard sad stories about him as a boy and a young man, and when I was with him I always thought of them, and I was cautious, as if the injuries might still be tender.

It may be that I did know my grandfather very well *because* I thought of him as a boy and a young man, and explained his silence to myself in such terms. My memory of him allows me to interpret the dignity of his shrinking height and stooping back as an effort of composure of the kind people make when the shock of cruelty is still new to them, when resignation is still a novel labor. I interpret the memory of his polished shoes and his habit of gardening in his oldest suit and his worst necktie as evidence that I sensed in him diligent pride in the face of sadness not otherwise to be borne. Perhaps he himself could not have told me how near the truth I was.

His gardening was uncanny. The flourishing he set in motion brought admirers from other counties. I remember once following him down a row of irises, not sure whether I was invited, whether the irises were being shown to me. He would hold one blossom and another in the tips of his fingers, at arm's length, and tilt his face up and back to look at them. It was an old man's method of scrutiny, but to me it seemed as if he were revealing prodigy or sleight, the way a magician opens his hand to reveal a dove. I looked carefully at every blossom he appeared to commend to me, noting how they were made of cell and capillary, whisker and freckle, frail skin tented on white bone, and how they were chill to the touch, and how they curled on themselves like smoke, and how, till the life was wrung out of it, each one accomplished a small grandeur of form.

In those mountains there is a great constant silence surrounding any brief local silence, and one is always aware of it. When I was a child it seemed to me sometimes it might be emptiness that would tease my soul out of my body, with some intention too huge even to notice my fragile flesh. I knew that the mountains and the lakes and the woods brought people's lives to disastrous conclusions, often too frightening to repeat in the hearing of children. There were people whose loss could hardly be borne no matter the years that passed, and whose names were spoken rarely, and then softly, with rue and grief — Steven and Lewis and the precious Virgie, a woman or girl I have mourned my whole life in the absence of all particulars, just for the way they said her name. I lived so as to be missed with bitterness, and I learned to be good at the things they praised, preparing and refining their regret. I poured myself into the vessel of their memories, which are mine now. I save all those people in myself by regretting the loss of them in the very way they taught me.

Oddly, perhaps, in the circumstances, no one so far as I remember ever spoke to me of heaven. Certainly no one ever spoke to me of hell. Though absentmindedly they sometimes murmured hymns to themselves, among my kindred religion was rarely mentioned. I believe I ascribed this fact to the power of it, since it was characteristic of them to be silent about things that in any way moved them. It never occurred to me to wonder if they were devout, nor have I any great reason to wonder, looking back. Religion was simply among the burdened silences I pondered and glossed, feeling no need to inquire, assuming an intimacy with the thoughts of those around me which may well have been entirely real.

Among my family, my training in the right conduct of life seemed to assume that left to myself I would rather not break a commandment, and to bend its coercive energies to improving my grammar. The patient old women who taught me Presbyterianism taught in parables. God spoke to Moses from a burning bush, Pharaoh dreamed a dream of famine, Jesus said, Take up your bed and walk. We drew or colored pictures of these events, which were, I think, never explained to us. No intrusion on the strangeness of these tales was ever made. It was as if some old relative had walked me down to the lake knowing an imperious whim of heaven had made it a sea of gold and glass, and had said, This is a fine evening, and walked me home again. I am convinced it was all this reticence, in effect this esotericism, which enthralled me.

Surely it is not true to say that the gospel stories were written in the hope that they would be believed; rather that, by the time they were written down, they were the cherished possession of the early church and had taken forms many had already found to be persuasive, and also beautiful and moving. It seems wrong to suggest that in their accounts of the resurrection the intent of the writers is to persuade their readers and hearers of the truth of an incredible event, simply because there is so much evidence that resurrection would not have been considered incredible. The prophet Elijah had brought a child back from the dead. He himself ascended into heaven without dying, and his return was awaited in Jesus' time. John the Baptist was believed to be Elijah. Jesus was believed to be Elijah. Herod thought Jesus was John the Baptist back from the dead. Jesus restored to life Lazarus and the temple official's daughter. Before the resurrection of Lazarus, his sister Martha dutifully misinterprets Jesus' assurance that he will live again to refer to a general resurrection of the dead. The Sadducees are described as those "who do not believe in the resurrection," a phrase which surely implies that the idea was abroad independently of Jesus. At the moment Jesus died, graves are said to have opened and the dead to have walked in the streets.

In the world the Gospels describe there seems to be no skepticism about miracles as such, only about the authenticity or origins of particular miracles. Indeed, where in the premodern world would one find such skepticism? The restoration of the dead to life is not only anticipated but reported, with, if anything, less astonishment than the healing of those born blind or lame.

It seems to me that the intent of the gospel writers is not to make the resurrection seem somehow plausible or credible — this could hardly be done without diminishing its impressiveness as miracle — but instead to heighten its singularity, when, as event, it would seem by no means unexampled. I believe it is usual to say that the resurrection established who Jesus was and what his presence meant. Perhaps it is truer to say the opposite, that who Jesus was established what his resurrection meant, that he seized upon a narrative familiar or even pervasive and wholly transformed it.

When, in the Gospel of John, weeping Mary Magdalene stoops to look into the tomb and sees the angels, they ask her, "Woman, why weepest thou?" The text creates the dreamy impression that the two angels speak together. Then she turns and sees a man standing behind her, Jesus, whom she mistakes for a gardener. He speaks the same words as the angels did, "Woman, why weepest thou?" and he asks, "Whom seekest thou?" Does he see and hear the angels, too? Or does he know her thoughts? Or was it his voice she heard in the first place? Mary herself would not have known. Jesus seems to be teasing her toward delight and recognition, ready to enjoy her surprise, in something like the ordinary manner of a friend. The narrative asserts that he is a figure of unutterable holiness, only pausing to speak to Mary before he ascends to heaven, yet it is his very ordinariness that disguises him from her. Splendor is very well for youths and angels, but when Jesus takes up again for a little while the life he had wept to leave, it is the life of a plain man.

If Jesus was not a messiah after the manner of David, neither was he a spiritual leader after the manner of Elijah, though his resurrection, if it were not insistently interpreted in the light of his life and teaching, might well have encouraged that association, which was clearly very available to his followers. The great difference is simply embrace. Elijah's ascent expressed God's love toward him. Jesus' resurrection expressed God's love toward humankind. Jesus tells Mary, "Go to my brethren, and say unto them, I ascend unto my Father, and your Father; and to my God, and your God."

This moment is surely full of implication. Imagine Jesus as an ordinary man, the sort to fall prey to the penalty of crucifixion, by means of which Roman law terrified the humble by depriving offenders of their dignity together with their lives. Then if, after his ordeal, Jesus had gathered around himself just the composure of an ordinary man, so that he could be mistaken for someone going about his work, that would seem like miracle and grandeur, that would be an astonishing beauty. It seems to me that the narrative, in its most dazzling vision of holiness, commends to us beauty of an altogether higher order than spectacle, that being mere commonplace, ineffable humanity.

"What is man that thou art mindful of him?" A question is more spacious than a statement, far better suited to expressing wonder. The method of the Psalmist is exuberant. He offers the heavens to our consideration, than which nothing vaster can be imagined, then diminishes them in relation to God by describing them as the work, not of his will or even of his hands, but of his fingers. There is a wonderful implication that the great moon and the innumerable stars are astonishing not for the vastnesses they fill so sparsely and illuminate so slightly, but because God should delight in making anything so small and fine as the heavens and their adornments, in every way exceeding them as he does. I have always imagined the trace of a gesture of conjuration or display left in the clouds of stars curling on themselves like smoke.

The strategy of the Psalmist is to close the infinite distance between God and humankind by confounding all notions of scale. If the great heavens are the work of God's fingers, what is small and mortal man? The poem answers its own question this way: Man is *crowned* with honor and glory. He is in a singular sense what God has made him, because of the dignity God has conferred upon him, splendor of a higher order, like that of angels. The Hebrew Scriptures everywhere concede: yes, foolish; yes, guilty; yes, weak; yes, sad and bewildered. Yes, resistant to cherishing and rebellious against expectation. And yes, forever insecure at best in his vaunted dominion over creation. Then how is this dignity manifest? Surely in that God is mindful of man, in that he "visits" him — this is after all the major assertion of the whole literature. "What is man?" is asked in awe — that God should be intrigued or enchanted by him, or loyal to him. Any sufficient answer would go some way toward answering "What is God?" I think anxieties about anthropomorphism are substantially inappropriate in a tradition whose main work has been to assert and ponder human theomorphism.

When, in the Gospel of John, Jesus says to Mary Magdalene, "Woman, why weepest thou?" he is using, so scholarship tells me, a term of great respect and deference. Elsewhere he addresses his mother as "woman." I know of no other historical moment in which this word is an honorific. Of course Jesus, however he is understood, whatever powers are ascribed to him, could only use the words he found ready for use, and this must mean that over generations the culture in which he was to live his life had been preparing a certain improbable consensus about the meaning of this one word, which, in the narrative, is the first one he speaks in the new world of his restored life.

How much speculation should detail such as this be asked to bear? It is as true of these old texts as it is of anything that we do not really know what they are. I would suggest their peculiarities reflect problems of art, more than they do discrepant memory or uncertain transmission. I would suggest that they attempt to preserve a sense of Jesus' presence, that they are evocation and portraiture first of all, meant to achieve likeness rather than precision, in the manner of art. The Old Testament is full of characterization, of great Moses, especially. But in those narratives the nature of the hero and the nature of God are separate mysteries, the second vastly overshadowing the first. In the Jesus narratives they are the same mystery, so attention dwells on him in a manner entirely unique in Scripture.

The agreement among the varying accounts is profound,

more strikingly so because they differ in their particulars. For example, in all the varying accounts of his encounters with his followers after the resurrection, Jesus is concealed from them by his ordinariness — as, for that matter, he had been in life. In every instance he is among them on terms of friendship, once even making a fire and cooking supper for them. If, let us say, memories were transposed to provide eloquent detail, or even if some details were invented, it would be in the service of creating a likeness, not a history, and discrepancies would matter not at all.

To say that literal representation is different from portraiture is to make a distinction like this: Jesus, even in the interval before his ascent into heaven, did in fact address a woman with courtesy and deference. Or, it would have been *like* Jesus, even in the interval before his ascent into heaven, to address a woman with courtesy and deference. A statement of the second kind could easily be truer, and is certainly more meaningful, than a statement of the first kind.

How to describe the powerful old life of Scripture? As a pious child, Jesus must at some time have heard the words, "What is man, that thou art mindful of him?" and also the psalm that begins "My God, my God, why hast thou forsaken me?" These narratives seize their occasion. They flourished in the perception and memory of those near Jesus, and in the stories they told about him. They were clearly in his mind. More is meant by prophecy, and more by fulfillment, than that narratives shape and recur. But without them there would be neither prophecy nor fulfillment.

"Woman," Jesus, when he had lived and died, said or would have said, using a word perhaps not used so gently since Adam was a gardener — "Woman, why weepest thou?" Mary Magdalene could hear this as the question of a kindly stranger, but it means, in fact, There is no more cause for weeping. It means, perhaps, God will wipe away all tears. "Who seekest thou?," a question of the same kind, means, She need not look farther. To Jesus, or to the writer whose account renders what he took to be implicit in the moment, these questions might be wider altogether, full of awe. How did sorrow enter the world? What would be the nature of comfort or of restitution? The scene we are given answers its own questions, and does not answer them at all. Here is Jesus, by great miracle an ordinary man, except that he carries in his body the marks of mortal injury. From whatever cosmic grandeur the moment claims for him, he speaks to the friend of his humanity with joy and kindness but also with deference, honoring her. When Mary looks at Jesus, knowing who he is, what does she see? A more amazing question — when Jesus looks at Mary, and whenever he has looked at her, what does *he* see? We are told that, in the days before death and sorrow, God walked of an evening in the garden he had made, that he saw his likeness in the gardeners, that he spoke with them. What can these strange stories mean? After so much time and event and so much revelation, the mystery is only compounded.

So I have spent my life watching, not to see beyond the world, merely to see, great mystery, what is plainly before my eyes. I think the concept of transcendence is based on a misreading of creation. With all respect to heaven, the scene of miracle is here, among us. The eternal as an idea is much less preposterous than time, and this very fact should seize our attention. In certain contexts the improbable is called the miraculous.

What is eternal must always be complete, if my understanding is correct. So it is possible to imagine that time was created in order that there might be narrative — event, sequence and causation, ignorance and error, retribution, atonement. A word, a phrase, a story falls on rich or stony ground and flourishes as it can, possibility in a sleeve of limitation. Certainly time is the occasion for our strangely mixed nature, in every moment differently compounded, so that often we surprise ourselves, and always scarcely know ourselves, and exist in relation to experience, if we attend to it and if its plainness does not disguise it from us, as if we were visited by revelation.

WILDERNESS

ENVIRONMENTALISM poses stark issues of survival, for humankind and for all those other tribes of creatures over which we have exercised our onerous dominion. Even undiscovered species feel the effects of our stewardship. What a thing is man.

The oldest anecdotes from which we know ourselves as human, the stories of Genesis, make it clear that our defects are sufficient to bring the whole world down. An astonishing intuition, an astonishing fact.

One need not have an especially excitable or a particularly gloomy nature to be persuaded that we may be approaching the end of the day. For decades, environmentalists have concerned themselves with this spill and that encroachment, this depletion and that extinction, as if such phenomena were singular and exceptional. Our causes have even jostled for attention, each claiming a special urgency. This is, I think, like quarreling over which shadow brings evening. We are caught up in something much larger than its innumerable manifestations. Their variety and seriousness are proof of this.

I am an American of the kind whose family sought out wilderness generation after generation. My great-grandparents finally settled in Idaho, much of which is wilderness now, in terms of its legal status, and is therefore, theoretically, protected. In the heart of this beloved, empty, magnificent state is the Idaho Nuclear Engineering Laboratory, among other things a vast repository for radioactive waste. Idaho, Utah, Nevada, New Mexico, beautiful names for vast and melancholy places. Europeans from time to time remark that Americans have no myth of landscape. In fact we have many such myths. People who cherish New England may find it difficult to imagine that Utah is cherished also. In fact, I started writing fiction at an eastern college, partly in hopes of making my friends there understand how rich and powerful a presence a place can be which, to their eyes, is forbidding and marginal, without population or history, without culture in any form recognizable to them. All love is in great part affliction. My bond with my native landscape was an unnamable yearning, to be at home in it, to be chastened and acceptable, to be present in it as if I were not present at all.

Moses himself would have approved the reverence with which I regarded my elders, who were silent and severe and at their ease with solitude and difficulty. I meant to be like them. Americans from the interior West know what I am describing. For them it is, or is like, religious feeling, being so powerful a reference for all other experience.

Idaho, Utah, Nevada, New Mexico. These names are all notorious among those who know anything at all about nuclear weapons. Wilderness is where things can be hidden, from foreign enemies, perhaps, but certainly from domestic critics. This effect is enhanced by the fact that wilderness dwellers everywhere are typically rather poor and scattered, not much in the public mind, not significant as voters. Wilderness is where things can be done that would be intolerable in a populous landscape. The relative absence of human populations obscures the nature and effect of programs which have no other object than to be capable of the most profound injury to human populations. Of course, even wilderness can only absorb such insult to the systems of life to a degree, for a while. Nature is very active — aquifers so vast, rivers so tireless, wind so pervading. I have omitted to mention the great Hanford Reservation in Washington State, with its ominous storage tanks, a whole vast landscape made an archaeological history of malign intent, and a great river nearby to spread the secret everywhere.

Russia is much more generously endowed with wilderness than America. Turn the globe, and there is an expanse that puts our little vastness in perspective. It is my impression that depredations of the kind we have been guilty of have been carried farther in Russia and its former territories, at least in proportion to the permission apparently implied by empty spaces. But wilderness can be borrowed, as the coast and interior of Australia and, of course, Nevada have been by the British for their larger nuclear weapons projects, and wilderness can be relative, like the English Lake District and the northwest coast of France. And then there is the sea. We have all behaved as if there were a place where actions would not have consequences.

Wilderness is not a single region, but a condition of being of the natural world. If it is no longer to be found in one place, we assume it exists in other places. So the loss of wilderness always seems only relative, and this somewhat mitigates any specific instance of abuse. Civilization has crept a little farther; humankind has still to learn certain obvious lessons about living in the world. We regret and we repent and we blame, and we assume that things can be different elsewhere. Again, the very idea of wilderness permits us to evade in some degree a recognition of the real starkness of precisely the kind of abuse most liable to occur outside the reach of political and economic constraints, where those who have isolation at their disposal can do as they will.

Utah is holy land to a considerable number of American people. We all learn as schoolchildren how the Mormons, fleeing intolerance and seeking a place where they could live out their religion, walked into the wilderness, taking their possessions in handcarts, wearing a trail so marked that parts of it are visible to this day. We know they chose barren land by a salt lake, and flourished there.

It is a very pure replication of the national myth. So how did we make the mistake we made, and choose this place whose very emptiness and difficulty were a powerful proof to the Mormons of the tender providence of God — how could we make Utah the battleground in the most furious and terrified campaigns in our long dream of war? The choice kept casualties to a minimum, which means that if the bombs were dropped in populous places the harm would have been clearly intolerable. The small difference between our fantasies of war and war itself would be manifest. As it is, there are many real casualties, and no doubt there would be far more if all the varieties of injury were known and acknowledged.

This is a potent allegory. It has happened over and over again that promised land or holy land by one reckoning is wasteland by another, and we assert the sovereign privilege of destroying what we would go to any lengths to defend. The pattern repeats itself so insistently that I think it is imbedded not merely in rational consciousness but also in human consciousness. Humankind has no enemy but itself, and it is broken and starved and poisoned and harried very nearly to death.

Look at England. They have put a plutonium factory and nuclear waste dump in the Lake District, a region so beautiful that it was set aside, spared most of the marring burdens of population. And what a misfortune that has been. Relatively small populations result in relatively small bases for interpreting public health effects, so emptiness ensures not safety so much as deniability. Wilderness and its analogues seem to invite denial in every form. In Utah and in Cumbria, it was the urgent business of years to produce weapons capable of inflicting every extreme of harm on enemy populations. Do they harm people who live where they are made and tested? If the answers "no," or "not significantly," or "it is too difficult to tell" were ever given in good faith, then clearly some mechanism of denial had come into play. The denial was participated in at a grand enough scale to make such answers sufficient for most of the public for a very long time, even though one effect was to permit methods of development and testing that assured widespread public contact with waste or fallout, and that will assure it into any imaginable future.

Denial is clearly a huge factor in history. It seems to me analogous to a fractal, or a virus, in the way it self-replicates, and in the way its varieties are the grand strategy of its persistence. It took, for instance, three decades of the most brilliant and persistent campaign of preachment and information to establish, in the land of liberty, the idea that slavery was intolerable. Strange enough. These antislavery agitators were understandably given to holding up Britain's ending of slavery in her colonies as the example of enlightened Christian behavior. But at the same time, British slave ships used the old slave routes to transport British convicts to Australia. Every enormity was intact, still suffered by women and children as well as men. Of course the color of the sufferer had changed, and it is always considered more respectable in a government to ravage its own population than others'. To this objection, I will reply that the arrival of the British was an unspeakable disaster to the native people of Australia and Tasmania. Slavery and genocide were only rechanneled, translated into other terms, but for the American abolitionists, and for the British abolitionists as well, this was nothing to pause over. It is understandable that Americans should wish to retain all the moral leverage that could be had from the admirable side of the British example. Still, this is another potent allegory, something to unriddle, or at least to be chastened by. After our terrible war, the people who struggled out of bondage, and were won out of bondage, found themselves returned to a condition very much resembling bondage, with the work all before them of awakening public awareness, in the land of the free, to the fact that their situation was intolerable.

Reform-minded Americans still depend on the idea that other countries are in advance of us, and scold and shame us all with scathing comparison. Of course they have no tolerance for information that makes such comparison problematic. The strategy, however generous in impulse, accounts in part for the perdurable indifference of Americans to actual conditions in countries they choose to admire, and often claim to love.

I have begun to consider Edgar Allan Poe the great interpreter of Genesis, or perhaps of Romans. The whole human disaster resides in the fact that, as individuals, families, cities, nations, as a tribe of ingratiating, brilliant, momentarily numerous animals, we are perverse, divided against ourselves, deceiving and defeating ourselves. How many countries in this world have bombed or poisoned their own terrain in the name of protecting it from its enemies? How many more would do so if they could find the means? Do we know that this phenomenon is really different in kind from the Civil War, or from the bloodbaths by which certain regimes have been able to legitimate their power? For a long time we have used dichotomies, good people/bad people, good institutions/bad institutions, capitalist/communist. But the universality of self-deceptive and self-destructive behavior is what must impress us finally.

Those who are concerned about the world environment are, in my view, the abolitionists of this era, struggling to make an enlightened public aware that environmental depredation is an axe at the root of every culture, every freedom, every value. There is no group in history I admire more than the abolitionists, but from their example I conclude that there are two questions we must always ask ourselves — what do we choose not to know, and what do we fail to anticipate? The ultimate success of the abolitionists so very much resembled failure that it requires charity, even more than discernment, to discover the difference. We must do better. Much more is at stake.

I have heard well-meaning people advocate an environmental policing system, presided over by the member governments of the United Nations Security Council. I think we should pause to consider the environmental practices and histories of those same governments. Perhaps under the aegis of the United Nations they do ascend to a higher plane of selflessness and rationality and, in this instance, the cowl will make the monk. Then again, maybe it will not. Rich countries that dominate global media look very fine and civilized, but, after all, they have fairly ransacked the world for these ornaments and privileges and we all know it. This is not to say that they are worse than other nations, merely that they are more successful, for the moment, in sustaining wealth and prestige. This does not mean they are well suited for the role of missionary or schoolmaster. When we imagine they are, we put out of mind their own very grave problems — abandoning their populations, and the biosphere, in the very great degree it is damaged by them, to secure moral leverage against whomever they choose to designate an evildoer. I would myself be willing to give up the hope of minor local benefits in order to be spared the cant and hypocrisy, since I have no hope that the world will survive in any case if the countries represented on the Security Council do not reform their own governments and industries very rigorously, and very soon.

I think it is an indulgence to emphasize to the extent we do the environmental issues that photograph well. I think the peril of the whole world is very extreme, and that the dolphins and koalas are finally threatened by the same potentialities that threaten every thing that creeps on the face of the earth. At this time, we are seeing, in many, many places, a decline in the wealth, morale, and ethos whose persistence was assumed when certain features of modern society were put in place, for example, nuclear reactors and chemical plants. If these things are not maintained, or if they are put to cynical uses by their operators or by terrorists, we can look forward to disaster after disaster. The collapse of national communities and economies very much enhances the likelihood that such things will happen.

We have, increasingly, the unsystematic use of medicine in the face of growing populations of those who are malnourished and unsheltered and grossly vulnerable to disease. Consider the spread of tuberculosis in New York City. Under less than ideal circumstances, modern medicine will have produced an array of intractable illnesses. In the absence of stability and wealth, not to mention a modicum of social justice, medicine is liable to prove a curse and an affliction. There are those who think it might be a good thing if we let ourselves slip into extinction and left the world to less destructive species. Into any imaginable future, there must be people to maintain what we have made, for example, nuclear waste storage sites, and there must be human civilizations rich and sophisticated enough to know how this is done and to have the means to do it. Every day this seems less likely.

And only consider how weapons and weapons materials have spread under cover of this new desperation, and how probable truly nihilistic warfare now appears. These are environmental problems, fully as much as any other kind.

Unless we can reestablish peace and order as values, and learn to see our own well-being in our neighbor's prosperity, we can do nothing at all for the rain forests and the koala bears. To pretend we can is only to turn our backs on more painful and more essential problems. It is deception and self-deception. It stirs a sad suspicion in me that we are of the Devil's party, without knowing it.

I think we are desperately in need of a new, chastened, self-distrusting vision of the world, an austere vision that can postpone the outdoor pleasures of cherishing exotica, and the first-world pleasures of assuming we exist to teach reasonableness to the less fortunate, and the debilitating pleasures of imagining that our own impulses are reliably good. I am bold enough to suggest this because, to this point, environmental successes quite exactly resemble failure. What have we done for the whale, if we lose the sea? If we lose the sea, how do we mend the atmosphere? What can we rescue out of this accelerating desperation to sell — forests and weapons, even children — and the profound deterioration of community all this indicates? Every environmental problem is a human problem. Civilization is the ecology being lost. We can do nothing that matters if we cannot encourage its rehabilitation. Wilderness has for a long time figured as an escape from civilization, and a judgment upon it. I think we must surrender the idea of wilderness, accept the fact that the consequences of human presence in the world are universal and ineluctable, and invest our care and hope in civilization, since to do otherwise risks repeating the terrible pattern of enmity against ourselves, which is truly the epitome and paradigm of all the living world's most grievous sorrows.

THE TYRANNY OF PETTY COERCION

COURAGE SEEMS TO ME to be dependent on cultural definition. By this I do not mean only that it is a word that blesses different behaviors in different cultures, though that is clearly true. I mean also, and more importantly, that courage is rarely expressed except where there is sufficient consensus to support it. Theologians used to write about a prevenient grace, which enables the soul to accept grace itself. Perhaps there must also be a prevenient courage to nerve one to be brave. It is we human beings who give one another permission to show courage, or, more typically, withhold such permission. We also internalize prohibitions, enforcing them on ourselves—prohibitions against, for example, expressing an honest doubt, or entertaining one. This ought not to be true in a civilization like ours, historically committed to valuing individual conscience and free expression. But it is.

Physical courage is remarkably widespread in this population. There seem always to be firefighters to deal with the most appalling conflagrations and doctors to deal with the most novel and alarming illnesses. It is by no means to undervalue courage of this kind to say it is perhaps expedited by being universally *recognized* as courage. Those who act on it can recognize the impulse and act confidently, even at the greatest risk to themselves.

Moral and intellectual courage are not in nearly so flourishing a state, even though the risks they entail — financial or professional disadvantage, ridicule, ostracism — are comparatively minor. I propose that these forms of courage suffer from the disadvantage of requiring new definitions continually, which must be generated out of individual perception and judgment. They threaten or violate loyalty, group identity, the sense of *comme il faut*. They are, intrinsically, outside the range of consensus.

Social comity is no doubt dependent on a degree of likemindedness in a population. It does sometimes help when we are in general agreement about basic things. Indeed, consensus is so powerful and so effectively defended that I suspect it goes back to earliest humanity, when our tribes were small and vulnerable, and schism and defection were a threat to survival. But it should never be forgotten how much repression and violence consensus can support, or how many crimes it has justified.

It is true that in most times and places physical courage and moral and intellectual courage have tended to merge, since dungeons, galleys, and stakes have been extensively employed in discouraging divergent viewpoints. For this reason our own society, which employs only mild disincentives against them and in theory positively admires them, offers a valuable opportunity for the study of what I will call the conservation of consensus, that is, the effective enforcement of consensus in those many instances where neither reason nor data endorse it, where there are no legal constraints supporting it, and where there are no penalties for challenging it that persons of even moderate brio would consider deterrents.

Let us say that the sort of courage I wish to consider can be defined as loyalty to truth. I am not entering any epistemological thicket here. The kind of truth that interests me is of the type sometimes represented in the statement "the house is on fire." It is consensus that conceals from us what is objectively true. And it is consensus that creates and supports "truths" that are in fact culturally relative. And, interestingly, it is consensus that is preserved when the objective truth is disallowed on the grounds that "truth" is merely the shared understanding of a specific group or culture.

Here is an instance: for some time the word "bashing" has been used to derail criticism of many kinds, by treating as partisan or tendentious statements that are straightforwardly true or false. To say that the disparity between rich and poor in this country exceeds any previously known in American history (putting aside the marked economic disparity between plantation owners and slaves) is to say something falsifiable — that is, for practical purposes, verifiable, and in any case arguable. But such statements are now routinely called "Bush bashing." In other words, something that is objectively true or false is dismissed as the slur of a hostile subgroup. Perfectly sensible people flinch at the thought that they might sound a trifle Jacobin, and they are shamed out of saying what they believe to be true in the plainest sense of the word "true." Nor is it the critics alone who lose their bearings when these strategies are employed. Those who identify with the group toward whom the criticisms are directed — in this case, the present administration — can hear irrational attack where they might otherwise hear a challenge to their values or to their theories and methods.

So the exchanges that political life entirely depends on, in which people attempt in good conscience to establish practical truth and then candidly assign value to it, simply do not take place. This is a failure of courage on both sides. I assume many apologists for the administration would find it painful to say that radical economic polarization is a good thing. So they are relieved to learn that they are only being "bashed," and therefore need not consider the issue on its merits.

Why critics are so flummoxed I can only speculate. Perhaps it is because most of the people in this country who take on public issues are educated and middle class. As is true of their kind anywhere, they are acculturated to distrust strong emotion, so they are effectively rebuked when they are accused of harboring it. Oddly, they seem often to be shamed out of defending the poor and vulnerable on the grounds that they themselves are neither poor nor vulnerable, as if there were properly no abstract issues of justice, only the strategies of interest groups or, more precisely, of self-interest groups. That their education and experience prepare them to think in terms larger than their own immediate advantage makes them an "elite," and ipso facto they are regarded as a self-interested subgroup of a particularly irksome kind. Even when they benefit, materially, from the policies they deplore and wish to change, their position is dismissed as nothing more than elitist, though the pols and pollsters who use the term have identical credentials and much greater power. To be intimidated in this way is a failure of courage, and to abandon democracy from an excess of self-doubt and good manners is no different, in its effect, than to abandon it out of arrogance or greed.

I am myself a liberal. By that I mean I believe society exists to nurture and liberate the human spirit, and that large-mindedness and openhandedness are the means by which these things are to be accomplished. I am not ideological. By that I mean I believe opportunities of every kind should be seized upon to advance the well-being of people, especially in assuring them decent wages, free time, privacy, education, and health care, concerns essential to their full enfranchisement.

I am very critical of liberalism, not in principle but as a movement. This distinction seems never to be made, and it is not at all subtle. As a principle, liberalism is essential to the sanity and humanity of this civilization. As a movement, it is virtually defunct. Those who have espoused it have failed it, in a way and to a degree that has allowed the very word to become a term of opprobrium. Some authoritative consensus turned against it, and, obedient to that consensus, its allies have abandoned the cause, if not gone over to the other side, into the embrace of illiberalism. The oddness as well as the potency of this phenomenon is certainly to be seen in the capitulation of the Democratic Party in Congress to a president whose mandate to govern was so weak as to be nonexistent. These solons were cowed not so much by being out of power as by being out of style. Perhaps so honorable a thing as courage should not be named in such a context, even to describe its own absence.

In all fairness, the capitulation of liberalism to illiberalism (a word I use advisedly — there is nothing conservative about this new politics) occurred along the whole broad progressive front, not just in Congress. Suddenly people were avoiding the word, trying to find a new name for their political convictions and failing, in part because they were not quite sure what their convictions were, or if they ought to deal in politics at all. Best leave it to the cynics and the bullies.

It is sad to consider how much first-rate courage must be devoted in this world to struggling out of the toils of sheer pettiness. The Saudi women who first drove automobiles risked and suffered penalties, overcame inhibitions, and shattered norms, heroic in their defiance of an absurd convention. We have our own Rosa Parks. That such great courage should have been required to challenge such petty barriers is a demonstration of the power of social consensus. How many minor coercions are required to sustain similar customs and usages? How aware are any of us, absent direct challenge, of how we also deal in trivial coercion?

This is a time when it actually requires a certain courage to declare oneself a liberal, even among presumptively like-minded people. That might seem a minor act after the instances I have just cited, in which people defied prejudice, custom, and law. But the purely arbitrary nature of this little coercion isolates the impulse to enforce consensus, even when absolutely nothing is at stake for the enforcers and the one subject to coercion risks no penalty — except the embarrassment of seeming not to know that a word is passé, that a posture is, well, as of now a little ridiculous. A great part of learning the argot of a peer group, which is a great part of claiming and assuming membership in it, is the self-editing that deletes disfavored language. All of us learn this skill in adolescence — learn it so well, perhaps, that we practice it unconsciously through life. This editing reaches deeper than mere language, and of course there is no such thing as mere language. The banishment of the word "liberal" was simultaneous with the collapse of liberalism itself. And however these events were related, the patient smile that precludes conversation on the subject means the matter is closed. To be shamed out of the use of a word is to make a more profound concession to opinion than is consistent with personal integrity. What is at stake? Our hope for a good community. Liberalism saw to the well-being of the vulnerable. Now that it has ebbed, the ranks of the vulnerable continuously swell. If this seems too great a claim to make for it, pick up a newspaper. Trivial failures of courage may seem minor enough in any particular instance, and yet they change history and society. They also change culture.

To illustrate this point, I will make a shocking statement: I am a Christian. This ought not to startle anyone. It is likely to be at least demographically true of an American of European ancestry. I have a strong attachment to the Scriptures, and to the theology, music, and art Christianity has inspired. My most inward thoughts and ponderings are formed by the narratives and traditions of Christianity. I expect them to engage me on my deathbed.

Over the years many a good soul has let me know by one means or another that this living out of the religious/ethical/aesthetic/intellectual tradition that is so essentially compelling to me is not, shall we say, cool. There are little jokes about being born again. There are little lectures about religion as a cheap cure for existential anxiety. Now, I do feel fairly confident that I know what religion is. I have spent decades informing myself about it, an advantage I can claim over any of my would-be rescuers. I am a mainline Protestant, a.k.a. a liberal Protestant, as these same people know. I do not by any means wear my religion on my sleeve. I am extremely reluctant to talk about it at all, chiefly because my belief does not readily reduce itself to simple statements.

Nevertheless, I experience these little coercions. Am I the last one to get the news that this religion that has so profoundly influenced world civilization over centuries has been ceded to the clods and the obscurantists? Don't I know that J. S. Bach and Martin Luther King have been entirely eclipsed by Jerry Falwell? The question has been put to me very directly: Am I not afraid to be associated with religious people? These nudges would have their coercive effect precisely *because* those who want to put me right know that I am not a fundamentalist. That is, I am to avoid association with religion completely or else be embarrassed by punitive association with beliefs I do not hold. What sense does that make? What good does it serve? I suspect it demonstrates the existence of a human herding instinct. After all, "egregious" means at root "outside the flock." There are always a great many people who are confident that they recognize deviation from group mores, and so they police the boundaries and round up the strays.

This is only one instance of a very pervasive phenomenon, a pressure toward concessions no one has a right to ask. These are concessions courage would refuse if it were once acknowledged that a minor and insidious fear is the prod that coaxes us toward conforming our lives, and even our thoughts, to norms that are effective markers of group identity precisely because they are shibboleths, a contemporary equivalent of using the correct fork. These signals of inclusion and exclusion, minor as they seem, have huge consequences historically because they are used to apportion the benefits and the burdens of collective life. The example of coercion I have offered, the standing invitation to sacrifice one's metaphysics to one's sense of *comme il faut,* has had the effect of marginalizing the liberal churches and elevating fundamentalism to the status of essential Christianity. The consequences of handing over the whole of Christianity to one momentarily influential fringe is clearly borne out in the silencing of social criticism and the collapse of social reform, both traditionally championed by American mainline churches, as no one seems any longer to remember.

The present dominance of aspersion and ridicule in American public life is a reflex of the fact that we are assumed to want, and in many cases perhaps do want, attitude much more than information. If an unhealthy percentage of the population gets its news from Jay Leno or Rush Limbaugh, it is because they are arbiters of attitude. They instruct viewers as to what, within their affinity groups, it is safe to say and cool to think. That is, they short-circuit the functions of individual judgment and obviate the exercise of individual conscience. So it is to a greater or lesser degree with the media in general. It is painful to watch decent and distinguished people struggle to function politically in this non-rational and valueless environment.

Finally, granting that consensus enforcement, and the endless small concessions made to endless small coercions, are no doubt universal in human civilization, they cannot be without cost, precisely because they disable courage. No one can truly submit to unreasonable coercion — by suppressing one's thinking, one's identity, one's metaphysics — without falling a little in one's own estimation. And no one can deal in coercion without cynicism. Both sides of the transaction compromise.

Cultures commonly employ the methods of cults, making their members subject and dependent. And nations at intervals march lockstep to enormity and disaster. A successful autocracy rests on the universal failure of individual courage. In a democracy, abdications of conscience are never trivial. They demoralize politics, debilitate candor, and disrupt thought.